FAITH & WORD EDITION
BLEST ARE WE

*Faith comes from what is heard,
and what is heard comes through the word of Christ.*

Romans 10:17

Series Authors

Rev. Richard N. Fragomeni, Ph.D.
Maureen Gallagher, Ph.D.
Jeannine Goggin, M.P.S.
Michael P. Horan, Ph.D.

Scripture Co-editor and Consultant
Maria Pascuzzi, S.S.L., S.T.D.

Multicultural Consultant
Angela Erevia, M.C.D.P., M.R.E.

The Subcommittee on the Catechism, United States Conference of Catholic Bishops, has found this catechetical series, copyright 2010, to be in conformity with the *Catechism of the Catholic Church*.

This book reflects the new revision of the

ROMAN MISSAL
THIRD EDITION

Cincinnati, Ohio

FAITH & WORD EDITION

BLEST ARE WE®

Contributing Writers

Ellen Marconi
Catholic Schools in America: Robert Kealey, Ph.D.
Faith in Action: Kathleen N. Burke
Feasts and Seasons: Marianne K. Lenihan, Louise Timko, Ph.D.
Our Catholic Heritage: Joyce A. Crider

Advisory Board

William C. Allegri, M.A., Patricia M. Feeley, S.S.J., M.A., Edmund F. Gordon, Patricia A. Hoffmann, Rev. Daniel Kelly, Cris V. Villapando, D.Min.

Consultants

Margaret J. Borders, M.R.S., Kelly O'Lague Dulka, M.S.W., Diane Hardick, M.A., Debra Schurko, Linda S. Tonelli, M.Ed., Joy Villotti-Biedrzycki

Music Advisor

GIA Publications: Michael A. Cymbala, Alec Harris, Robert W. Piercy

Nihil Obstat

M. Kathleen Flanagan, S.C., Ph.D.
Censor Librorum

Imprimatur

† Most Reverend Arthur J. Serratelli
Bishop of Paterson

April 28, 2008

The *nihil obstat* and *imprimatur* are official declarations that a book or pamphlet is free of doctrinal and moral error. No implication is contained therein that those who have granted the *nihil obstat* and *imprimatur* agree with the contents, opinions, or statements expressed.

Acknowledgments

Excerpts from the *New American Bible* with Revised New Testament and Psalms Copyright © 1991, 1986, 1970 Confraternity of Christian Doctrine, Inc., Washington, DC. Used with permission. All rights reserved. No portion of the *New American Bible* may be reprinted without permission in writing from the copyright holder.

All adaptations of Scripture are based on the *New American Bible* with Revised New Testament and Psalms Copyright © 1991, 1986, 1970 Confraternity of Christian Doctrine, Inc., Washington, DC.

Excerpts from the English translation of the *Rite of Marriage* © 1969, International Committee on English in the Liturgy, Inc. (ICEL); excerpts from the English translation of the *Rite of Baptism for Children* © 1969, ICEL; excerpts from the English translation of the *Rite of Penance* © 1974, ICEL; excerpts from the English translation of *Eucharistic Prayers for Masses with Children* © 1975, ICEL; excerpts from the English translation of the *Rite of Confirmation*, Second Edition © 1975, ICEL; excerpts from the English translation of the *Liturgy of the Hours* © 1976, ICEL; excerpts from *Pastoral Care of the Sick: Rites of Anointing and Viaticum* © 1982, ICEL; excerpts from the English translation of *The Roman Missal*, Second Edition © 2010, ICEL; excerpts from the English translation of the *Rite of Christian Initiation of Adults* © 1985, ICEL. All rights reserved.

Excerpts from *Catholic Household Blessings and Prayers* (revised edition) © 2007, United States Conference of Catholic Bishops, Washington, D.C.

Music selections copyrighted and/or administered by GIA Publications are used with permission of GIA Publications, Inc., 7404 So. Mason Avenue, Chicago, IL 60638-9927. Please refer to songs for specific copyright dates and information.

In Appreciation: Blessed Kateri Church, Sparta, NJ; Church of the Assumption, Morristown, NJ; Our Lady of Mercy Church, Whippany, NJ; Our Lady of the Lake Church, Sparta, NJ; St. Ann's Church, Parsippany, NJ; St. Joseph's Church, Croton Falls, NY; St. Peter the Apostle Church, Parsippany, NJ; St. Thomas More Church, Convent Station, NJ; GIA Publications, Inc., Chicago, IL; WLP Publications, Franklin Park, IL; Rev. Michael W. Cichon (Sign Language Advisor); Rev. George Hafemann

Credits

COVER: Gene Plaisted, OSC/The Crosiers

SCRIPTURE ART: Tim Ladwig

ALL OTHER ART: 20, 21 Elizabeth Wolf; 28 Tim Ladwig; 30 Scott Cameron; 31 Barb Massey; 33 Tom Sperling; 38 Tim Ladwig; 39 Lusignan Design; 42 Tim Ladwig; 44 (L) Roman Dunets; 47 Reggie Holladay; 50 Tim Ladwig; 52 Scott Cameron; 54 Tim Ladwig; 56 Roman Dunets; 57 Amanda Harvey; 62, 64 Tim Ladwig; 69, 70 (Inset), 71 Tom Sperling; 76 Bernadette Lau; 77 Ginna Magee; 83 Lusignan Design; 84 Bernadette Lau; 86 Tim Ladwig; 89 Barb Massey; 90 Roman Dunets; 93 (TC) Ginna Magee; 96 Tim Ladwig; 97 Bernard Adnet; 99 Jack McMaster; 100 Tim Ladwig; 101 Barb Massey; 108, 110 Tim Ladwig; 111 David Bathurst; 112 Tim Ladwig; 115 Bernadette Lau; 120 Tim Ladwig; 121 Morella Fuenmayor; 122 Tim Ladwig; 123 Teresa Beraski; 126, 127, 129 Tom Sperling; 135 Ginna Magee; 142 Tim Ladwig; 143, 143(B) David Helton; 144 Tim Ladwig; 145 Heather Holbrook; 146 Tim Ladwig; 149 Freddie Levin; 154 Tim Ladwig; 155 Marion Eldridge; 158 Tim Ladwig; 161 Marcie Hawthrone; 166 Tim Ladwig; 167 Linda Howard Bittner; 168 Tim Ladwig; 171 Jack McMaster; 175 Reggie Holladay; 178, 180 Tim Ladwig; 185 Tom Sperling; 193 Hal Just; 200 Bernadette Lau; 201 Diana Magnuson; 202 Tim Ladwig; 206 Patti Green; 207 Lusignan Design; 212 Tim Ladwig; 213 Chris Reed; 214 Tim Ladwig; 215 David Bathurst; 218 Roman Dunets; 218 (B) Gershom Griffith; 219 Bernard Adnet; 224 Tim Ladwig; 225 Amanda Harvey; 226 Tim Ladwig; 227 Bernadette Lau; 228 Tim Ladwig; 229 Anne Stanley; 230, 233 Diana Magnuson; 236, 238 Tim Ladwig; 241 Deborah Pinkney; 243, 245 Tom Sperling; 251 Hal Just; 258 Tim Ladwig; 259 Sandy Rabinowitz; 260 Tim Ladwig; 262 Heather Graham; 263 Amy Vangsgard; 264 Roman Dunets; 270, 272 Tim Ladwig; 273 Bernadette Lau; 277 Terra Muzick; 282 Tim Ladwig; 283 Claude Martinot; 284, 286, 287 Tim Ladwig; 289 Chris Reed; 294 Tim Ladwig; 295 Elizabeth Wolf; 296 Tim Ladwig; 299 Teresa Berasi; 300 Tim Ladwig; 301 Tom Sperling; 309 Hal Just; 313 Robin DeWitt; 314 David Bathurst; 319 Heather Holbrook; 321 Deborah Pinkney; 322, 323 Barb Massey; 327 David & Chrissie Wysotski; 329 Donna Perrone; 333 Cindy Rosenheim; 335 Deborah Pinkney; 337 Karen Bell; 341 Paula Wendland; 345 Cindy Rosenheim; 347 Reggie Holladay; 351 Heather Holbrook; 353 Heather Graham; 355 David Bathurst; 359 Kelly Kennedy; 361 Donna Perrone; 363 Barb Massey; 364 Tim Ladwig; 365 Jean & Mou-Sien Tseng; 367 Jackie Snider; 373 Donna Perrone; 375 Jun Park; 377 Bernadette Lau; 381 David Coulson; 385 Craig Terlson; 387 Dave Whamond; 408 Tom Sperling; 409 Burgandy Beam; 417 D. Hurst/Alamy

PHOTOS: Every effort has been made to secure permission and provide appropriate credit for photographic material. The publisher deeply regrets any omission and pledges to correct errors called to its attention in subsequent editions.

9 (B) Gene Plaisted, OSC/The Crosiers; 12 © Richard Cummins/Folio, Inc.; 13 Durham Street Methodist Church, New Zealand/SuperStock; 14 © Tony Freeman/PhotoEdit; 23 (Bkgd) © Robert F. Sisson/NGS Image Collection; 23 (Inset)/Yavneh Publishing House,Ltd.; 26 © Rob Crandall/The Image Works, Inc.; 27 © Frank Siteman/Index Stock Imagery; 32 (R) Alfred Eisenstaedt/LIFE/TimePix; 34 Tom Brakefield/Image Works; 38 © Myrleen Ferguson Cate/PhotoEdit; 40 Chris Sheridan/Catholic New York; 44 © Rykoff Collection/Corbis; 46 (Bkgd) A. Tjagny-Rjadno; 49 © William Johnson/Stock Boston; 50 Photofest; 51 © Mike Brinson/Getty Images; 56 SuperStock; 58 © Aliki Sapountzi/Aliki Image Library/Alamy Images; 62 © Morton Beebe, S.F./Corbis; 63 © Lawrence Migdale/Stock Boston; 63 © David Young-Wolfe/PhotoEdit; 70 (Bkgd) © Paul Edmondson/Getty Images; 81 (Bkgd) © Sonia Halliday Photographs; 81 (Inset) Bridgeman Art; 84 © Richard Barenholtz/Corbis; 85 William Zdinak, Artist; 90 (CR) Sarah Johnson; 90 (BR) June Jamison Thorne; 91 (TL) David Young-Wolff/PhotoEdit; 91 (R) © John Welzenbach/Corbis; 92 (Bkdg) © William Waterfall/Pacific Stock; 92 (Inset) © Richard Hutchings/PhotoEdit; 97 © Myrleen Ferguson Cate/PhotoEdit; 98 Chris Sheridan/Catholic New York; 103 Jim Whitmer; 104 (L) Richard Lord; 104 (Bkgd) Bob Daemmrich/Stock Boston; 108 Sean Sprague/© CNEWA, New York; 109 © Bill Wittman; 114 Corbis; 116 (Bkgd) © H. David Seawall/Corbis; 124 Gene Plaisted, OSC/The Crosiers; 127 (TL) © Roger Ball/Corbis Stock Market; 127 (TR) © A. Lichtenstein/Corbis Sygma; 128 (Bkgd) Getty Images; 140 (Bkgd) (Inset) © Sonia Halliday Photographs; 142 © The Art Archives/Corbis; 150 (Bkgd) Stefano Amantini/Atlantide/Bruce Coleman, Inc.; 154 Meyer-Vogelpohl; 155 © Myrleen Ferguson Cate/PhotoEdit; 156 Gene Plaisted, OSC/The Crosiers; 162 © David Young-Wolfe/PhotoEdit; 165 R. Barry Levy/Index Stock Imagery; 166 Little Sisters of the Poor; 170 The Nicholas Green Foundation; 170 The Nicholas Green Foundation/sculpted and designed by Bruce Hasson; 173 Index Stock Imagery; 174 © E.R. Degginger/Bruce Coleman, Inc.; 177 (L) Jim Cummins; 177 (R) © Mary Kate Denny/Getty Images; 178 GIA Publications; 179 Gene Plaisted, OSC/The Crosiers; 179 © Tom McCarthy/Photri, Inc.; 186 (Bkgd) Index Stock Imagery; 197 (Bkgd) © Richard T. Nowitz; 197 (Inset) © The British Museum/Photo/© Dorling Kindersley; 200 Joe Rimkus, Jr./Catholic News Service; 204 © Barbara Stephenson/Catholic Campaign for Human Development; 205 (CL, C) © Bill Wittman; 205 (CR) © James L. Shaffer; 208 (Bkgd) SuperStock; 208 (Inset) © Arthur Tilley/Getty Images; 212 © Francis G. Mayer/Corbis; 220 (Bkgd) John Shaw/Bruce Coleman, Inc.; 224 The Printery House of Conception Abbey; 232 (Bkgd) Thomas Winz/Panoramic Images; 232 (BL) Myrleen Ferguson Cate/PhotoEdit; 240 © Arturo Mari/Catholic News Service; 244 (Bkgd) Thomas Winz/Panoramic Images; 244 (BL) W.P. Wittman; 255 (Bkgd) © Sonia Halliday Photographs; 255 (Inset) Erich Lessing/Art Resource, NY; 258 Scala/Art Resource, NY; 264 The Granger Collection, New York; 265 (TL) © W.P. Wittman; 265 (TR) James L. Shaffer; 266 © Bonnie Kamin/PhotoEdit; 270 Franco Origlia/Getty Images; 271 © Bill Horsman/Stock Boston; 274 AP/Wide World; 276 © Stephen R. Swan/Comstock Images, Inc./Index Stock Imagery; 278 (Bkgd) Gene Plaisted, OSC/The Crosiers; 278 (CR) The Cummer Museum of Art and Gardens, Jacksonville, FL/SuperStock; 282 Everett Collection, Inc.; 288 © Bettmann/Corbis; 289 Bob Daemmrich/Stock Boston; 289 Spencer Grant/Stock Boston; 290 © Robert Frerck/Getty Images; 294 Musee d'Orsay, Paris, France/Erich Lessing/Art Resource, New York; 295 © Peter Turnley/Corbis; 298 Canossian Sisters; 302 © Ed Honowitz/Getty Images; 318 © Bill Wittman; 320 Jim Whitmer; 324 Fr. Carl B. Trutter, O.P.; 326 © Bill Wittman; 334 SuperStock; 334 © Bill Wittman; 339 © A. Ramey/PhotoEdit; 342 (Bkgd) CLEO; 344 © Bill Wittman; 346 Danielle L. Dipre; 348 Brian Leatart/Food Pix; 350 © W.P. Wittman; 354 © Hanan Isachar/Corbis; 356 H. Isachar/Art Directors & TRIP Photo Library; 358 © Bill Aron Photography; 362 Richard Lord; 363 Lawrence Migdale/Stock Boston; 368 AP/Wide World Photos; 372 Fr. Carl B. Trutter, O.P.; 374 Gene Plaisted, OSC/The Crosiers; 378 Gene Plaisted, OSC/The Crosiers; 379 Jim Whitmer; 380 Gene Plaisted, OSC/The Crosiers; 382 Corbis Sygma; 383 CLEO; 384 © Ann Ball; 386 Catholic News Service; 388 AP/Wide World Photos; 394 Chris Sheridan/Catholic New York; 395 Gene Plaisted, OSC/The Crosiers; 396 Gene Plaisted, OSC/The Crosiers; 397 © W. P. Wittman; 402 Mary Kate Denny/PhotoEdit; 405 Myrleen Cate/Index Stock Imagery; 407 Jim Whitmer; 410 Beniaminson/Art Resource, New York; 411 Courtesy of Saint Patrick's School; 412 Courtesy: Sisters of Providence Archives, Seattle, WA; 414 Eileen Ryan, courtesy of Christo Rey Jesuit High School, Chicago, IL 60608; 416 © Gary Gardiner/Small Town Stock; 418 Getty Images; 420 (BL) Chris Sheridan/Catholic New York; 420 (CR) AP/World Wide; 421 (BR) Chris Sheridan/Catholic New York; 422 Angelo Cavalli/Getty Images

CONTENTS

UNIT 1

CHAPTER	PAGE	CATECHISM PILLARS

Faith in Action

WHAT CATHOLICS BELIEVE

HOW CATHOLICS WORSHIP

HOW CATHOLICS LIVE

HOW CATHOLICS PRAY

WHAT CATHOLICS BELIEVE

HOW CATHOLICS WORSHIP

HOW CATHOLICS LIVE

HOW CATHOLICS PRAY

FEASTS AND SEASONS

OUR CATHOLIC HERITAGE

Organized according to the four pillars of the Catechism

LET US PRAY

The Sign of the Cross

In the name of the Father,
and of the Son,
and of the Holy Spirit.

        Amen.

Signum SIHG-noom
Crucis KROO-chees

Line 1. In nómine Patris,
    ihn NOH-mee-nay PAH-trees

2. et Fílii,
    et FEE-lee-ee

3. et Spíritus Sancti.
    et SPEE-ree-toos SAHNK-tee.

        Amen.
        AH-men.

Glória Patri

GLOR-ee-ah PAH-tree

Lines 1.–2. Glória Patri et Fílio
    GLOR-ee-ah PAH-tree et FEE-lee-oh

3. et Spirítui Sancto.
    et spee-REE-too-ee SAHNK-toh.

4. Sicut erat in princípio,
    SEE-koot AIR-aht ihn prihn-CHEE-pee-oh,

5. et nunc et semper
    et noonk et SEM-pair

6. et in saecula saeculórum.
    et ihn SAY-koo-lah say-koo-LOR-oom.

        Amen.
        AH-men.

Glory Be

Glory be to the Father
and to the Son
and to the Holy Spirit,
as it was in the beginning
is now, and ever shall be
world without end. Amen.

* The lines in the Latin prayers are numbered to match the lines in the English prayers.

The Hail Mary

Hail, Mary, full of grace,
the Lord is with thee.
Blessed art thou among women
and blessed is the fruit of thy
     womb, Jesus.
Holy Mary, Mother of God,
pray for us sinners,
now and at the hour of our death.

Amen.

Ave, María
AH-vay, mah-REE-ah

Lines 1.–2. Ave, María, grátia plena, Dóminus tecum.
AH-vay, mah-REE-ah, GRAHT-see-ah PLAY-nah,
DOH-mee-noos TAY-koom.

3. Benedícta tu in muliéribus,
bay-nay-DEEK-tah too ihn moo-lee-AIR-ee-boos,

4.–5. et benedíctus fructus ventris tui, Iesus.
et bay-nay-DEEK-toos FROOK-toos VEN-trees TOO-ee,
YAY-zoos.

6. Sancta María, Mater Dei,
SAHNK-tah mah-REE-ah, MAH-tair DAY-ee,

7. ora pro nobis peccatóribus,
OR-ah proh NOH-bees pek-uh-TOR-ee-boos,

8.–9. nunc et in hora mortis nostrae.
noonk et ihn OR-ah MOR-tees NOHS-tray.

Amen.
AH-men.

The Lord's Prayer

Our Father, who art in heaven,
hallowed be thy name;
thy kingdom come
thy will be done
on earth as it is in heaven.
Give us this day our daily bread,
and forgive us our trespasses,
as we forgive those who trespass
     against us;
and lead us not into temptation,
but deliver us from evil.

Amen.

Oratio Dominica
oh-RAHT-see-oh doh-MEE-nee-kah

Lines 1.–2. Pater noster, qui es in caelis:
PAH-tair NOHS-tair kwee es ihn CHAY-lees:

3. sanctificétur nomen tuum;
sahnk-tee-fee-CHAY-tor NOH-men TOO-oom;

4. advéniat regnum tuum;
ahd-VEH-nee-aht REG-noom TOO-oom;

5.–6. fiat volúntas tua, sicut in caelo, et in terra.
FEE-aht voh-LOON-tahs TOO-ah, SEE-koot ihn
CHAY-loh, et ihn TAIR-ah.

7.–8. Panem nostrum cotidiánum da nobis hódie;
PAH-nem NOH-stroom koh-tee-dee-AH-noom dah
NOH-bees OH-dee-ay;

9.–10. et dimítte nobis débita nostra,
et dih-MEET-tay NOH-bees DEH-bee-tah NOH-strah,

11.–12. sicut et nos dimíttimus debitóribus nostris;
SEE-koot et nohs dih-MIHT-ee-moos
day-bee-TOR-ee-boos NOH-strees;

13.–14. et ne nos indúcas in tentatiónem;
et nay nohs ihn-DOO-kahs ihn ten-taht-see-OH-nem;

15. sed líbera nos a malo.
sed LEE-bair-ah nohs ah MAH-loh.

Amen.
AH-men.

The Apostles' Creed

I believe in God,
the Father almighty,
Creator of heaven and earth,
and in Jesus Christ, his only Son, our Lord,
who was conceived by the Holy Spirit,
born of the Virgin Mary,
suffered under Pontius Pilate,
was crucified, died and was buried;
he descended into hell;
on the third day he rose again from the dead;
he ascended into heaven,
and is seated at the right hand of God the Father almighty;
from there he will come to judge the living and the dead.

I believe in the Holy Spirit,
the holy catholic Church,
the communion of saints,
the forgiveness of sins,
the resurrection of the body,
and life everlasting.

Amen.

The Nicene Creed

I believe in one God,
the Father almighty,
maker of heaven and earth,
of all things visible and invisible.

I believe in one Lord Jesus Christ,
the Only Begotten Son of God,
born of the Father before all ages.
God from God, Light from Light,
true God from true God,
begotten, not made, consubstantial with the Father;
through him all things were made.
For us men and for our salvation
he came down from heaven,
and by the Holy Spirit was incarnate of the Virgin Mary,
and became man.

For our sake he was crucified under Pontius Pilate,
he suffered death and was buried,
and rose again on the third day
in accordance with the Scriptures.
He ascended into heaven
and is seated at the right hand of the Father.
He will come again in glory
to judge the living and the dead
and his kingdom will have no end.

I believe in the Holy Spirit, the Lord, the giver of life,
who proceeds from the Father and the Son,
who with the Father and the Son is adored and glorified,
 who has spoken through the prophets.

I believe in one, holy, catholic and apostolic Church.
I confess one Baptism for the forgiveness of sins
and I look forward to the resurrection
of the dead and the life of the world to come.

Amen.

Act of Contrition

My God,
I am sorry for my sins with all my heart.
In choosing to do wrong
and failing to do good,
I have sinned against you
whom I should love above all things.
I firmly intend, with your help,
to do penance,
to sin no more,
and to avoid whatever leads me to sin.
Our Savior Jesus Christ
suffered and died for us.
In his name, my God, have mercy.

Rite of Penance

Hail, Holy Queen

Hail, holy Queen, Mother of Mercy:
Hail, our life, our sweetness, and our hope.
To you do we cry,
poor banished children of Eve.
To you do we send up our sighs,
mourning and weeping
in this valley of tears.
Turn then, most gracious advocate,
Your eyes of mercy toward us;
and after this our exile
show unto us
the blessed fruit of your womb, Jesus.
O clement, O loving, O sweet Virgin Mary.

Amen.

Prayer to Jesus Christ in the Eucharist

Lord Jesus Christ, I believe that
you are truly present in
the Eucharist.
As I receive you in Holy Communion,
help me to love as you loved,
and serve as you served,
so I can be the Body of
Christ to others.

Amen.

Vocation Prayer

Lord, show me how to be of service, in
your Church and in the world.
Help me see what you want me to do.
Give me vision, courage, and friends who
encourage me to do your work.

Amen.

The Rosary

The **Rosary** is a prayer that honors Mary, the Mother of Jesus, and helps us meditate on the life of Christ. We pray the Rosary using a set of beads. A group of ten beads is called a decade. Before each decade, recall one of the mysteries, or important times in the lives of Mary and Jesus. There are twenty mysteries, shown at right. The prayers for the beads are shown below.

The Mysteries of the Rosary

The Joyful Mysteries

1. The Annunciation
2. The Visitation
3. The Nativity
4. The Presentation in the Temple
5. The Finding of the Child Jesus After Three Days in the Temple

The Luminous Mysteries

1. The Baptism at the Jordan
2. The Miracle at Cana
3. The Proclamation of the Kingdom of God and the Call to Conversion
4. The Transfiguration
5. The Institution of the Eucharist

The Sorrowful Mysteries

1. The Agony in the Garden
2. The Scourging at the Pillar
3. The Crowning with Thorns
4. The Carrying of the Cross
5. The Crucifixion and Death

The Glorious Mysteries

1. The Resurrection
2. The Ascension
3. The Descent of the Holy Spirit at Pentecost
4. The Assumption of Mary
5. The Crowning of the Blessed Virgin Mary as Queen of Heaven and Earth

Fourth Mystery Lord's Prayer

Ten Hail Marys, Glory Be

Third Mystery Lord's Prayer

Ten Hail Marys, Glory Be

Ten Hail Marys, Glory Be

Fifth Mystery, Lord's Prayer

Second Mystery Lord's Prayer

Ten Hail Marys, Glory Be

Three Hail Marys, Glory Be

Ten Hail Marys, Glory Be

Sign of the Cross and Apostles' Creed

Lord's Prayer

First Mystery Lord's Prayer

Hail, Holy Queen (pray at the end)

The Stations of the Cross

1. Jesus is condemned to death.

2. Jesus accepts the cross.

3. Jesus falls the first time.

4. Jesus meets his mother.

5. Simon helps Jesus carry the cross.

6. Veronica wipes the face of Jesus.

7. Jesus falls the second time.

8. Jesus meets the women of Jerusalem.

9. Jesus falls the third time.

10. Jesus is stripped of his garments.

11. Jesus is nailed to the cross.

12. Jesus dies on the cross.

13. Jesus is taken down from the cross.

14. Jesus is buried in the tomb.

15. Jesus Christ is risen.

The Bible

The Word became flesh
and made his dwelling
among us.

John 1:14

The Bible

The Bible is the Word of God. The Bible is the story of God and his people.

We believe that God is truly the author of the Bible because the Holy Spirit inspired the people who wrote it.

The Bible is a collection of seventy-three books. It is divided into two parts. The first is called the Old Testament. There are forty-six books in the Old Testament. These books include stories, laws, history, poetry, and prayers. We read the Old Testament to learn about God's people before Jesus was born.

The second part of the Bible is called the New Testament. There are twenty-seven books in the New Testament, which includes the four Gospels, the letters of Saint Paul, and other writings of the Apostles and early Christians. We read the New Testament to learn about the life of Jesus and the early Christians.

The Bible is very important for Catholic worship. At Sunday Mass and on holy days, we hear a reading from the Old Testament and two readings from the New Testament. The second reading from the New Testament is always from the Gospel.

Activity

Finding a Bible Text

Finding passages in the Bible is not like finding something in a story book or a textbook. Each book of the Bible is divided into chapters, and each chapter has a number. The chapters are divided into verses, which may contain one or more sentences. Verses also have numbers.

The following example will help you learn how to look up passages from the Bible.

Book	Chapter	Verse
Sirach	6	14

Using the Bible

The following Bible references relate to stories you will read about this year. Using your Bible, look up these passages. In the space next to each reference, write the title of the Scripture story.

Exodus 20:1–17 _____

Matthew 6:9–13 _____

Matthew 5:3–10 _____

John 13:31–35 _____

Luke 15:11–32 _____

_____

Matthew 20:1–16 _____

Activity

1. Use your Bible to look up each Scripture passage shown below. Draw a line to connect each Scripture passage to its corresponding image from the map on page 21.

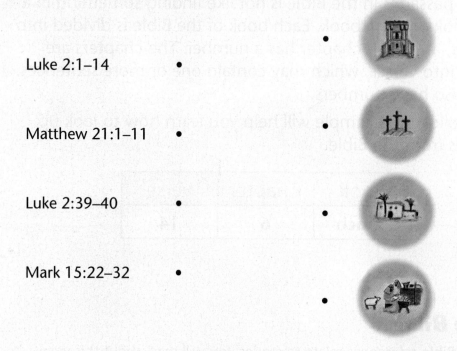

Luke 2:1–14

Matthew 21:1–11

Luke 2:39–40

Mark 15:22–32

2. Read the story about the Samaritan Woman from John 4:4–42. There is no image for Samaria on the map on page 21. In the space below, draw your own image that describes what took place in this story.

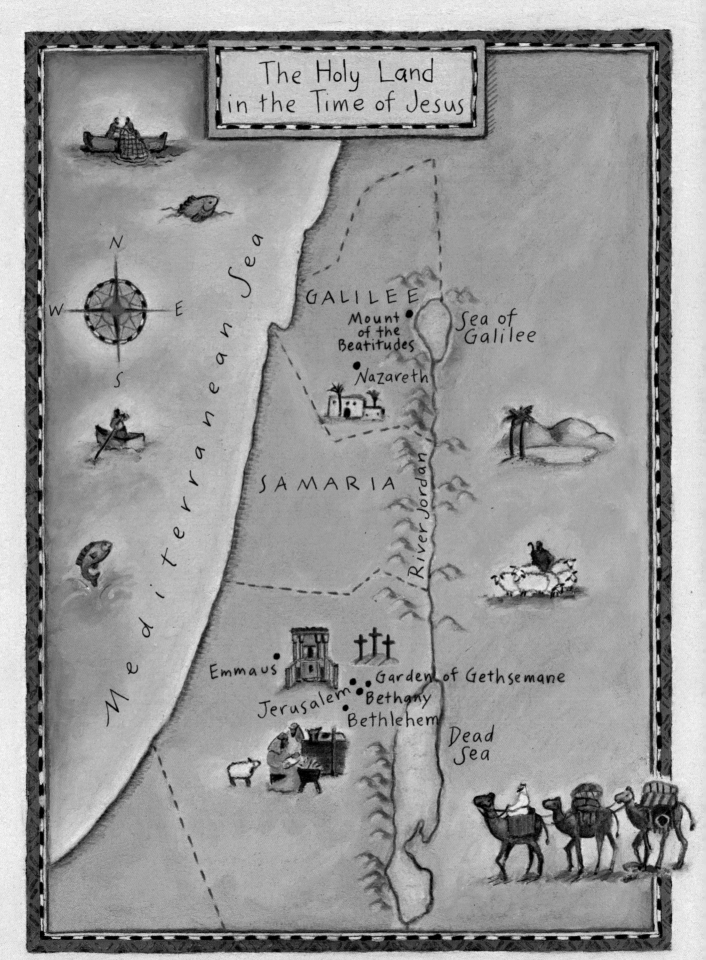

The Holy Land
in the Time of Jesus

N
W E
S

Mediterranean Sea

GALILEE

Mount
of the
Beatitudes

Sea of
Galilee

Nazareth

SAMARIA

River Jordan

Emmaus

Garden of Gethsemane

Jerusalem

Bethany

Bethlehem

Dead
Sea

BLEST ARE WE

Words and Music by David Haas
Spanish translation by Ronald F. Krisman

REFRAIN

Blest are we, ho-ly chil-dren of light— are we!——
¡Ben-de-ci-dos, so-mos san-tos hi-jos de la luz!——

Blest are we, cho-sen peo-ple of God!——
¡Ben-de-ci-dos y e-le-gi-dos por Dios!——

Blest are we, God has plans— for you and me!
¡Ben-de-ci-dos, Dios nos quie-re ser cual Je-sús!

Fine

Blest— are we!— We are the chil-dren of God!——
¡Ben-de-ci-dos, so-mos los hi-jos de Dios!——

VERSE

1. For our world,— each sis-ter and broth-er:
1. Por el mun-do, por to-dos sus pue-blos:

We— are called,— called— to serve!——
¡So-mos lla-ma-dos pa-ra ser-vir!——

We are here to love— one an-oth-er:
Nos a-me-mos los u-nos a los o-tros;

D.C.

We— are called,— called— to serve!
¡So-mos lla-ma-dos pa-ra ser-vir!——

2. For the poor, the meek and the lowly:
   We are called, called to serve!
   For the weak, the sick and the hungry:
   We are called, called to serve!

2. Por los pobres, los mansos y humildes:
   ¡Somos llamados para servir!
   Por los enfermos, hambrientos, y débiles:
   ¡Somos llamados para servir!

3. For all those who yearn for freedom:
   We are called, called to serve!
   For the world, to be God's kingdom:
   We are called, called to serve!

3. Por los que sufren y quieren ser librados:
   ¡Somos llamados para servir!
   Venga a nosotros el Reino de los Cielos:
   ¡Somos llamados para servir!

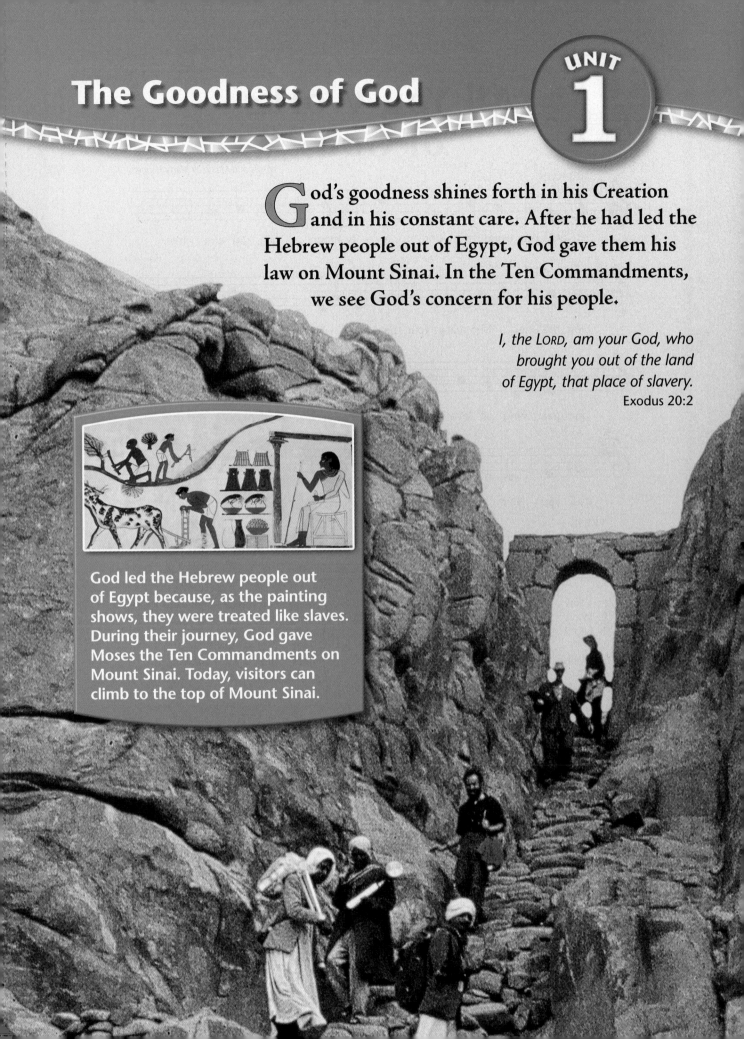

The Goodness of God

God's goodness shines forth in his Creation and in his constant care. After he had led the Hebrew people out of Egypt, God gave them his law on Mount Sinai. In the Ten Commandments, we see God's concern for his people.

I, the LORD, am your God, who brought you out of the land of Egypt, that place of slavery.
Exodus 20:2

God led the Hebrew people out of Egypt because, as the painting shows, they were treated like slaves. During their journey, God gave Moses the Ten Commandments on Mount Sinai. Today, visitors can climb to the top of Mount Sinai.

All You Works of God

Words and Music by Marty Haugen

REFRAIN

All you works of God, ev-'ry moun-tain, star and tree,

bless the One— who shapes your beau-ty, who has caused you all to be

one great song of love and grace, ev-er an - cient, ev-er new.

Fine

Raise your voic - es, all you works of God!———

VERSE

Cantor   *All*   *Cantor*

1. Sun and moon:		Stars of heav - en:——
2. Winds of God:		Cold and win - ter:——
3. Night and day:		Light and dark - ness:——
4. All the earth:	Bless your Mak - er!	Hills and moun-tains:——
5. Wells and springs:		Seas and riv - ers:——
6. Fly - ing birds:		Beasts and cat - tle:——
7. All who live:		Men and wom - en:——

All   *Cantor*

Chant your praise!

Show - ers——	and	dew:
Snow - storms——	and	ice:
Light - nings——	and	clouds:
Green things——	that	grow:
Whales in——	the	deep:
Chil - dren	at	play:
Ser - vants——	of	God:

All   *D.C.*

Raise up— your joy - ful song.———

Take Home

FAMILY TIME

God's Goodness

The history of our faith goes back to Abraham and his descendants, the people of Israel. At the time when much of the Old Testament was written, belief in many gods was common. The Israelites came to know that there was only one God and that this God was all good. Out of this goodness, God created the earth and all creatures. We are loved because we have been created in the image and likeness of God.

ACTIVITY

You Are Good!   For each family member, fold a piece of cardstock in half. Invite family members to identify one way that God has been good to them. Then have each person write a prayer of thanks on the front of the card and decorate it. During the week, read the prayers before the family eats together.

From Brett:
Thank you, God, for my mother who takes care of me!

WEEKLY PLANNER

On Sunday

Listen to God speaking about his love for you and how you can bring his message to others. Share with your family what you heard.

On the Web

blestarewe.com

Visit our Web site for the saint of the day and the reflection question of the week.

Saint of the Week

 Saint Thomas Aquinas (c.1225–1274)

Saint Thomas Aquinas was a Dominican priest who loved learning and teaching. A Doctor of the Church, he wrote volumes about the greatness of God. The works of Saint Thomas are still being studied today.

Patron Saint of: colleges, learning, schools, students
Feast Day: January 28

 A Prayer for the Week

Lord, Saint Thomas Aquinas lived life for the joy of learning. Bless all those who help us learn more about you as Father, Son, and Holy Spirit. Amen.

Take Home

FAMILY TIME

 ## ✝ Scripture Background

Before the Time of Jesus

Genesis The Hebrew name for the Book of Genesis is *bereshith* which means "in the beginning." With these opening words, the story of Creation unfolds. In later chapters, we meet Abraham and Noah and other people who play an important role in the history of the Israelites. Genesis concludes with a story about Joseph and his brothers. Scholars believe the stories in Genesis are based on the oral traditions of the Hebrew people.

Read the two stories of Creation in Genesis 1:1–31, 2:1–4; 2:5–23

OUR CATHOLIC TRADITION in Architecture

Antoni Gaudí Antoni Gaudí (1852–1926) was one of the great modernist architects of the twentieth century. Born in Catalonia, Spain, Gaudí was a devout Roman Catholic whose work was inspired by his deep faith in God and love of nature. Gaudí once said that his task as an architect was one of "collaboration with the Creator." His innovative and imaginative designs blended elements of the Neo-Gothic, art nouveau, and surrealist schools of art. His most celebrated work is the unfinished church *La Sagrada Família* ("The Holy Family") in Barcelona.

1 God's Goodness

 God looked at everything he had made, and he found it very good.

Genesis 1:31

Share

Enjoying God's Creation

God created a beautiful world for us to explore and enjoy with others.

Activity

In the space below, write about one way you enjoy God's creation with your family or friends.

_____

_____

_____

_____

How do we learn about God's goodness?

Hear & Believe

Scripture The Story of Creation

*The first story in the **Bible** is about the Creation of the world. People knew that God had created everything in the universe. This is the story about how it happened.*

In the beginning, everything was dark. Then God sent his Spirit over the darkness. And through his Word, God said, "Let there be light!" And there was light! Then, God said, "Let there be sky!" Blue sky appeared.

God separated dry land from the waters. Trees and plants of every kind sprang up. Then God called into the world great lights for the sky, and named them the sun, the moon, and the stars.

God made swimming creatures, flying creatures, and all the animals that live upon the land. Then our God created people in his own image—a man and a woman who lived in perfect friendship with God.

God blessed everything he had made and he found it very good.

Based on Genesis 1:1–31; 2:1–4

God in Creation

God cares for our needs by giving us the gift of Creation. We see God's goodness in the world around us. God wants us to respect and care for others and for all of Creation.

Activity

You are a special part of God's Creation. Tell about yourself on the lines below. Be sure to include some information about your talents and the good things you do.

I am interested in _____

_____.

My favorite subject is _____.

I really care about _____.

I care for others by _____

_____.

I try to _____

_____.

How can we come to know God's goodness?

Hear & Believe

Saint Thomas Teaches About the Trinity

Thomas Aquinas was a great scholar who lived in Italy and France 700 years ago. He spent a great deal of time learning about God and his goodness.

From the time he was five years old, Thomas attended school in a **monastery**. He had an excellent memory and learned quickly. His teachers were amazed at the many questions he asked about God. Thomas eagerly listened to stories from the Bible and grew in his love for God. When he was about nineteen years old, Thomas became a Dominican priest. Thomas prayed, "Give me, Lord, a mind to know you, a heart to seek you, and wisdom to find you."

Thomas wrote many books as well as hymns and prayers. He wrote about the **mystery** of the **Holy Trinity** —God the Father, God the Son, and God the Holy Spirit. He taught that the Trinity is the central mystery of the Catholic faith. Thomas also helped people understand the wonders of God and Creation.

Thomas spent his life studying about God and helping others understand the Catholic faith. For this reason, in 1323, Pope John XXII named him a saint, and in 1567, Pope Pius V named him a Doctor of the Church. Although Thomas lived long ago, people continue to learn from his writings. Because of his great intelligence, he is the patron saint of schools and students.

Our Church Teaches

God and everything he creates is good. In the Bible, we read about God and the Creation of the world. Through God's Son, who is the Word of God, and through the Holy Spirit, we learn that there is one God in Three Divine Persons—the Father, the Son, and the Holy Spirit. One God in Three Divine Persons is called the Holy Trinity.

Jesus taught us to call God our Father. Jesus Christ, God's only Son, sent us the Holy Spirit. The Spirit guides the Church to do the work of Christ. Throughout the Bible, we learn more about the work of the Trinity in our lives.

 GO TO **page 392 to read more about the Holy Trinity.**

We Believe

God reveals himself as one God in Three Divine Persons—the Father, the Son, and the Holy Spirit.

Faith Words

Holy Trinity
One God in Three Divine Persons is called the Holy Trinity. The Three Divine Persons are the Father, the Son, and the Holy Spirit.

Activity

Look at each scrambled word. Cross out the two extra letters in each word to reveal a word that tells something about the Trinity. Write the word on the line. A star tells you that the word begins with a capital letter.

1. *efateher _____

2. gorodnesls _____

3. *njelsus _____

4. lrodving _____

5. *crelatpor _____

6. *srpiorit _____

How can we help others to see God's goodness?

31

Respond

Rachel Carson and Caring for Creation

We are all part of God's Creation. He gives us the responsibility to care for people and our environment. One person who showed concern for God's Creation was the American writer Rachel Carson.

Rachel Carson was born in Springdale, Pennsylvania. As an adult, she worked for the U.S. Fish and Wildlife Service. In her writings, Rachel Carson explained that all creation must be respected. She wrote that if pesticides are not used properly, animals and fish could die. She also said that using pesticides on crops could poison our food. Because of her statements, the use of pesticides was restricted in many parts of the world. In 1963, she won an award for her books about respecting life and the environment.

Activities

1. Think about how you respect people and care for the environment. Design a button that shows others one way you do this. When you are finished, share your design with a partner.

2. Look at the picture below. Circle the places that show God's Creation not being respected.

3. Write about one way we can show our thanks to God. Tell how we can take care of the gifts we have been given.

_____

_____

_____

_____

_____

How can we praise God for the gift of Creation?

Prayer Celebration

A Prayer of Praise

We can see God's goodness all around us. Let us give thanks and praise to God for giving us everything that is good.

Leader: All you waters above the heavens,

All: bless the Lord.

Leader: Sun and moon,

All: bless the Lord.

Leader: All you winds,

All: bless the Lord.

Leader: You dolphins and all water creatures,

All: bless the Lord.

Leader: All the birds of the air,

All: bless the Lord.

Leader: Let us bless the Father, and the Son, and the Holy Spirit.

All: Let us praise and exalt him above all forever.

From Daniel 3:59–80, in the Liturgy of the Hours

A **Complete** the sentences with words from the box.

1. Everything that God created is _____.

2. The Holy Spirit guided people to write all that
   is contained in the _____.

3. Jesus taught us to call God our _____.

4. The Holy Spirit guides the Church to do the work
   of _____.

5. Saint Thomas Aquinas wrote about the mystery
   of the _____.

Holy Trinity
truth
good
Father
Bible
Christ

B **Respond** to the following.

1. Name or draw five things the story of Creation tells us that God created.

2. Write about one way you can care for God's Creation.

_____

_____

_____

_____

C Circle the letter of the best answer.

1. The first story in the Bible is about the _____.

   a. birth of Jesus

   b. Creation of the world

   c. first Christian community

   d. Resurrection

2. One God in the Three Divine Persons is called the _____.

   a. holy Catholic Church

   b. Communion of Saints

   c. Holy Trinity

   d. Holy Eucharist

3. Rachel Carson wrote books about _____.

   a. world travel

   b. respecting life and the environment

   c. stories of Creation

   d. world peace

4. We are to take care of all that _____.

   a. we want

   b. is around us

   c. our friends give us

   d. God creates

D Respond to the following questions.

1. Who are the Three Divine Persons of the Holy Trinity?

   _____

   _____

   _____

2. What can someone your age do to give thanks and praise to God for the gifts of Creation?

   _____

   _____

   _____

Take Home

FAMILY TIME

Praise and Thanksgiving

It is natural to express your thanks when you are given a wonderful gift. When you are in the presence of someone great, it is natural to praise that person. The parish community gathers regularly to praise and thank God the Father who loves us so much that he sent his Son, Jesus, and remains with us through the Holy Spirit.

ACTIVITY

Partners Is there someone you know whom you want to thank and praise? This person could be a teacher, someone you work with, a relative, or a friend. Take a few minutes to send him or her a note of thanks or praise.

WEEKLY PLANNER

On Sunday
Listen carefully to the Lord's Prayer. What parts of it are a prayer of praise, and what parts of it are a prayer of thanksgiving?

On the Web
blestarewe.com

Visit our Web site for the saint of the day and the reflection question of the week.

Saint of the Week

Saint Pius X
(1835–1914)

For nearly 19 centuries, Catholics first received Holy Communion around the age of 13, after being confirmed. Saint Pius X, less than 100 years ago, changed the rule allowing children "at age of reason" (about 7 years old) to receive their First Communion.

Patron Saint of: first communicants
Feast Day: August 21

A Prayer for the Week

Lord, Saint Pius X taught that you gave us the precious gift of your own self in the Eucharist. We need you in our lives. Help us stay close to you always. Amen.

FAMILY TIME

✝ Scripture Background

In the Time of Jesus

Sabbath On Friday evening, the Jews of Palestine listened for the sound of the ram's horn that signaled the start of the Sabbath. After the sixth blast, every family gathered for their evening meal. Dressed in their best clothes, they ate special food reserved for the Sabbath. This included freshly baked bread called *challos*. Afterwards, the family recited the benediction. The head of the family then raised a cup of wine and chanted the blessing of sanctification.

In 1 Corinthians 11:23–26, Paul reminds us about Jesus sharing bread and wine with his disciples at the Last Supper.

Our Catholic Tradition in Prayer

Bead-prayers We think of the Most Holy Rosary with its sets of beads as unique among Catholic devotions. Yet, there are many bead-prayers in the Roman Catholic tradition. Early Christians recited the Lord's Prayer many times during the day to keep focused on their beliefs. Some tied a knot on a string each time they recited the prayer. The term *prayer bead* come from the Middle English word *bede*, meaning 'prayer.'

2 Praise and Thanksgiving

 It is right and just.

Preface of the Mass

Share

Debra and Michael were excited. They had just given their grandmother a very special gift for her birthday. It was a picture frame they had made in art class. The frame held a picture of Debra and Michael with their grandmother.

"I love it! It is the best gift I have ever received," their grandmother said.

A few weeks later, Debra and Michael went with their parents to visit their grandmother. Michael asked Debra, "Do you think Nana really liked her gift?" Debra said, "Let's see what she did with it when we get there."

When they arrived at their grandmother's house, they found the picture in a special place in her living room.

"I will treasure it forever. I am very grateful for your gift," their grandmother said.

Activity

God blesses you with family and friends who give you special gifts. Complete the note to thank someone for a gift you have received.

Thank you

---

for

How can we praise and thank God?

Hear & Believe

 Worship We Give Thanks and Praise

God gives us many gifts. We can thank God for these gifts
by praying each day. The most important way Catholics pray and
give thanks is the Sunday **Eucharist**. The **Mass** is the most perfect
prayer of thanksgiving and praise to God. At Mass we joyfully sing
and praise God as a community. We gather together as God's holy
people. Together we pray:

Papal Mass, Cuba, 1998

> God our Father, you have brought us here together
> so that we can give you thanks and praise
> for all the wonderful things you have done.
>
> We thank you for all that is beautiful in the world
> and for the happiness you have given us.
>
> We praise you for daylight
> and for your word which lights up our minds.
>
> We praise you for the earth,
> and all the people who live on it,
> and for our life which comes from you.
>
> We know that you are good.
> You love us and do great things for us.
>
> *Eucharistic Prayer for Masses with Children I*

The Gift of Jesus

Through the Mass we give thanks and praise to God for blessing us with his greatest gift, his Son, Jesus. We show our love for God by accepting this gift and inviting Jesus to enter our hearts. The thanks and praise we give to God show him how much this gift means to us.

The two main parts of the Mass are the **Liturgy of the Word** and the **Liturgy of the Eucharist**. In the Liturgy of the Word, Christ is present as we listen to God's Word from the Bible. In the Liturgy of the Eucharist, Christ is present when, through the power of the Holy Spirit, the bread and wine become the Body and Blood of Christ.

Activity

The celebration of the Eucharist is the Church's prayer of thanksgiving to God. Write two ways we thank God at Mass.

_____

_____

_____

_____

_____

_____

_____

Faith Words

Mass

The celebration of the Eucharist is called the Mass. At Mass we share in the life, Death, and Resurrection of Jesus Christ.

Liturgy of the Word

The Liturgy of the Word is the part of the Mass in which we hear the Word of God in the Scriptures.

Liturgy of the Eucharist

The Liturgy of the Eucharist is the part of the Mass in which the bread and wine become the Body and Blood of Christ.

When did Jesus first celebrate the Eucharist?

41

Hear & Believe

✝ The Last Supper

On Holy Thursday we remember Jesus Christ giving us the Eucharist at the meal we call the Last Supper. We listen to the following Scripture story read during the Mass of the Lord's Supper on Holy Thursday.

When Jesus knew that his enemies would soon arrest him, he gathered with his disciples for a special meal. They met together in Jerusalem in a large room that was prepared just for them. Jesus began the meal by giving thanks to the Father for his many blessings. Then he took the bread and broke it. As Jesus did this, he said, "This is my body that is given up for you." Jesus then shared the bread with his disciples.

At the end of the supper, Jesus took the cup that was filled with wine. He said, "This is the cup of my blood that is given up for you."

Jesus told his disciples how much he loved them. He asked them to share this meal often, until he returned at the end of time.

Based on 1 Corinthians 11:23–26

Our Church Teaches

We respond to God's goodness by celebrating the Mass. Through the **priest**, we are united with the Father. We also remember the Sacrifice Jesus made to save us from our sins. Through the Holy Spirit our gifts of bread and wine become the Body and Blood of Jesus Christ. When we receive the Body of Christ, we think about God's goodness and want to share it with others. All of the prayers and actions at Mass make up one complete celebration.

Activity

Use the secret code to find a special response we use at Mass. Fill in the blank with the letter that matches the number.

1	2	3	4	5	6	7	8	9	10	11	12	13
A	B	C	D	E	F	G	H	I	J	K	L	M

14	15	16	17	18	19	20	21	22	23	24	25	26
N	O	P	Q	R	S	T	U	V	W	X	Y	Z

___ ___ ___ ___ ___ ___ ___ ___ ___
9   20   9   19   18   9   7   8   20

___ ___ ___ ___ ___ ___ ___.
1   14   4   10   21   19   20

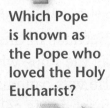

Which Pope is known as the Pope who loved the Holy Eucharist?

Respond

Saint Pius X

Giuseppe (jeh-SEP-ee) Sarto grew up in a little village in northern Italy. His father was a mailman, and his mother was a seamstress. Even though his family was poor, Giuseppe did not mind. He liked growing up in a large family with his nine brothers and sisters. One thing that Giuseppe did not like was that he had to wait until he was twelve years old to receive Holy Communion.

As Giuseppe grew up, he felt that God was calling him to be a priest. When he was old enough, he left his village and entered a seminary. One day, Giuseppe read in the Bible that Jesus said, "Let the children come to me." Giuseppe thought a lot about these words and about all the parishes filled with young children. He remembered how when he was a child, he had wanted so much to receive Jesus in the Eucharist but had to wait until he was older. From that day on, Giuseppe dreamed about making it possible for younger children to receive the Eucharist.

In 1858, Giuseppe became a priest. For many years, he worked in poor parishes, helping the people. He later became a bishop, and in 1903 he was chosen to be the Pope. He took the name Pius X, and he remembered his dream about helping the children. Pope Pius X encouraged a change in church custom, allowing children as young as seven years old to receive the Eucharist. The Pope also encouraged all Catholics to attend Mass often and receive Holy Communion. Because of this, Pope Pius X became known as the Pope who loved the Holy Eucharist. He was canonized a saint in 1954. His feast day is celebrated on August 21.

Activities

1. Match each sentence with the correct photograph that shows a way you exprerience Christ at Mass. Draw a line to each picture.

Christ is present in the assembly at Mass.

Christ is present in the words from Scripture.

Christ is present in the Eucharist.

2. Think back to the day you made your First Communion. How did you feel about receiving Jesus in the Eucharist for the first time?

_____

_____

_____

How can we give thanks and praise to God?

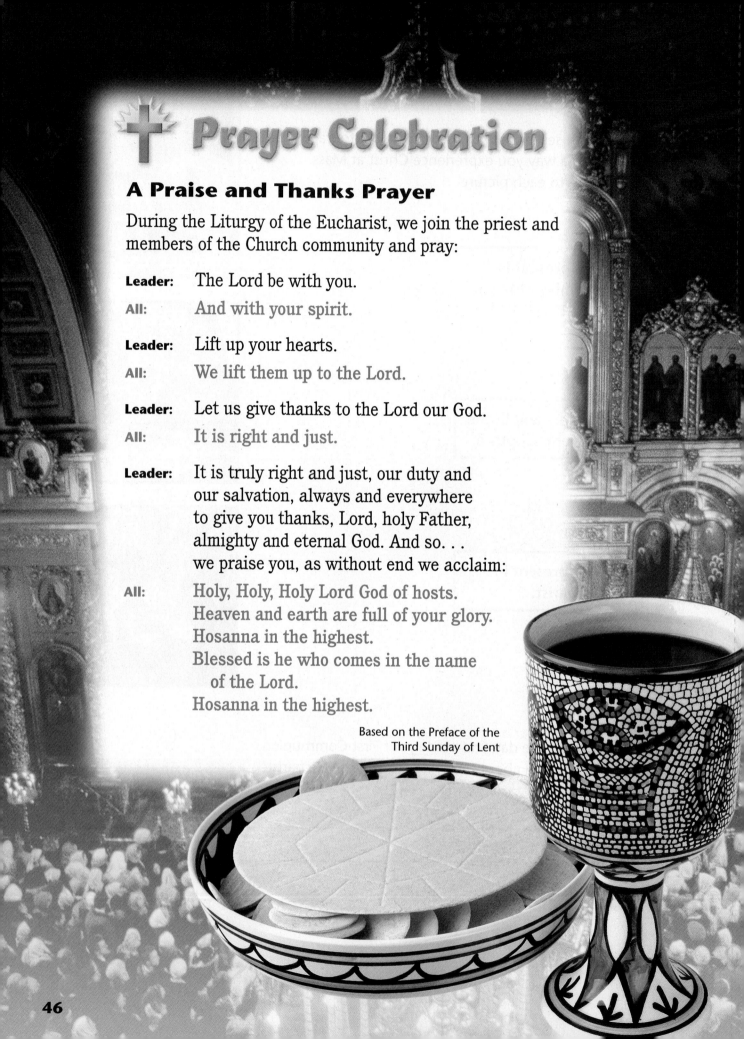

✝ Prayer Celebration

A Praise and Thanks Prayer

During the Liturgy of the Eucharist, we join the priest and members of the Church community and pray:

Leader: The Lord be with you.

All: And with your spirit.

Leader: Lift up your hearts.

All: We lift them up to the Lord.

Leader: Let us give thanks to the Lord our God.

All: It is right and just.

Leader: It is truly right and just, our duty and our salvation, always and everywhere to give you thanks, Lord, holy Father, almighty and eternal God. And so. . . we praise you, as without end we acclaim:

All: Holy, Holy, Holy Lord God of hosts.
Heaven and earth are full of your glory.
Hosanna in the highest.
Blessed is he who comes in the name
 of the Lord.
Hosanna in the highest.

Based on the Preface of the
Third Sunday of Lent

A **Choose** a word from one of these picture frames to complete each sentence.

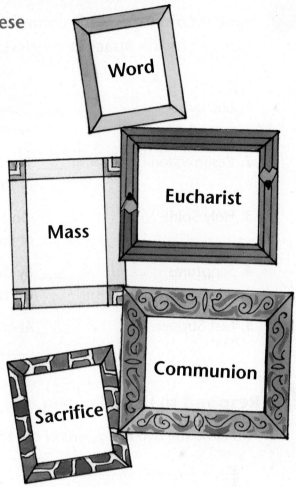

1. Through the _____, we give thanks and praise to God.

2. The part of the Mass in which God speaks to us through Scripture is called the Liturgy of the _____.

3. Through the power of the Holy Spirit, the bread and wine become the Body and Blood of Jesus Christ during the Liturgy of the _____.

4. We receive Jesus Christ in Holy _____ at Mass.

5. At the celebration of the Mass, we remember the _____ Jesus made to save us from our sins.

Word

Eucharist

Mass

Communion

Sacrifice

B **Circle** the correct words to complete the prayer we pray during the Liturgy of the Eucharist.

Holy, Holy, Holy Lord God of *(wonder, hosts, strength, wisdom).*

Heaven and *(Earth, sky, moon, stars)* are full of your glory.
Hosanna in the highest.

Blessed is he who *(loves, comes, helps, heals)* in the name of the Lord.

Hosanna in the highest.

Chapter Review

C **Match** column A with column B by writing the correct number in the space provided.

A

1. Eucharist

2. Resurrection

3. Holy Spirit

4. Scriptures

5. Last Supper

B

_____ Christ is present at Mass when we listen to the words from the _____.

_____ The Mass is another name for the celebration of the _____.

_____ On Holy Thursday, we remember the actions of Jesus at the _____.

_____ By the power of the _____, Christ is present in the Eucharist.

_____ At Mass, we share in the life, Death, and _____ of Jesus Christ.

D **Respond** to the following.

1. Name the two main parts of the Mass.

_____

_____

2. Write one thing you would tell a seven-year-old who is preparing to receive Holy Communion for the first time.

_____

_____

_____

_____

_____

FAMILY TIME

The Commandments and God's Covenant

A covenant binds together two or more people for their entire life. The people of Israel used the word *covenant* to describe the relationship God established with them. In the Bible a covenant is more serious than a contract and is entered into more out of love and commitment than out of obligation.

ACTIVITY

Rainbows God made an everlasting covenant with Noah and with all living things. God told Noah that the rainbow was the symbol of his promise never again to destroy all the living with a flood. Look in your house for things that can cause a rainbow such as a soap bubble, or a prism. How many can you find?

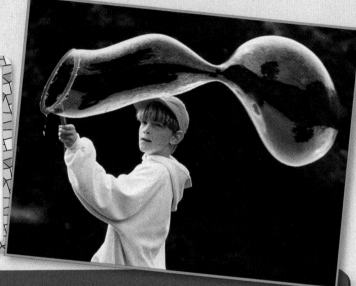

WEEKLY PLANNER

On Sunday

How will you bring home the sense of holiness that you experience at church and share it with others?

On the Web

blestarewe.com

Visit our Web site for the saint of the day and the reflection question of the week.

Saint of the Week

Saint Justa
(first century)

Saint Justa was a potter. She was also the sister of Saint Ruffina. Someone offered to purchase a significant amount of her pottery at a high price. When the sisters discovered that the pieces of pottery were to be used in pagan rituals, they smashed them all.

Patron Saint of: potters, Seville, Spain
Feast Day: July 19

A Prayer for the Week

You have given us the greatest gift, Lord, by inviting us into a covenant with you. Like Saint Justa, help us to learn to live faithfully with you and with others. Amen.

Take Home

FAMILY TIME

✝ Scripture Background

Before the Time of Jesus

Signs of God's Presence   In the Old Testament, God sometimes appeared to others through forces of nature, such as fire, lightning, or storms. Moses experienced God's presence through the burning bush and later as a pillar of fire leading the Israelites through the wilderness. These dramatic sights signaled God's presence and revealed his power and authority. They are most common in Genesis and Exodus, the first two books of the Bible.

Read Exodus 19:16–25 to find out how God made his presence known to Moses and the Israelites on Mount Sinai.

OUR CATHOLIC TRADITION in Film

Bible Movies   Many movies have been based on events in the Bible. Two of the most famous are *The Ten Commandments* and *Jesus of Nazareth*. These movies portrayed larger-than-life Bible characters and brought the story of Salvation to the movies. You may want to rent them and watch them with your family. You can then contrast *The Ten Commandments* with the more recent animated movie *The Prince of Egypt*.

3 The Commandments and God's Covenant

 I am the LORD, your God. You shall not have other gods besides me.

Based on Exodus 20:2–3

Share

God loves us and promises to be present in our lives. We make promises to God, our friends, and our family to show them how important they are to us. When we keep our promises, we make others happy.

Activity

Think of two special people in your life. In the boxes below, write a promise to each person. Then try to keep your promises.

Dear _____,

I promise to _____

_____

_____

_____

Dear _____,

I promise to _____

_____

_____

_____

What did God give to his people to show them how to live?

Hear & Believe

✝ Scripture The Ten Commandments

More than 3,000 years ago, God led the Hebrew people out of slavery in Egypt. God promised to lead them to their own land where they would be free. This land was known as the Promised Land.

Moses and the Hebrew people were in the desert, traveling to the Promised Land. One day, God told Moses to gather the people near a mountain. There they saw lightning flash and heard thunder rumble and a trumpet sound. God sent these signs. He wanted the people to know that he would always be with them.

Moses climbed up the mountain. There God spoke to him. God gave Moses ten laws written on two slabs, or tablets, of stone. The laws showed how the people were to live with fairness and kindness. "If the people follow these rules, I will protect them," God told Moses. "I will give them long and rich lives."

Moses went down the mountain. He read the people the laws, which we call the **Ten Commandments**. The people said, "We will do all God asks."

Based on Exodus 19:16–25; 20:1–26; 24:12

1. I am the LORD, your God. You shall not have other gods besides me.
2. You shall not take the name of the LORD, your God, in vain.
3. Remember to keep holy the Sabbath day.
4. Honor your father and mother.
5. You shall not kill.
6. You shall not commit adultery.
7. You shall not steal.
8. You shall not bear false witness against your neighbor.
9. You shall not covet your neighbor's wife.
10. You shall not covet anything that belongs to your neighbor.

We Worship God

God made the **Covenant**, or sacred agreement, with the Hebrew people. The Hebrew people were bound by the Covenant to obey the Ten Commandments. These laws are part of the natural world that God created. As Catholics, we too must follow the laws contained in the Ten Commandments.

God's Laws of Love

God gave the Hebrew people the Commandments to help them remain close to him and to one another. The Ten Commandments are God's laws. They are ways of showing love for God and for other people. They are rules to help us live together in peace.

The first three Commandments tell us how to love God. The Fourth through Sixth Commandments guide us in respecting the gift of life. The Seventh Commandment guides us in respecting other people's property. The Eighth Commandment helps us to be honest and truthful. The Ninth and Tenth Commandments remind us to be satisfied with the gifts God gives us. Jesus tells us that to be his disciples, we must follow the Ten Commandments.

Activity

Why do you think the Ten Commandments are called God's laws of love?

_____

_____

_____

Faith Words

Ten Commandments
The Ten Commandments are the laws God gave to Moses to help us live in peace with God and others.

Covenant
A covenant is an agreement between people or groups of people. God made the Covenant, or sacred agreement, with the Hebrew people.

How can we follow God's laws?

Hear & Believe

 ## Understanding the 1st, 2nd, and 3rd Commandments

The First Commandment teaches us to put God first in our lives and to love and serve him as the one true God. At church or in our homes, we may have **sacred images**, statues or pictures of God, Mary, and the saints, to help us pray. We treat these sacred images with respect and care. However, we do not worship them. We **worship** only God. In the Second Commandment, we are told to respect the name of God. This means that we never say the name of God or Jesus in anger. The Third Commandment says that we should keep holy the LORD's Day. Because of this, we set aside a whole day to honor God.

GO TO page 404 and read the right-hand column of the Ten Commandments chart to learn more about how to live the commandments.

Activity

1. Put the story of Moses and the Ten Commandments in the correct order from 1 to 7.

   ____ Moses read the laws to the people.

   ____ They saw lightning flash and heard thunder rumble.

   ____ The Hebrew people gathered near a mountain.

   ____ Moses climbed up the mountain.

   ____ God led Moses and the Hebrew people out of slavery.

   ____ God gave Moses ten laws written on two tablets of stone.

   ____ Moses went down the mountain.

Our Church Teaches

Through the ages, God made his covenants with Noah, Abraham, and Moses. We honor God's law today. God asks us to serve him and place him first in our lives. God asks us to speak his name with reverence rather than anger. We show our love for God by spending time with him, especially at Mass on Sundays and holy days. The Church guides us as we try to honor God's law.

Activity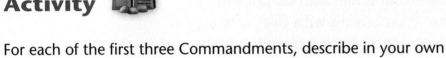

For each of the first three Commandments, describe in your own words how you think God wants us to act.

First Commandment

_____

_____

_____

_____

Second Commandment

_____

_____

_____

_____

Third Commandment

_____

_____

_____

_____

How can we learn from Saint Teresa?

Respond

Saint Teresa and Becoming Closer to God

Saint Teresa was born in Ávila, Spain, in 1515. As a child, she loved to read about the saints with her brother, Rodrigo. When she was eighteen, Teresa became a nun in a Carmelite convent. At that time the nuns in her order led a very social life. Teresa enjoyed talking to the other nuns and entertaining visitors who came to the convent.

As time went on, Teresa felt that material things were distracting her from a close relationship with God. She taught the Carmelite nuns to live simply, spending more time in prayer. Teresa wanted to place God first in her life.

She learned to pray in silence for many hours. She even wrote books about prayer and how to worship God.

We honor Saint Teresa on October 15. She showed us how to draw closer to God through prayer.

By following the Commandments, we choose to grow closer to God. When we place God first in our lives, we are responding to God's covenant with love.

The famous walled city of Ávila, Spain, as it looks today.

Activities

1. Read the sentence below. Each sentence refers to one of the first three Commandments. Write the number of the Commandment that each sentence matches.

    a. Juan went to Mass last Sunday even though he stayed up late the night before. _____

    b. Maryellen and her family pray before each meal. They thank God for their food and for his love. _____

    c. Stephen believes that money is not the most important thing in life. _____

    d. Caitlin told her friend Jake not to use Jesus' name when he gets mad. _____

2. How does your parish live out the first three Commandments?

_____

_____

_____

_____

Prayer Celebration

A Prayer of Petition

The word *petition* means "to ask God for something that is needed." We can pray that God will help us follow his laws of love. In the following prayer, the Leader reads petitions based on the Ten Commandments.

Leader: That we may live the first three Commandments by showing our love for God,

All: help us, Lord, to follow your Commandments.

Leader: That we may live the Fourth through Sixth Commandments by respecting the gift of life,

All: help us, Lord, to follow your Commandments.

Leader: That we may follow the Seventh Commandment by respecting other people's property,

All: help us, Lord, to follow your Commandments.

Leader: That we may follow the Eighth Commandment by being honest and truthful,

All: help us, Lord, to follow your Commandments.

Leader: That we may follow the Ninth and Tenth Commandments by being satisfied with the gifts God gives us,

All: help us, Lord, to follow your Commandments.

3 Chapter Review

A **Match** the words in column A with the definitions in column B.

A	B
1. Covenant	___ received the Ten Commandments from God.
2. worship	___ the sacred agreement between God and the Hebrew people.
3. sacred images	___ are the laws that God gave to Moses.
4. Ten Commandments	___ means to give honor and praise God.
5. Moses	___ are statues or pictures that remind us of God, Mary, and the saints.

B **Respond** to these questions.

1. How did Saint Teresa place God first in her life?

_____

_____

_____

_____

_____

_____

2. Why is it important to keep the promises we make to God and other people?

_____

_____

_____

_____

3 Chapter Review

C Circle the letter of the best answer.

1. God made a _____ with Moses.
   a. covenant
   b. sign
   c. meeting
   d. symbol

2. The _____ are God's rules that help us live in peace.
   a. Scriptures
   b. Ten Commandments
   c. Rules for Living
   d. Petitions

3. The _____ Commandment tells us to set aside a whole day to honor God.
   a. First
   b. Second
   c. Third
   d. Fourth

4. The Ten Commandments guide us in _____ the one, true God.
   a. explaining
   b. ignoring
   c. serving
   d. defending

5. The _____ Commandment tells us to place God first in our lives.
   a. First
   b. Second
   c. Third
   d. Fourth

6. A prayer in which we ask God for something that is needed is called a _____.
   a. blessing
   b. petition
   c. thanksgiving
   d. request

D Respond to the following questions.

1. What do the first three Commandments tell us?

_____

2. How does the Eighth Commandment help us?

_____

Take Home

FAMILY TIME

The Commandments and the Lord's Prayer

One of the ways we express our relationship with God is through prayer. The prayer that Jesus taught us, the Lord's Prayer, should be the model for all the praying that we do. This prayer is an example of the relationship that God invites us into—one of the closest of relationships, that of parent and child. This lesson features the Lord's Prayer and its meaning for us as Christians.

ACTIVITY

Prayer Card Take a large index card or a piece of colored posterboard, about six inches long by two inches wide and write the words to the Lord's Prayer on it. Decorate it with stickers or drawings. Seal it with clear-plastic contact paper. Punch a hole in the top and run a piece of ribbon or yarn through it. Now you have a prayer card that you can use as a bookmark.

WEEKLY PLANNER

On Sunday
Pray the Lord's Prayer at Mass with a special feeling of gratitude that God invited us to call him Father.

On the Web
blestarewe.com

Visit our Web site for the saint of the day and the reflection question of the week.

Saint of the Week

 Saint Peter of Alcantara (1499–1562)

Saint Peter became a Franciscan when he was 16 and an ordained priest at 25. He was known for his preaching and lived a private life in deep prayer when he wasn't conducting missions. Saint Peter helped reform his religious order and helped Saint Teresa of Ávila do the same for the Carmelite community.

Patron Saint of: Brazil
Feast Day: October 19

A Prayer for the Week

We are your children, Lord, because you told us to call you Father. Help us pray deeply to you like Saint Peter of Alcantara did. Amen.

Take Home

FAMILY TIME

✝ Scripture Background

Before the Time of Jesus

Father In Bible times, a father had certain responsibilities toward his family. As head of the household, he protected his children and provided for their spiritual and physical needs. It was a father's duty to discipline his children and to oversee their religious studies. He had special obligations to his sons, such as having them circumcised and helping them learn a trade.

Jesus taught us to address God as Father in the Lord's Prayer found in Matthew 6:5–13.

OUR CATHOLIC TRADITION in Music

Sung Prayer The Lord's Prayer has been set to music many times. Perhaps the best-known rendition is by Albert Hay Malotte. Perry Como, host of a TV show in the 1950s and 1960s, sang this prayer on his show. Since then, gifted composers such as Leonard Bernstein and Dave Brubeck have written and recorded new musical versions of the Lord's Prayer.

Dave Brubeck, composer of the Mass setting *To Hope!*

4 The Commandments and the Lord's Prayer

 Your Father knows what you need before you ask him.

Matthew 6:8

Share

God created the many wonderful people in our lives. We grow close to others when we share our thoughts and feelings with them.

Activity

Look at the pictures below. Write what thoughts or feelings you think these people are sharing.

How do we share our thoughts and feelings with God?

✝ Scripture The Lord's Prayer

Jesus prayed often. He taught people how to pray so that they could speak to God, too. He said, "When you pray, do not be like those who pray where everyone will see them. Instead, go to a private place in your home. Pray in secret. Your heavenly Father will know you are praying and will reward you. Do not pray like those who talk by using many words. Your Father knows what you need even before you ask. This is how you should pray:

> Our Father who art in heaven,
> hallowed be thy name.
> Thy kingdom come.
> Thy will be done
> on earth, as it is in heaven.
> Give us this day our daily bread,
> and forgive us our trespasses,
> as we forgive those who trespass against us,
> and lead us not into temptation,
> but deliver us from evil."

Based on Matthew 6:5–13

Prayer

Prayer is opening ourselves to God, who is all-loving. God wants us to share our thoughts and feelings with him. Through prayer we can grow closer to God and grow strong in our **faith**. God answers us when we listen with our hearts.

When we pray the Lord's Prayer, we praise and thank God for his goodness, **mercy**, and love. We ask for God's help in spreading the message of the **Kingdom of God**. As the first three Commandments tell us, we praise God, we respect God's name, and we honor sacred and holy times in our lives. God, Father, Son, and Holy Spirit, guides us toward his Kingdom.

Activity

Think about how you have experienced God's goodness today and write a special prayer of thanks.

Our Father,

_____

_____

_____

_____

Amen.

GO TO page 409 to read more about the Lord's Prayer.

Faith Words

faith
Faith is belief in God.

mercy
Mercy is the loving kindness that God shows to sinners.

Kingdom of God
The Kingdom of God is God's promise of justice, peace, and joy that all his people will share at the end of time.

How should we pray?

Hear & Believe

Praying to Our Father in Heaven

Mrs. Brodie said to her class, "Before we gather in the prayer corner, think about how God listens to your deepest thoughts and feelings." As the class reflected on this, Mrs. Brodie passed out sheets of paper. She continued, "Write one thing you would like to change about yourself to help you become a better person. When you're finished, we'll pray for God's help in making these changes."

Matt didn't have to think long about what he might write. Just this morning, his friend Pete had said, "Do you realize how often you find fault with someone or something? Your comments really can hurt." Matt was surprised by his friend's words, but after some thought, he realized Pete made an important point. Just this morning, he had complained when classmates forgot their lines during play practice. He had made a few mistakes during the practice, too, but no one had criticized him.

Matt wrote on his paper "I'd like to be less judgmental and more accepting of others." He put his paper in the basket on the prayer table. His classmates did the same. Then they joined hands and prayed the Lord's Prayer.

Our Church Teaches

God knows everything about us. Yet God still wants us to share our lives with him through prayer. When we pray, we show our love for God. God lovingly hears our prayers and guides us to him.

The Lord's Prayer is a special prayer in which we honor God and thank him for his goodness. We believe in God's promise of a loving Kingdom filled with peace and joy. The Lord's Prayer sums up the Gospel message of Jesus.

Activity

The circle contains a hidden message that describes an important way to stay close to God. To find the message, write the letter under the arrow in the circle in the first blank space. Continuing clockwise, write every third letter in the remaining blank spaces.

__ __ __ __   __ __ __ __ __ __ __ __ __ __ __

Based on 1 Thessalonians 5:17

How should we live to be happy in the Kingdom of God?

Respond

Responding to the Commandments in Prayer

When God made the Covenant with the Hebrew people, he reminded them that his great love is forever. He asked them to respond to his love by showing love for him in return, and by sharing his goodness with others. Through the Lord's Prayer, we learn how to respond to the Ten Commandments in prayer.

Activities

1. The first three Commandments require us to give proper worship and respect to God. Complete the chart below by writing ways you can obey the Commandments and follow the Lord's Prayer. You can refer to pages 404 and 409 for help.

The Ten Commandments	The Lord's Prayer	My Response
I — I am the LORD, your God. You shall not have other gods besides me.	Our Father who art in heaven	List one way you can worship God. _____ _____
II — You shall not take the name of the LORD, your God, in vain.	Hallowed be thy name	List two ways you can respect the name of God. _____ _____
III — Remember to keep holy the LORD's Day.	Our Father who art in heaven	List a second way you can worship God. _____ _____

2. Using American Sign Language, learn to sign the following phrase from the Lord's Prayer.

Our   Father   who art

in   heaven,   hallowed be

thy   name.

How can we use sign language as a way to pray?

Prayer Celebration

Signing the Lord's Prayer

Leader: Let us show our love and respect for God as we sign the Lord's Prayer.

All:
Our Father who art in heaven,
hallowed be thy name.
Thy kingdom come.
Thy will be done
on earth, as it is in heaven.
Give us this day our daily bread,
and forgive us our
trespasses, as we
forgive those who trespass against us,
and lead us not into temptation,
but deliver us from evil.
Amen.

Father

4 Chapter Review

A **Circle** the letter of the best answer.

1. In the Lord's Prayer, we give _____ to God.
   a. mercy and forgiveness
   b. praise and thanks
   c. gifts and talents
   d. thoughts and prayers

2. Belief in God is called _____.
   a. love
   b. thanks
   c. hope
   d. faith

3. We pray the Lord's Prayer to share our hope for the coming of _____.
   a. the Holy Spirit
   b. the Kingdom of God
   c. Creation
   d. Moses

4. The loving kindness that God shows to sinners is called _____.
   a. goodness
   b. mercy
   c. peace
   d. kindness

5. Through the _____, we learn how to respond to the Commandments in prayer.
   a. world
   b. Lord's Prayer
   c. Church
   d. Kingdom of God

B **Write** the word from the Lord's Prayer that is being signed in each picture.

_____   _____   _____

Chapter Review

C **Match** column A with column B by writing the correct number in the space provided. Use page 409 for help.

A

1. hallowed be thy name
2. forgive us our tresspasses
3. lead us not into temptation
4. Amen
5. Our Father
6. Thy kingom come
7. Give us this day our daily bread
8. deliver us from evil

B

_____ We pray that God will protect us from what is harmful.

_____ I believe.

_____ We pray for our needs.

_____ We respect God's name.

_____ We ask God for forgiveness.

_____ We pray that everyone will live as Jesus teaches us to live.

_____ We ask God to help us do what is right.

_____ God is our Father.

D **Respond** to the following.

1. Write two things Jesus taught us about prayer.

_____

_____

_____

_____

2. What advice about prayer would you give to someone your age who wants to pray?

_____

_____

_____

Faith in Action

Good Stewards   A steward is someone who is given the responsibility of caring for something. God calls us to be stewards of his Creation. In the places where we live, learn, and play, God wants us to make a difference as we care for Creation. When we work together and all do our part, we can carry out this important responsibility. One way we can care for Creation is by writing letters to government officials who make decisions that help protect and preserve the environment.

In Everyday Life

Activity   Unscramble the words and use them to fill in the blank spaces. Then write about how you can help care for each place. The first one is started for you.

h r c u c h   1. In the c h u r c h , I can _____.

h l c o o s   2. In __ __ __ o __ __, I can _____.

e h m o   3. At __ __ __ e, I can _____.

In Your Parish

Activity   After each statement, write what you could do to be a good steward of creation.

1. Write what you would say in a letter to your parish council asking if the plates, glasses, and eating utensils used at parish dinners could be recyclable and biodegradable.

   _____

   _____

2. Write what you would say to your principal asking if your school can recycle paper products, glass and plastic.

   _____

   _____

Faith in Action

Altar Servers   To assist at Mass as an altar server is both a privilege and a responsibility. It is a chance to be an example and to set a tone of dignity and reverence before, during, and after Mass. The altar server encourages everyone to participate with appropriate gestures, such as sitting, standing, kneeling, bowing, and genuflecting. Helping to prepare the altar, assisting with the bread and wine, and holding the prayer book, or *Sacramentary* are just some of the duties of the altar server.

In Everyday Life

Activity   We can honor and respect those we meet in our daily life. Read the puzzle pieces. Then write how someone who hears each message from you might feel about himself or herself.

Do you much   know how I love you?

Keep up the   good work!

_____   _____

_____   _____

_____   _____

In Your Parish

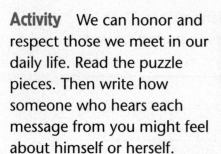

P
R
A
I
S
E

_____

_____

_____

_____

_____

_____

Activity   Think of someone you admire in your parish community whose name begins with one of the letters in the word *praise*. Write the name of the person and some words to describe why the person is praiseworthy.

Faith in Action

Teachers Catechists are people who teach us about our Catholic faith. Religion teachers in Catholic schools are also catechists. They share their faith with us. They invite us to trust God's promises and obey his commandments. Through their example, teachers help us love as Jesus did. We, too, can be an example to our friends and younger brothers and sisters. When they see how we love others, honor and respect our parents, and pray to God, they will be encouraged to do the same.

In Everyday Life

Activity For each day on the timeline, write a word that describes one way that you set a good example for others last week.

LAST WEEK

Sunday	Monday	Tuesday	Wednesday	Thursday	Friday	Saturday
_____	_____	_____	_____	_____	_____	_____

On the line below, write what you will do to set a good example in the week ahead.

_____

_____

In Your Parish

Activity Think about a teacher you admire. Write about the things you most admire about him or her.

_____

_____

_____

_____

Faith in Action

Honoring God through Music Ministries   When we think about God's many gifts to us, our hearts and minds turn to words of praise and thanksgiving. Over the centuries, composers have set words of praise and thanksgiving to music in sacred hymns and songs. The many people who sing in choirs, play musical instruments, and serve as cantors or song leaders make up the music ministry of the parish. These people use their talents to make the Mass a beautiful and prayerful experience for everyone.

In Everyday Life

Activity   What is the title of a favorite song you sing at Mass? Write why you like this particular song. Indicate what it means to you.

In Your Parish

Activity   Look at the words to the right that are often sung at Mass. What does each word express?

_____

_____

Amen

Alleluia

Unit Wrap-up

Take a walk through the garden to find the hidden words you will need to answer the questions below.

1. God wants us to care for his _____.

2. It is right to give God _____ and _____.

3. God made a _____ with the Hebrew people.

4. We pray to our Father in _____.

A **Match** column A with column B by writing the correct number in the space provided.

A

1. Father

2. Word

3. Kingdom of God

4. Holy Spirit

5. sins

6. Bible

7. Eucharist

8. Christ

9. Mass

10. Holy Trinity

B

_____ At Mass, we remember that Jesus saved us from our _____.

_____ The Holy Spirit guided people to write all that is contained in the _____.

_____ Saint Thomas Aquinas helped people learn more about the _____.

_____ We give thanks and praise to God through the celebration of _____.

_____ The Church does the work of _____ through the guidance of the Holy Spirit.

_____ God speaks to us through Scripture in the Liturgy of the _____.

_____ By the power of the _____, Christ is present in the Eucharist.

_____ Jesus taught us to call God our _____.

_____ God's promise of justice, peace, and joy at the end of time is the _____.

_____ In the Liturgy of the _____, the bread and wine become Christ's Body and Blood.

B **Name** the ways Jesus Christ is present at Mass.

_____

_____

_____

_____

C **Complete** the sentences with words from the box.

covenant	Creation	Ten Commandments
Holy Trinity	First	Second
Third	serving	petition

1. The _____ Commandment tells us to place God first in our lives.

2. The first story in the Bible is about the _____ of the world.

3. The _____ Commandment tells us to set aside a whole day to honor God.

4. The Commandments guide us in _____ the one true God.

5. The Ten Commandments are part of God's _____ with us.

6. A prayer in which we ask God for something that is needed is called a _____.

7. The _____ are God's rules that help us live in peace.

8. One God in the Three Divine Persons is called the _____.

D **Write** the First, Second, and Third Commandments.

I _____

_____

II _____

_____

III _____

_____

E **Circle** the letter of the best answer.

1. Statues or pictures that remind us of God, Mary, and the saints are called _____.

   a. holy pictures

   b. memorabilia

   c. sacred images

   d. relics

2. The Mass is another name for the celebration of the _____.

   a. holy orders

   b. Eucharist

   c. Anointing of the Sick

   d. catechumenate

3. On Holy Thursday, we remember the words and actions of Jesus at the _____.

   a. Last Supper

   b. Council of Jerusalem

   c. Wedding of Canaa

   d. Sermon of the Mount

4. At Mass, we share in the life, Death, and _____ of Jesus Christ.

   a. Ascension

   b. Resurrection

   c. ministry

   d. Church

5. Our belief in God is called _____.

   a. hope

   b. faith

   c. temperance

   d. fortitude

6. The loving kindness that God shows to sinners is called _____.

   a. healing

   b. patience

   c. temperance

   d. mercy

F **Respond** to the following questions.

1. What are the names of the Three Divine Persons of the Holy Trinity?

   _____

2. What can someone your age do to care for God's Creation?

   _____

Jesus Is the Son of God

Through his life and teaching, Jesus showed us what it means to be made in the image of God. Through his Death and Resurrection, Christ gave us a share in his divine life forever.

Father, forgive them, they know not what they do.

Luke 23:34

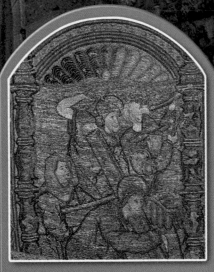

This embroidery on a priest's chasuble shows the Via Dolorosa, the street along which Jesus carried the cross.

Blest Are They

Matthew 5:3–12, Adapted by David Haas

Music by David Haas

VERSE

1. Blest are they, the poor in spir-it,
2. Blest are they, the low-ly ones,

theirs is the king-dom of God.
they shall in-her-it the earth.

Blest are they, full of sor-row,
Blest are they who hun-ger and thirst,

they shall be con-soled.
they shall have their fill.

REFRAIN

Re-joice and be glad!

Bless-ed are you, ho-ly are you!

Re-joice and be glad!

Yours is the king-dom of God!

3. Blest are they who show mercy,
   mercy shall be theirs.
   Blest are they, the pure of heart,
   they shall see God!
   Refrain

4. Blest are they who seek peace;
   they are the children of God.
   Blest are they who suffer in faith,
   the glory of God is theirs.
   Refrain

5. Blest are you who suffer hate,
   all because of me.
   Rejoice and be glad,
   yours is the kingdom; shine for all to see.
   Refrain

Take Home

FAMILY TIME

Jesus, the Image of God

Mirrors give us a representation of ourselves. They reflect back our physical appearance. We speak of Jesus being a "true mirror" of God. Jesus in his words and actions is the true Revelation of God. Jesus makes known to us what God is like and what God expects of us. In following Jesus, we are called to be true images of what God is like.

Ellen cares about people.

ACTIVITY

Mirror Message Make a mirror out of a piece of silver paper or aluminum foil. In the center, write how someone in your family reflects God's image. Give it to that person as a gift!

WEEKLY PLANNER

On Sunday

Remember that Jesus is our true friend and role model. Listen to the words of the Scripture readings at Mass that illustrate Jesus' role in our lives.

On the Web

blestarewe.com

Visit our Web site for the saint of the day and the reflection question of the week.

Saint of the Week

Saint Catherine of Bologna (1413–1463)

Saint Catherine of Bologna traded in a courtly life to join the Poor Clares religious community. She was known for her holiness, piety, and charity. Saint Catherine was also a painter and manuscript illuminator.

Patron Saint of: artists
Feast Day: March 9

A Prayer for the Week

Jesus, we thank you for your example. Like Saint Catherine of Bologna, help us to use our talents, to always give praise to you, our perfect role model. Amen.

Take Home

FAMILY TIME

✝ Scripture Background

In the Time of Jesus

Burial Jewish burials usually took place within a day after the person's death. An important part of the burial custom was the preparation of the body. Family members and friends washed the body, anointed it with spices, and wrapped it in linen. The mourners then carried the body in a procession to the tomb. Rock-cut tombs that were sealed with large stones were common burial sites. After Jesus died on the cross, his body was placed in this type of tomb.

Read about Jesus' Crucifixion in Luke 23:33–56.

OUR CATHOLIC TRADITION in America

City Names Saints are people who have tried to live like Jesus. They are examples for us, as Jesus was an example. They showed us how to be human and also images of God. In our country we have many cities that have been named after saints, for example: St. Louis, San Francisco, St. Paul, and Santa Barbara. They are daily reminders of saints in our midst.

Golden Gate Bridge, San Francisco, CA

5 Jesus, the Image of God

LET US PRAY

Whoever has seen me has seen the Father.

John 14:9

Share

In His Image

There are people in our lives who set a good example for us by being kind, helpful, and loving as Jesus was. We call these people role models. Role models show us how to bring God's goodness into our world. We admire them and try to follow in their footsteps.

Activity

Who do you think is a good role model in your life? On the lines below, write the name of your role model. Then write how this person is kind or helpful.

My role model is: _____

_____

This person is a role model for me because: _____

_____

_____

_____

_____

_____

_____

How did Jesus show us his love?

Hear & Believe

✝ Scripture The Crucifixion

Jesus was God and at the same time human like us. We look to Jesus as an example of how best to live our own lives as Christians. Even in the moments before he died, Jesus showed us how to forgive those who hurt us.

Soldiers hung Jesus upon a wooden cross. Many people watched him suffering. Some leaders watched too, mocking him by saying, "He saved others! Let him save himself now!" The soldiers played games to see who would get his clothes. They also made fun of Jesus. As Jesus was suffering, he said, "Father, forgive them. They do not know what they are doing."

Based on Luke 23:33–37

Jesus Is God's Divine Son

Jesus was sent by God to live among us. Being a man, he experienced pain, suffering, and death.

Jesus is also the Second Divine Person of the Holy Trinity. He is **divine** because he is God's Son. Jesus saved us from our sins by his life, Death, Resurrection, and **Ascension** into Heaven. This is known as the **Paschal Mystery**. The Paschal Mystery is the greatest way Jesus could show God's deep love for each of us. We celebrate the Paschal Mystery and our new life with Jesus every Sunday at Mass.

Faith Words

divine

The word *divine* means "of God." Jesus Christ is both human and divine—that is, he is both true man and true God.

Ascension

The Ascension is the moment when Jesus, in his resurrected body, entered Heaven.

Paschal Mystery

The Paschal Mystery is the life, Death, Resurrection, and Ascension of Jesus Christ.

Activity

Below are two examples of how we should live as Jesus did. Write four other words to describe followers of Jesus. Then circle the word that is the most difficult for you. On the lines below, write a sentence telling why.

considerate _____ _____

forgiving _____ _____

_____

_____

_____

_____

_____

_____

Who is our role model?

Mrs. Griffin Helps Others

Jackie was excited as she waited for Mrs. Griffin to arrive at Holy Cross School. Mrs. Griffin was a volunteer for Jackie's class. She came every week to help Jackie's class with special projects. Jackie also saw Mrs. Griffin every Sunday at Mass. Mrs. Griffin was active in the Church, giving of her time to help others. Jackie knew that Mrs. Griffin visited patients in the hospital and made telephone calls to elderly people who were homebound with no family nearby.

Jackie really liked Mrs. Griffin because she was such a kind and giving person. Mrs. Griffin made Jackie feel important, especially when she complimented her artwork. "You have a very special talent," Mrs. Griffin always told Jackie.

A knock at the door interrupted Jackie's thoughts. Mrs. Griffin entered along with a lively black puppy named Gabe. Mrs. Griffin told the class how she was helping to train the little Labrador puppy. "When this puppy is older, he will become a friend and guide for a person who is blind," Mrs. Griffin said. She explained how she brings Gabe to places such as parks or stores. Mrs. Griffin said, "It's important for him to feel comfortable around people."

As Jackie listened, she thought about what a caring person Mrs. Griffin was.

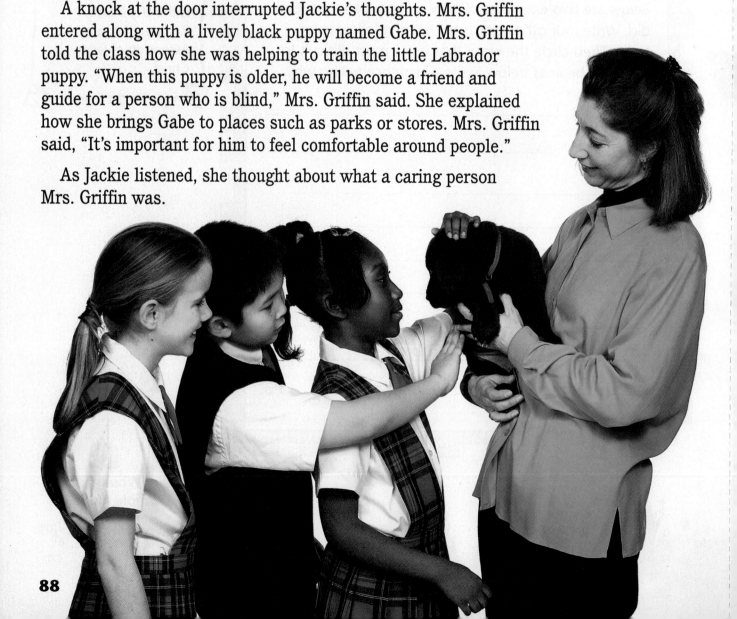

Jesus, Our Role Model

We are special because we are created in the image of God. If we live the way Jesus taught us to live, we will be showing God's goodness to others.

Jesus is our role model. During his life on earth, Jesus showed us how to treat others with respect and to care for God's world. God wants us to follow the example of Jesus.

Our Church Teaches

Jesus is God's Son. He is both human and divine. He was born to Mary by the power of the Holy Spirit. During his life, Jesus showed God's love to others. We try to live as Jesus did.

Jesus died and then rose from the dead to save us from our sins and to give us new life. Jesus is present in our lives today in Scripture, the Sacraments, and through the witness of the Christian community. We celebrate the Paschal Mystery each week at Mass.

Activity

Write the names of two people who give their time to help others. How do they help others? What sacrifices will you make?

_____

_____

_____

_____

_____

_____

How do I follow Jesus?

Respond

Saint Catherine of Bologna and Seeing the Face of God

Catherine de'Vigri was born in Bologna, Italy, on September 8, 1413. When she was eleven, she learned to paint tiny statues. A few years later, Catherine became a religious sister.

One Christmas Eve night, she had a vision of Mary holding Baby Jesus. In the vision, Mary let Catherine hold Jesus in her arms. This vision has been painted by many artists.

Catherine led a group of religious women that became part of the community of sisters called the Poor Clares. She once wrote that she would do her very best to follow Jesus.

Catherine is known today as Saint Catherine of Bologna. She is honored as the patron saint of artists. We celebrate her feast day on March 9.

Activities

1. Many artists have tried to paint the face of Jesus. What do you think Jesus looked like?

   Draw your own picture of the face of Jesus.

2. Read each story. Rewrite the part that is underlined. Keep in mind what Christ, our role model, might say.

a. Megan's team is playing basketball and the score is tied. During the last minutes of play, her teammate Dina, passes the ball to her. Megan misses the pass, and the other team gets the ball and scores. The game ends with the other team winning by a point. Dina yells at Megan and calls her names. She shouts, "How could you miss such an easy pass?"

_____

_____

b. Every day Jessica practices on her clarinet. She has a solo part in the spring concert. On the night of the concert, Jessica is very nervous. As she walks on stage, she trips and falls. Although Jessica is embarrassed, she walks to her seat and plays her piece beautifully. After the concert her classmate, Tim, says, "I can't believe how clumsy you are!"

_____

_____

_____

3. Find a word hidden in the line of letters. Then complete the message.

M T R S G X U Q F O L L O W D C G T M

Jesus says, "___ ___ ___ ___ ___ ___ me."

Based on Mark 1:17

How do we see the image of God in others?

Prayer Celebration

A Prayer of Reflection

Leader: Each of us is called to follow Jesus' example and continue doing God's will. Look at the picture that you drew of Jesus. Use it to help you pray. Think about what Jesus said: "Whoever has seen me has seen the Father" (John 14:9).

Reader: Christ has no body now on earth but yours.
No hands but yours. No feet but yours.
Christ must look out on the world with your eyes.
He needs to move around doing good things by using your feet. And he uses your hands to bless his people.

Based on the Prayer by Saint Teresa of Ávila

Leader: Jesus, teach us to speak kind words. Teach us to do good deeds. Help us to follow you.

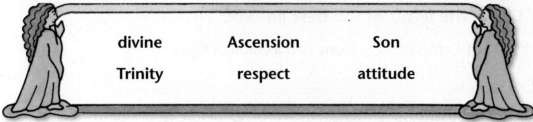

divine   Ascension   Son

Trinity   respect   attitude

A **Complete** each statement about Jesus by choosing one of the words above. You will not have to use all the words.

1. Jesus Christ is both human and _____.

2. Jesus is the Second Divine Person of the Holy _____.

3. The moment when Jesus, in his resurrected body, entered Heaven

   is known as his _____.

4. Jesus is God's _____.

5. Jesus showed us how to treat others with _____.

B **Match** column A with column B by writing the correct number in the space provided.

A	B
1. role models	_____ We celebrate our new life with Jesus at every _____.
2. image	_____ Jesus died and rose from the dead to save us from our _____.
3. of God	_____ We are special because we are created in God's _____.
4. Mass	_____ People who show us how to live like Jesus are called _____.
5. sins	_____ The word *divine* means _____.

C **Circle** the letter of the best answer.

1. Saint Catherine of Bologna had a vision of Mary
_____.

   a. on the cross

   b. holding the Baby Jesus

   c. before Jesus's birth

   d. at the Resurrection

2. The life, Death, Resurrection, and Ascension of Jesus Christ is known as the
_____.

   a. mystery of Christ

   b. Holy Trinity

   c. Paschal Mystery

   d. human mystery

3. Jesus was born to Mary by the power of the
_____.

   a. covenant

   b. holy Catholic Church

   c. Communion of Saints

   d. Holy Spirit

4. As Jesus suffered on the cross he said, "Father,
_____."

   a. forgive them

   b. remember me

   c. give me strength

   d. be with me

D **Respond** to the following.

1. Explain why we call Jesus our role model.
_____
_____

2. Write about one way someone you know has been a role model as a follower of Jesus.
_____

Take Home

FAMILY TIME

Baptism in Christ

John the Baptist, Jesus' cousin, baptized him in the Jordan River. Jesus' baptism announced his vocation to reveal God to the world. Our Baptism calls us to help others come to know God.

ACTIVITY

Celebrate Look for the baptismal candles of family members. Light the candles as a remembrance of that special day. Celebrate by looking at the pictures or the video from each of the ceremonies. You may want to do this on the anniversary of your Baptism, too!

WEEKLY PLANNER

On Sunday

As you pray the Nicene Creed listen for the things we believe as Catholics.

On the Web

blestarewe.com

Visit our Web site for the saint of the day and the reflection question of the week.

Saint of the Week

Saint John the Baptist (first century)

Saint John the Baptist was a Prophet and fearless preacher of repentance. He prepared the way for his cousin, Jesus. Several of his followers were chosen to be among the Apostles of Jesus.

Patron Saint of: Baptism, converts
Feast Day: June 24 & August 29

A Prayer for the Week

Lord, John the Baptist in his day prepared for Jesus. Help us prepare the way for Jesus today. Give us John's courage to be honest and to reach out to the poor and needy. Amen.

Getting ready for Chapter 6

Take Home

✝ Scripture Background

In the Time of Jesus

Jordan River The longest river in Palestine begins in the mountains of northern Galilee. It is appropriately named the Jordan, which means "descender." From the mountains it descends into the Sea of Galilee. The river eventually empties into the Dead Sea. The Dead Sea is more than a thousand feet below sea level. The river's direct course is sixty-five miles long, but with its winding path it covers two hundred miles. Jesus' ministry began when he was baptized in the Jordan River.

Read about the meaning of Baptism in Romans 6:3–4.

OUR CATHOLIC TRADITION in the Sacraments

Baptism The Sacraments are rich with signs. In Baptism, water is poured three times over the head of a person being baptized, a sign of our belief in the Three Divine Persons of the Trinity. Sacred Chrism is used on the forehead, signing us as priest, prophet, and king—the three roles of a Christian. The Oil of Catechumens is used to anoint those preparing for Baptism. It represents being protected by God. The white garment shows that we have "put on Christ" and are starting a new life as a follower of Jesus. The baptismal candle represents that, like Christ, we are to be a light in the world.

6 Baptism in Christ

LET US PRAY You have become a new creation, and have clothed yourself in Christ.

Rite of Baptism

Share

God gave you unique gifts that can help you cooperate with others. When you join a group or team, you work together to reach a common goal. You may wear similar outfits as a sign of belonging to the group.

Activities

1. How is the girl in the picture working with others toward a common goal? Write your answer on the lines under the picture.

_____

_____

_____

2. Think of a group that you belong to. It may be a club or a team. Perhaps you worked on a special project with family members or friends. In the chain, write the names of the people in your group. Then write below what your group did together.

_____

_____

_____

What signs are used at Baptism to show we are followers of Jesus?

Worship   The Sacrament of Baptism

At our Baptism, the Holy Spirit united us with Jesus Christ and with God's holy people, the Church. Being one with Christ and the Church, we can work together to show God's goodness to everyone.

Baptism and Anointing

There are many signs used in the Sacrament of **Baptism**. Water is poured three times over the head of the person being baptized, while the priest or deacon says:

"I baptize you in the name of the Father,
and of the Son,
and of the Holy Spirit."

Rite of Baptism

Being **immersed** in water is a sign of Jesus' Death and Resurrection. It shows that the person is cleansed of sin and ready to start a new life as a follower of Jesus. Each time we enter a church, we bless ourselves with holy water. We do this to remember our Baptism.

The person being baptized is also **anointed** with the **Sacred Chrism**. This is a sign that the baptized person will continue Jesus' mission of spreading God's goodness.

Baptismal Garment

A white robe is put on the person being baptized. This is a sign of starting a new life as a follower of Jesus Christ.

Then the priest or deacon says:

"You have become a new creation, and have clothed yourself in Christ.

See in this white garment the outward sign of your Christian dignity. With your family and friends to help you by word and example, bring that dignity unstained into the everlasting life of heaven."

The Rite of Baptism

Baptismal Candle

At the end of the celebration, a candle is lighted from the Easter candle. This is a sign that each baptized person is to be a light for the world just like Jesus.

Faith Words

Baptism
Baptism is the first Sacrament of Christian Initiation that welcomes us into the Church and frees us from all sin.

anointed
Being anointed means that the person receives God's grace to spread Christ's message.

Activity

Complete the following information about your baptism.

I, _____, was baptized on _____ in the church of _____. The person who baptized me was _____. My godparents are

_____.

Some of the people who attended my baptism are

_____

_____

_____

_____.

Why is the Sacrament of Baptism important?

Hear & Believe

✝ One in Christ

During the celebration of Baptism, we listen to some Scripture readings. In one of the readings, Paul, an important leader of the early Church, tells us what it means to be baptized in Christ.

> Through faith you are all children of God in Christ Jesus. All of you who were baptized into Christ have clothed yourselves with Christ. There is neither Jew nor Greek, there is neither slave nor free person, there is not male and female; for you are all one in Christ Jesus.

Based on Galatians 3:26–28

In another reading, Paul reminds us of the new life all Christians share with Christ as he speaks the following words to us.

> When we were baptized into Christ, we were baptized into his death. We were buried with Christ through Baptism, so that, just as Christ was raised from the dead by the glory of the Father, we too might live in newness of life.

Based on Romans 6:3–4

Our Church Teaches

Through Baptism, the Holy Spirit unites us with Christ and the Church. Our new life begins in the Risen Christ. In this new life **Original Sin** is wiped away and we are called to live as Christians. We receive strength from other members of the Christian community as we work together to spread God's goodness. As Christians, we bring true meaning to the signs used in Baptism when we try to live as Jesus did. We give thanks and praise to God for the gift of of the Holy Spirit.

Activity

As Christians, we share our faith with each other and work together as followers of Jesus.

Use the symbols to decode this message from Scripture. The words reveal something special about those who are baptized.

A = ♣   O = ☙   G = ♥
L = ❖   E = ✳   T = ✝   W = ❧
C = ✳   R = ◉   H = ✿   J = ★
N = ✴   F = ✺   U = ✛
D = ✿   S = ✢   I = ✚

How can I spread God's goodness to others?

Respond

Bringing New Life to Others

Tommy looked through the window of the school bus. He saw a new student in the first or second grade saying good-bye to his mom at the bus stop. What interested Tommy was that they were using sign language to speak to each other.

Other children noticed this, too, because no one spoke to the new boy on the bus. He rode in silence the rest of the way to school.

That evening, after finishing his homework, Tommy found information about American Sign Language on a Web site. He began to memorize some signs and letters. When the new boy boarded the bus the next day, Tommy motioned for him to share his seat. In sign language he said, "Hi. My name is Tommy." "I'm Jimmy," the boy signed. They both smiled at each other. Tommy and Jimmy sat together on the bus for the rest of the school year.

Activity

Zoom In!

Take a look at each close-up picture. Under each picture, write how you or the students in the photos could bring the light of Christ to each unhappy student.

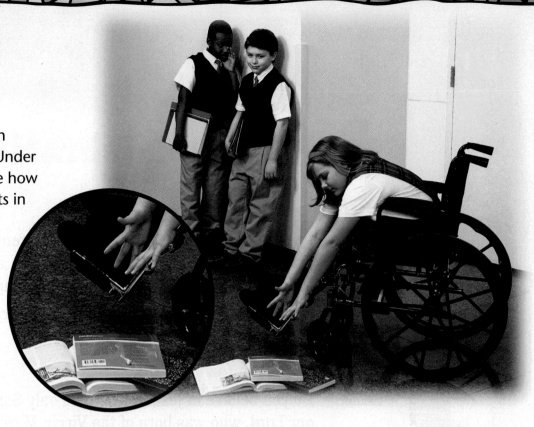

_____

_____

How can I renew the promises made at my Baptism?

_____

_____

Prayer Celebration

Our Profession of Faith

Leader: At our Baptism, our parents and godparents professed their faith in the Trinity. Let us stand and renew these promises made at our Baptism.

Leader: Do you believe in God, the Father Almighty, creator of heaven and earth?

All: I do.

Leader: Do you believe in Jesus Christ, his only Son, our Lord, who was born of the Virgin Mary, was crucified, died, and was buried, rose from the dead, and is now seated at the right hand of the Father?

All: I do.

Leader: Do you believe in the Holy Spirit, the holy Catholic Church, the Communion of Saints, the forgiveness of sins, the resurrection of the body, and life everlasting?

All: I do.

Leader: This is our faith. This is the faith of the Church. We are proud to profess it, in Christ Jesus, our Lord.

All: Amen.

Leader: Through Baptism, you have put on Christ. Let God's love within you shine.

Based on the Rite of Baptism

6 Chapter Review

A **Complete** the sentences with words from the list.

Christians	anointed	Baptism	oil
Original Sin	Water	goodness	

1. The first Sacrament of Christian Initiation is called

   _____.

2. Being _____ means that the baptized person
   will continue to spread Christ's message.

3. The Christian community works together to spread

   God's _____.

4. Through Baptism _____ is wiped away.

5. _____ is poured three times over the head of
   the person being baptized, while the priest or deacon says:
   "I baptize you in the name of the Father, and of the Son,
   and of the Holy Spirit" *(Rite of Baptism)*.

B **Match** column A with column B by writing the correct
number in the space.

A	B
1. clothed in a white garment	_____ a sign of Jesus' Death and Resurrection
2. immersed in water	_____ a sign that the baptized person receives God's grace to continue Jesus' misson of spreading God's goodness
3. anointed with Sacred Chrism	_____ a sign that the baptized person will be a light for the world
4. a lighted candle	_____ an outward sign of Christian dignity

C **Draw** a picture of one way you could let God's love and goodness shine within you.

D **Respond** to the following.

1. Explain what the Holy Spirit does for us through Baptism.

_____

_____

_____

2. Describe how someone your age can spread Christ's message.

_____

_____

_____

Take Home

The Commandments and the Beatitudes

Thinking about our blessings introduces this chapter on the Beatitudes, or ways to find true happiness. Share ideas at home about the blessings your family has received and the things that make you truly happy. Take some time this week to celebrate family members as blessings to each other.

ACTIVITY

Place Mats Prepare place mats for the dinner table that show the unique gifts of family members. Have the children make them for parents and the parents for children. Talk about these unique gifts at dinner.

WEEKLY PLANNER

On Sunday

Listen to the Gospel reading. Talk about the meaning of this Sunday's Scriptures.

On the Web

blestarewe.com

 Visit our Web site for the saint of the day and the reflection question of the week.

Saint of the Week

 Saint Matthew
(first century)

Saint Matthew was an Apostle of Jesus and a Gospel writer. Matthew left his job as a tax collector and followed Jesus. Matthew wrote his account of Jesus' life for Jewish converts, teaching that Jesus is Lord and King, the Messiah.

Patron Saint of: accountants and bankers
Feast Day: September 21

 **A Prayer for the Week**

Saint Matthew gave us a wonderful gift by writing one of the Gospels. Jesus, help us to read the Gospels with understanding and love. Teach us to follow you. Amen.

Take Home

FAMILY TIME

✝ Scripture Background

In the Time of Jesus

Horns of Hattin   In addition to teaching in the synagogues, Jesus often spoke to crowds gathered outdoors, particularly in Galilee. According to tradition, Jesus delivered his Sermon on the Mount from a hill called the Horns of Hattin. It was named for its two high peaks that resemble horns and for a nearby village. Located near Capernaum, the hill overlooks the Sea of Galilee and the Plain of Gennesaret. Today the Horns of Hattin is also called the Mount of Beatitudes.

Read about Jesus' teaching of the Beatitudes in Matthew 5:1–12.

OUR CATHOLIC TRADITION in Social Justice

CNEWA   The Catholic Near East Welfare Association (CNEWA) was founded in 1926 by Pope Pius XI to provide aid to people living in the Middle East, Northeast Africa, India, and Eastern Europe. CNEWA ministers to families, the disabled, the homeless, the elderly, and those affected by war. It also works to strengthen Eastern Catholic Churches by building schools, churches, rectories, and convents and by sponsoring seminarians and religious brothers and sisters. To learn more about CNEWA, visit www.cnewa.org.

7 The Commandments and the Beatitudes

 **In your right hand, happiness forever.**

Based on Psalm 16:11

Share

God wants each of us to be happy and the whole world to be a happy place in which to live. Some things we decide to do can help make us happy. Sometimes we decide to do things that can make us happy for a time, but then end up making us and others unhappy.

Activity

Read the list in the box and check those things you might decide to do that would end up making you and others happy.

_____ Talk about what you don't like about other people.

_____ Be fair.

_____ Put God first in your life

_____ Try to understand how others feel.

_____ Yell at your friends when you are angry.

_____ Forgive people. Make up.

_____ Don't worry about your friend's feelings.

_____ Try to respect everyone.

_____ Do not share. Keep all the good stuff for yourself.

_____ Laugh at people who make mistakes.

What do I need to do to be holy?

Hear & Believe

 **Scripture** The Story of the Rich Young Man

One day a rich man approached Jesus and asked, "Good Teacher, what must I do to find everlasting happiness?" Jesus answered, "You must follow the Commandments." Jesus then reminded the man of the Commandments: "You shall not commit adultery; you shall not kill; you shall not steal; you shall not lie; honor your father and your mother."

"I have followed these Commandments since I was a boy," the man said proudly.

"There is still one thing left for you to do," Jesus said. "Sell all that you have and give it to the poor. If you do this you will have a treasure in Heaven. Then come and follow me."

The man was disappointed with Jesus' answer and he became very quiet. He did not want to give away his money and the things that he owned.

Jesus looked at the man with sadness and said, "How hard it is for those who are attached to wealth to enter the Kingdom of God!"

Based on Luke 18:18–24

Living a Holy Life

In this Scripture story, Jesus tells us how we can live happy and holy lives. Jesus reminds us how important it is to follow God's commandments. The Ten Commandments guide us in worshiping God and treating others with respect. God gave us the Commandments to help us grow closer to him and to all his children.

In addition to keeping the Ten Commandments, Jesus said that we must be willing to share what we have. God wants us to be generous with others, especially with people who need our help. When we care for others as Jesus did, we help make the world a just and peaceful place.

God promises that if we follow the Ten Commandments and all that Jesus taught, we will be happy forever in the Kingdom of God.

GO TO page 404 to review the Ten Commandments.

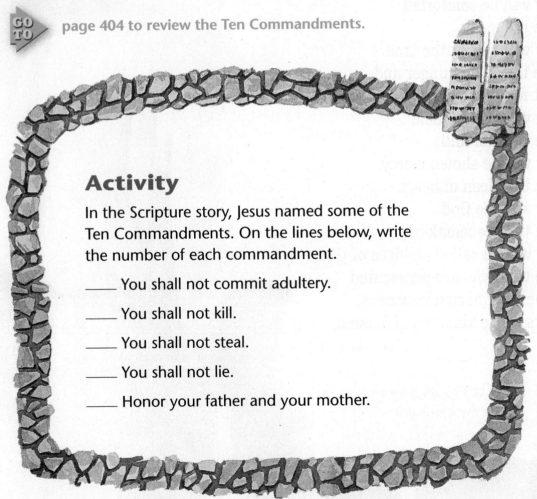

Activity

In the Scripture story, Jesus named some of the Ten Commandments. On the lines below, write the number of each commandment.

_____ You shall not commit adultery.

_____ You shall not kill.

_____ You shall not steal.

_____ You shall not lie.

_____ Honor your father and your mother.

What did Jesus teach us about the way to happiness?

Hear & Believe

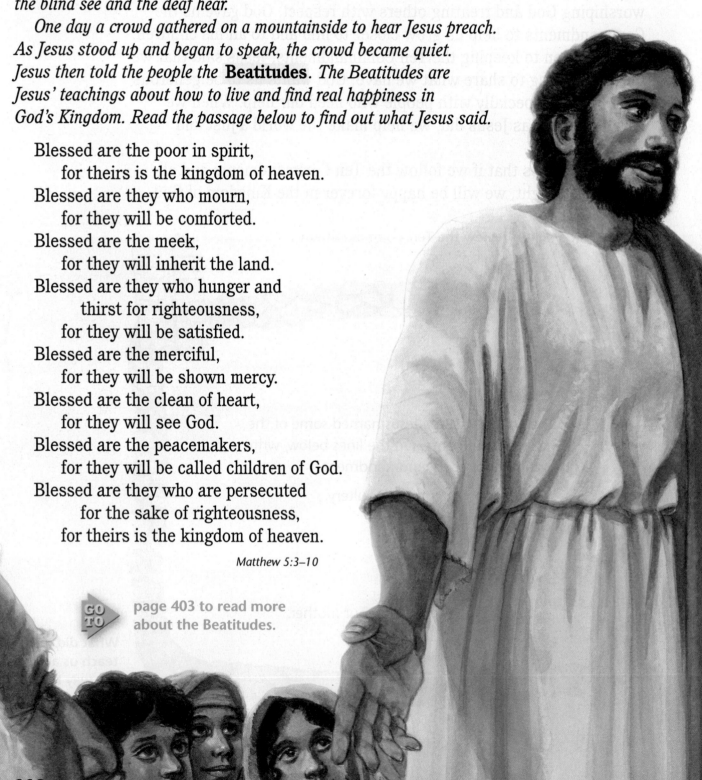

✝ The Beatitudes

For days, weeks, and months, Jesus had been busy telling people about God's Kingdom. He had traveled to many places, where he helped anyone who was in need. He helped those who were paralyzed to walk. He made the blind see and the deaf hear.

One day a crowd gathered on a mountainside to hear Jesus preach. As Jesus stood up and began to speak, the crowd became quiet. Jesus then told the people the **Beatitudes***. The Beatitudes are Jesus' teachings about how to live and find real happiness in God's Kingdom. Read the passage below to find out what Jesus said.*

Blessed are the poor in spirit,
　　for theirs is the kingdom of heaven.
Blessed are they who mourn,
　　for they will be comforted.
Blessed are the meek,
　　for they will inherit the land.
Blessed are they who hunger and
　　　thirst for righteousness,
　　for they will be satisfied.
Blessed are the merciful,
　　for they will be shown mercy.
Blessed are the clean of heart,
　　for they will see God.
Blessed are the peacemakers,
　　for they will be called children of God.
Blessed are they who are persecuted
　　　for the sake of righteousness,
　　for theirs is the kingdom of heaven.

Matthew 5:3–10

GO TO page 403 to read more about the Beatitudes.

Following the Commandments and the Beatitudes

When Jesus preached about the Beatitudes, he knew that the people were trying to keep God's laws. Like the rich young man in the Scripture story, they sought to obey the Ten Commandments. Jesus helped people understand that the Beatitudes are paths to true happiness in God's Kingdom. In keeping the Ten Commandments and living the Beatitudes, we will be happy forever in the Kingdom of God.

Activity

Write one of the Beatitudes in your own words.

_____

_____

_____

_____

Our Church Teaches

By listening to Jesus, we learn about the Kingdom of God. It is Jesus' promise of peace, justice, and fairness for all people. Jesus tells us that the Kingdom of God grows within our hearts if we try to live as Jesus teaches. For us to find real happiness, Jesus invites us to join him in the Kingdom.

God's Kingdom has come, but it is not here in its full glory yet. That is why, when we pray the Lord's Prayer, we pray, "Thy kingdom come."

How should we live to be happy in the Kingdom of God?

113

Respond

Living the Beatitudes Today

Mrs. Torrado's class was excited. They made a chart that explained the meaning of the Beatitudes for today. They decorated it with photographs showing young people, children, and even Mother Teresa helping other people. Their pastor decided that everyone in the parish should see it. He had it printed in the parish bulletin! This is what it looks like.

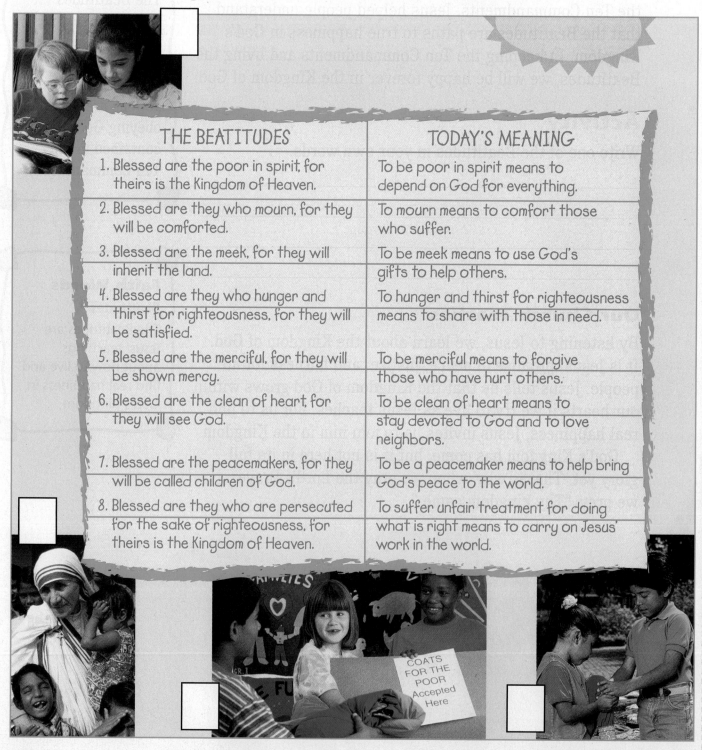

THE BEATITUDES	TODAY'S MEANING
1. Blessed are the poor in spirit, for theirs is the Kingdom of Heaven.	To be poor in spirit means to depend on God for everything.
2. Blessed are they who mourn, for they will be comforted.	To mourn means to comfort those who suffer.
3. Blessed are the meek, for they will inherit the land.	To be meek means to use God's gifts to help others.
4. Blessed are they who hunger and thirst for righteousness, for they will be satisfied.	To hunger and thirst for righteousness means to share with those in need.
5. Blessed are the merciful, for they will be shown mercy.	To be merciful means to forgive those who have hurt others.
6. Blessed are the clean of heart, for they will see God.	To be clean of heart means to stay devoted to God and to love neighbors.
7. Blessed are the peacemakers, for they will be called children of God.	To be a peacemaker means to help bring God's peace to the world.
8. Blessed are they who are persecuted for the sake of righteousness, for theirs is the Kingdom of Heaven.	To suffer unfair treatment for doing what is right means to carry on Jesus' work in the world.

COATS FOR THE POOR Accepted Here

Activity

Now make your own chart using page 114 as a guide. Write how each commandment could be written as a beatitude. The eighth commandment has been done for you.

The Ten Commandments

1. I am the LORD your God. You shall not have other gods besides me.

2. You shall not take the name of the LORD, your God, in vain.

3. Remember to keep holy the LORD's Day.

4. Honor your father and mother.

5. You shall not kill.

6. You shall not commit adultery.

7. You shall not steal.

8. You shall not bear false witness against your neighbor.

9. You shall not covet your neighbor's wife.

10. You shall not covet anything that belongs to your neighbor.

✝ Prayer Celebration

A Scripture Prayer

Leader: Dear God, we know that you created us to be happy. We remember that your Son, Jesus, showed us the way to happiness. He taught us the Beatitudes.

All: You show us the path of life. In your presence there is fullness of joy. In your right hand, happiness forever.

Leader: *(Read slowly from the Bible each Beatitude in Matthew 5:3–10.)*

All: *(Respond after each Beatitude.)* You show us the path of life.

Based on Psalm 16:11

Chapter Review

A **Circle** the letter of the best answer.

1. Jesus' teachings about finding real happiness are called the
   _____.

   a. Commandments   **c.** law

   b. Sacraments   **d.** Beatitudes

2. If we follow the _____ and the Beatitudes, we will be
   happy forever in the Kingdom of God.

   a. Lord's Prayer   **c.** Church

   b. Ten Commandments   **d.** Way

3. To hunger and thirst for righteousness means to _____.

   a. share with those in need   **c.** bring God's peace to the world

   b. help those in need   **d.** feed people in the world

4. To mourn means to _____.

   a. share with others   **c.** work with others

   b. help others   **d.** comfort those who suffer

5. To be merciful means to _____.

   a. depend on God   **c.** love others

   b. thank God   **d.** forgive others

B **Respond** to the following.

1. One thing that makes me happy is

   _____

   _____

   _____.

2. One thing that makes someone close to me happy is

   _____

   _____.

C **Complete** the sentences with words from the box.

meek	peacemakers	clean of heart
righteousness	persecuted	

1. Blessed are the _____, for they will see God.

2. Blessed are they who are _____ for the sake of righteousness, for theirs in the Kingdom of Heaven.

3. Blessed are the _____, for they will inherit the land.

4. Blessed are they who hunger and thirst for _____, for they will be satisfied.

5. Blessed are the _____, for they will be called children of God.

D **Respond** to the following.

1. Write one of the Beatitudes in your own words.

_____.

_____.

_____.

_____.

2. What can someone do to live this Beatitude?

_____.

_____.

_____.

_____.

FAMILY TIME

The Commandments and the Kingdom

We are called to be witnesses to the Kingdom of God. We do this each day by following the Ten Commandments and living the Beatitudes as Jesus did.

ACTIVITY

Bake a Cake On Epiphany, also known as Three Kings Day, some people bake a cake to remember the gifts of the three kings to Jesus at his birth. Baking a cake is a fun activity that the family can do to celebrate the life of the Church, including the presence of God's kingdom of justice and love.

WEEKLY PLANNER

On Sunday

At Mass, pray the Profession of Faith to affirm your Catholic beliefs and pray the General Intercessions for the special requests of your parish community.

On the Web

blestarewe.com

Visit our Web site for the saint of the day and the reflection question of the week.

Saint of the Week

Saint Teresa of Ávila
(1515–1582)

Saint Teresa of Ávila joined the Carmelite sisters and soon felt God's call to reform. She reformed her order by founding the "discalced" (without shoes) Carmelites. A great teacher and writer, she was the first woman named Doctor of the Church.

Patron Saint of: Spain, sick people
Feast Day: October 15

A Prayer for the Week

Lord, like Saint Teresa of Ávila, give us strength so that our thoughts may become courageous deeds. Help us do your will. Amen.

Take Home

FAMILY TIME

✝ Scripture Background

In the Time of Jesus

Vineyards   The long, hot summers of Palestine provided the perfect conditions for cultivating grapevines. They grew in abundance on the hillsides and were surrounded by stone walls for security. Family members helped guard against thieves and animals by acting as lookouts from a watchtower. Harvesting took place in September. While some grapes were dried for raisins or used to make a honey relish, most were crushed for wine.

In Matthew 20:1–16, Jesus uses a vineyard as the setting of his parable.

Our Catholic Tradition in Art

Hand-Copied Bibles   During the Middle Ages, monks from northern Africa, the Near East, and Europe made books by hand-copying every word. European monks became well known for copying the Bible many times. Painters, called illuminators, illustrated the Bibles using bright colors and lavish gold to create pictures called illuminations. These Bibles are treasures. They represent the monks' love for the Word of God. They are extraordinary works of art and holy keepsakes of our Catholic tradition.

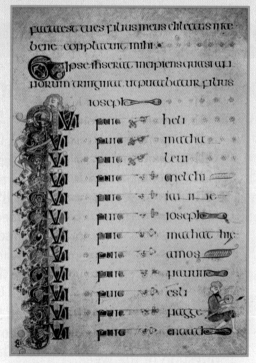

Genealogy of Christ from *The Book of Kells*, Trinity College, Dublin, Ireland

8 The Commandments and the Kingdom

The last will be first, and the first will be last.

Matthew 20:16

Share

When we treat others fairly, we are a sign of God's Kingdom.

Activities

It's Not Fair!

1. Melinda and Bob are having cake for dessert. Why is Bob upset?

   _____

   _____

   _____

   _____

2. Read the list of experiences that you might consider unfair. Put a check in front of the ones you have experienced. Then draw a cartoon for something unfair that has happened to you. Use an experience from the list or another one you remember.

_____ You were blamed for something you didn't do.

_____ An older brother or sister stayed up later than you.

_____ You didn't get the present you really wanted.

_____ Your teacher gave you too much homework.

_____ You did the most work on a group project.

What did Jesus teach us about God's justice?

Hear & Believe

✝ Scripture The Laborers in the Vineyard

*At times, God's ways are difficult to understand. God's **justice** can be different from our own. Jesus spoke of this when he told this story.*

A rich landowner owned a vineyard. At dawn he went out and hired laborers to work in his fields. The workers agreed on how much the landowner would pay them and then went to work. At nine o'clock the landowner saw some more workers. He said, "Go and work in my vineyard. I will pay you what is fair." He did the same at noon, at three o'clock, and at five o'clock. At the end of the day, all the workers came for their money. The landowner paid each worker the same amount no matter how long he had worked. Those who had worked longest said, "This is not fair! We worked much longer than the others!"

The landowner replied, "My friends, I am not cheating you. I paid you what we agreed on. Can I not do what I want with my own money? Are you jealous because I am generous?"

Jesus finished his story by saying, "The last will be first, and the first will be last."

Based on Matthew 20:1–16

God's Justice

We expect to be treated fairly. We want to receive what we deserve. In the Scripture story we learn that God's justice is not always the same as ours. God treats us differently than we may treat each other. He loves us and treats us equally. God always sees the goodness in each of us and fills us with everlasting love.

To help us understand God's justice, we look to Jesus, our role model. By the way he lived, Jesus showed us what the Kingdom of God is like. We follow his example by obeying the Ten Commandments and living the Beatitudes. The Ten Commandments and the Beatitudes lead to God's justice.

Faith Words

justice

Justice means treating everyone fairly and with respect by following Jesus' teachings.

Activity

Design a bumper sticker that encourages us to see the good in every person.

How can we live as people of the Kingdom of God?

Hear & Believe

Saint Francis de Sales and Living a Holy Life

We give witness to God's Kingdom when we imitate Jesus. Saint Francis de Sales was a disciple of Jesus. Because Francis was a gentle and caring person, he is called the "Gentleman Saint."

Born in France in 1567, Francis became a priest and then later a bishop. He traveled throughout his diocese caring for others. Francis loved children and taught them to be considerate and respectful of others. Francis found a way to communicate with people who were deaf. He created his own sign language!

Francis was an excellent writer. His most famous book is called *Introduction to the Devout Life*. In this work, Francis explained how all people could be close to God. Many people at that time thought that only priests, nuns, or monks could lead holy lives. Francis inspired all people to live as holy people of God's Kingdom.

To lead holy lives, Francis said that we must forgive ourselves when we make mistakes and be willing to try again. Then we will be more patient and understanding with others. Francis believed that every person is a valuable part of God's Kingdom. "Do not wish to be anything but what you are," Francis taught, "and try to be that perfectly."

The Church celebrates Saint Francis de Sales' feast day on January 24. He is the patron saint of writers and people who are hearing impaired.

Our Church Teaches

During Mass, we pray the Lord's Prayer. Jesus taught his first followers to pray this prayer for the coming of the Kingdom and God's justice. When we pray the words *thy kingdom come*, we ask for God's goodness and justice for all people. We believe that one day we will be fully joined with the Kingdom of God.

We Believe

When we pray the Lord's Prayer, we express our belief in God's Kingdom of justice and love.

Activity

Write a prayer for the coming of God's Kingdom.
Use at least four of the words in the border.

love   unity   joy

mercy

peace

justice   goodness

Respond

Send Us Forth

Christ is present at Mass and through him we come to experience the Kingdom of God.

At Mass we experience God's goodness and love. We feel the joy of being a part of God's Kingdom and are ready to share it with others.

Activities

1. Find and circle seven hidden words below that describe what we can experience at Mass.

justice   unity   joy   mercy   peace   goodness   love

```
a s d f g g h j k q l e r y l o v e
l m w j n b h v g c f x p z s d f h
k m r u r c x t o j s f t e i m b b
g v o s n n p j q c y n m s a t h w
p g b t c h f g o o d n e s s c f g
r u n i t y m k o y y m r o r x e c
t s n c b m r a e p z z c h f b p e
v o l e j c w x k l a o y j p h x r
```

Choose one of the words you circled. Write how you experience this at Mass.

_____

_____

Using the words you circled, select a word that describes what the people in each picture have experienced at Mass and are now sharing with others. Share your answers with a partner.

2. Using American Sign Language, learn to sign the following phrase from the Lord's Prayer. Review what you learned in Chapter 4 and sign all the phrases together.

| Thy | kingdom | come. |

How do we pray for the coming of the Kingdom of God?

Prayer Celebration

A Prayer of Praise

Leader: Together let us pray for our needs and the needs of the Church and sign "Thy kingdom come."

Reader 1: For all Christians, that we may always follow Jesus, our role model. We pray . . .

All: thy kingdom come.

Reader 2: For all Church leaders, especially the Pope, our bishops, and our pastor, that they may be true signs of Christ. We pray . . .

All: thy kingdom come.

Reader 3: For those who are persecuted for the sake of righteousness, for the Kingdom of Heaven is theirs. We pray . . .

All: thy kingdom come.

Reader 4: For all of us gathered here, that someday we will fully experience God's justice in the Kingdom of God. We pray . . .

All: thy kingdom come.

Leader: For our own special intentions that we now remember . . .

Leader: Together, let us sign the Lord's Prayer.

A **Complete** the sentences with words from the box.

praying	Mass	goodness
lead	justice	living

1. We bring _____ to others when we treat everyone with respect and follow Jesus' teachings.

2. During _____, we pray the Lord's Prayer.

3. The Ten Commandments and the Beatitudes _____ to God's justice.

4. We follow Jesus' example by obeying the Ten Commandments and _____ the Beatitudes.

5. In the Lord's Prayer, when we pray "thy kingdom come," we ask for God's _____ and justice.

B **Write** the word from the Lord's Prayer that is being signed in each picture.

_____ _____ _____

8 Chapter Review

C **Write or draw** about something you think is unfair.

D **Respond** to the following questions.

1. What happened in the Scripture story called "The Laborers in the Vineyard"? ______________________________

____

____

____

2. What does this Scripture story teach us about God's justice?

____

____

____

____

Faith in Action

The Cursillo Movement Jesus calls us all to be his disciples. Today, he calls each of us to follow him, to learn from him, and to continue his work in the world. The Cursillo Movement helps people learn and remember the most important beliefs and practices of their Catholic faith and live more like Jesus. *Cursillo* means "little course." As such, it is a little course in Christianity. People involved in Cursillo seek to be "Christlike," doing what Jesus did and acting as Jesus acted.

In Everyday Life

Activity Think about what most helps you to be like Jesus. Mark an ✗ next to the words that describe the most important way you have learned to be like Jesus. Put a check mark ✓ next to any other ways that have helped you. Add one of your own.

_____ Reading about Jesus in the Bible

_____ Praying about what to do and how to act

_____ Asking for guidance from someone I trust

_____ Seeing how someone I admire acts

_____ (in my own words) _____

_____

In Your Parish

Activity When we work, pray, and celebrate together and care for one another, we are living as Jesus calls us to live. Identify three opportunities in your parish in which you can learn more about what it means to live as brothers and sisters in Christ. One has been done for you.

We work together: _____

We pray together: _____

We celebrate together: _____

We care for one another: _____

Faith in Action

Godparents   Our godparents are people with a strong faith who promise to help us learn to believe in the same things they do. They love us and take the time to support us as we grow in faith. Godparents help us recognize the gifts that we can share with the Church. In this way, we give back to the Church the new life that we received at Baptism.

In Everyday Life

Activity   When Joey first moved in down the street, he made friends very quickly. He was always happy and did nice things for his new neighbors. One day, Christi got angry at Joey because he was spending more time with Susan than with her. So she started saying bad things about Joey to the other kids on the street. After a few days, Joey was feeling very left out. Everyone forgot about all the good things Joey had done for them. On the lines below, write an ending to the story that shows people welcoming Joey after all.

_____

_____

In Your Parish

Activity   Write down the first name of someone in your family or parish who was recently baptized. Then, write one reason for being thankful to God for that person. Conclude by saying a prayer of thanksgiving to God for the gift of the Sacrament of Baptism.

Name: _____

I thank God for this person because _____

_____

_____.

Faith in Action

The Holy Name Society   Begun in 1274, the Holy Name Society seeks to generate love and reverence for the Holy Name of God and Jesus Christ. Today, members of the Holy Name Society are active in parishes ministering to others and supporting the work of the Church.

In Everyday Life

Activity   Find your way through the maze to the happiness that Jesus promises those who follow his example and teachings.

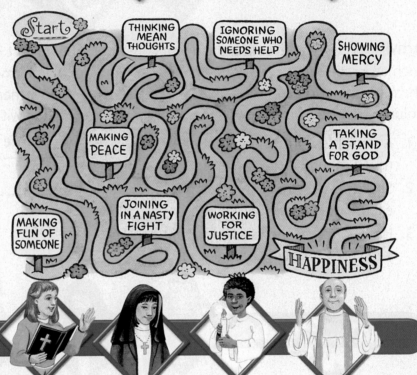

In Your Parish

Activity   The Junior Confraternity of the Holy Name Society welcomes youth from ages 9 through 18. Its members are committed to prayer, service, and witness. In each section below, underline one or two items that you can commit to doing over the next few months.

Prayer: Read God's Word more.   Pray the Rosary.   Go to Mass. Find a prayer partner.

Service: Help someone in need.   Support an organization that lives out the Gospel.   Perform random acts of kindness.

Witness: Always tell the truth.   Do not cheat.   Share the Gospel with someone. Make prayerful decisions.

Finance Committee Every parish and Catholic school has a group of valuable people who serve the Church by using their knowledge about finances. These people usually develop a budget, watch over spending, and generally look after the financial health of the parish or school. They are often involved in fundraising efforts that are held to meet expenses.

In Everyday Life

Activity Have you ever imagined you could get a head start on something, such as a race, to increase your chances of winning? Sometimes, just being in the race is enough of a reward. For each statement below mark an **X** in the column that best fits your opinion. Discuss your responses with a partner.

	Agree	Disagree	Not Sure
1. A person's worth is determined by how much money he or she makes.			
2. Saying "I don't have time" is a good excuse not to help someone.			
3. How you treat the least important person you know is how you treat Jesus.			

In Your Parish

Activity Think about the many people who make it possible for you to enjoy all that you have. Who cooks? Who buys the food? Who grows or packages the food you buy? What would happen if one of these people did not do his or her job? Choose one person who works or volunteers in your parish and list two things that could happen if this person did not do his or her job.

Name/Job Title: _____

1. _____

   _____

2. _____

   _____

Match the verse or phrase that best goes with each crown.

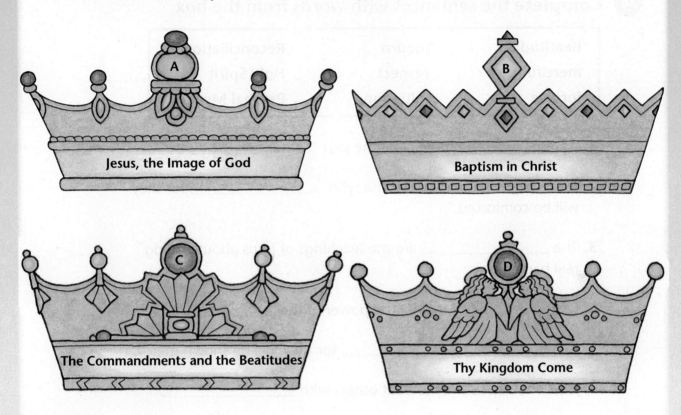

Jesus, the Image of God

Baptism in Christ

The Commandments and the Beatitudes

Thy Kingdom Come

1 _____ Blessed are the poor in spirit, for theirs is the kingdom of heaven (Matthew 5:3).

2 _____ The last will be first, and the first will be last (based on Matthew 20:16).

3 _____ I baptize you in the name of the Father, and of the Son, and of the Holy Spirit (*Rite of Baptism*).

4 _____ Whoever has seen me has seen the Father (John 14:9).

A **Complete** the sentences with words from the box.

Beatitudes	mourn	Reconciliation
merciful	respect	Holy Spirit
forgive	Initiation	Paschal Mystery

1. As Jesus suffered on the cross, he said "Father, _____ them."

2. Jesus taught, "Blessed are those who _____, for they will be comforted."

3. The _____ are the teachings of Jesus about finding real happiness.

4. Jesus was born to Mary by the power of the _____.

5. Blessed are the _____, for they will be shown mercy.

6. Jesus showed us how to treat others with _____.

7. Baptism is the first Sacrament of Christian _____.

8. We celebrate the _____ at every Mass.

B **Choose** one of the Beatitudes. What can someone do to live this Beatitude?

_____

_____

_____

_____

_____

_____

2 Unit Review

C **Match** column A with column B by writing the correct number in the space provided.

A

1. divine

2. peacemakers

3. righteousness

4. Original Sin

5. goodness

6. clean of heart

7. Holy Trinity

8. anointed

9. meek

10. Ascension

B

_____ Jesus is the Second Divine Person of the _____.

_____ The return of the resurrected Jesus to his Father in Heaven is known as the _____.

_____ Blessed are the _____, for they will see God.

_____ Blessed are the _____, for they shall inherit the land.

_____ In the Lord's Prayer, when we pray "thy kingdom come," we ask for God's _____.

_____ Being _____ means that the baptized person receives God's grace to continue to spread God's goodness.

_____ Jesus Christ is both human and _____.

_____ Through Baptism, _____ is wiped away.

_____ Blessed are the _____, for they will be called children of God.

_____ Blessed are they who hunger and thirst for _____, for they will be satisfied.

D **Explain** how Jesus is our role model.

_____

_____

_____

E **Circle** the letter of the best answer.

1. At Baptism, a sign that the baptized will be a light to the world is the _____.

   a. white garment

   b. lighted candle

   c. water

   d. Chrism

2. Wearing a _____ is a sign of starting a new life as a follower of Jesus.

   a. white garment

   b. oil of chrism

   c. cross

   d. white flower

3. At Baptism, a sign that the baptized will continue Jesus' mission is the

   _____.

   a. white garment

   b. candle

   c. water

   d. Sacred Chrism

4. Being _____ is a sign of Jesus' death and Resurrection.

   a. immersed in water

   b. save us from our sins

   c. signed with a cross

   d. called by name

F **Respond** to the following.

1. What does the Holy Spirit do for us through Baptism?

   _____

   _____

2. What is something you can do to spread Christ's message?

   _____

   _____

   _____

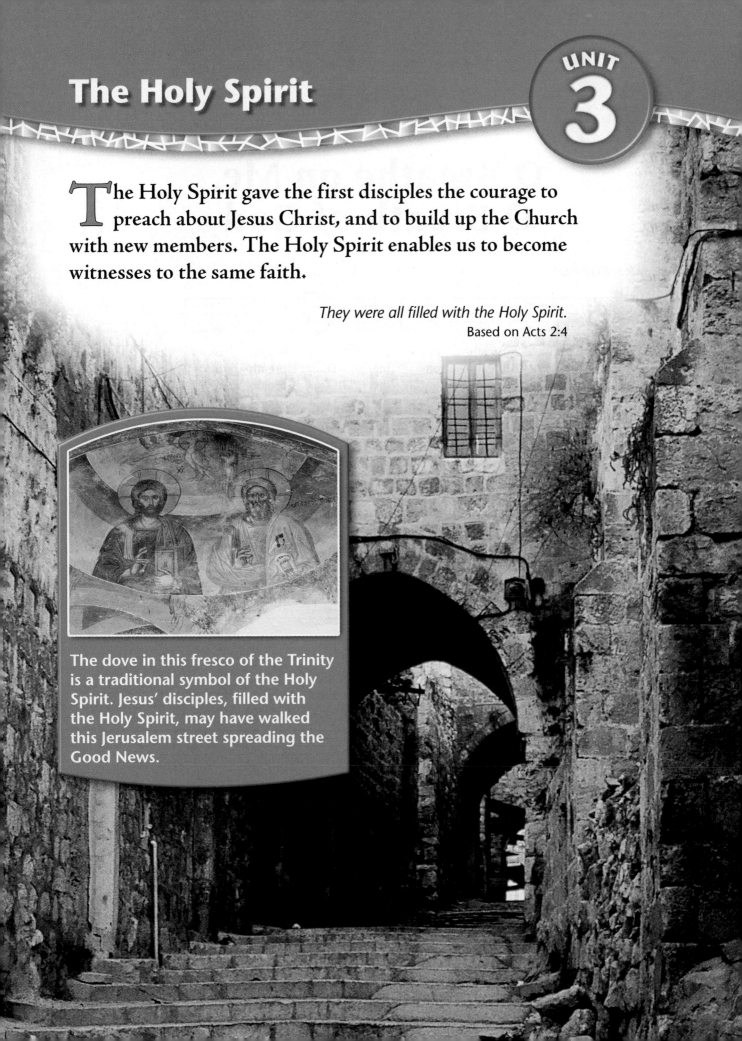

The Holy Spirit

The Holy Spirit gave the first disciples the courage to preach about Jesus Christ, and to build up the Church with new members. The Holy Spirit enables us to become witnesses to the same faith.

They were all filled with the Holy Spirit.
Based on Acts 2:4

The dove in this fresco of the Trinity is a traditional symbol of the Holy Spirit. Jesus' disciples, filled with the Holy Spirit, may have walked this Jerusalem street spreading the Good News.

O Breathe on Me, O Breath of God

Words by Edwin Hatch

ST. COLUMBA, CM

1. O breathe on me, O breath of God,
2. O breathe on me, O breath of God,
3. O breathe on me, O breath of God,
4. O breathe on me, O breath of God,

Fill me with life a - new,
Un - til my heart is pure;
My will to yours in - cline,
So shall I nev - er die,

That I may love the things you love,
Un - til my will is one with yours,
Un - til this self - ish part of me
But live with you the per - fect life

And do what you would do.
To do and to en - dure.
Glows with your fire di - vine.
Of your e - ter - ni - ty.

Take Home

FAMILY TIME

The Holy Spirit Guides Us

Jesus Christ sent the Holy Spirit to guide us after his Ascension to Heaven. The Spirit keeps the grace of the Sacraments alive and growing in us. Through the work of the Spirit, we become holy. In this chapter we will explore the way the Spirit guides our lives.

ACTIVITY

Signs and Symbols The Bible uses the images of a dove, wind, and fire to help us understand the Holy Spirit. Choose three events that are coming up and pick a symbol for each event. Using fabric or construction paper, place these symbols on a large piece of material to make a banner. Hang this banner in your home where it can be seen.

WEEKLY PLANNER

On Sunday

The disciples let go of their fears on Pentecost. During the General Intercessions at Mass, pray that the Holy Spirit will help you overcome your fears.

On the Web

blestarewe.com

 Visit our Web site for the saint of the day and the reflection question of the week.

Saint of the Week

 Saint Francis Solano (1549–1610)

Saint Francis Solano traveled from his native Spain in 1589 to become a missionary priest to the New World. He was able to speak many languages and used this talent to minister to Indians and Spanish colonists in Peru.

Patron Saint of: Argentina, Bolivia, Chile, Paraguay, Peru
Feast Day: July 14

A Prayer for the Week

Spirit of Wisdom and Spirit of Love, come and live in our family. Like Saint Francis Solano, give us the strength and courage to love one another as God loves us. Amen.

Take Home

✝ Scripture Background

In the Time of Jesus

Upper Room   In a Jewish home, the upper room was a spacious area on the second floor usually reserved for guests. In a one-story home, the upper room may have been a structure on the flat roof. Jesus chose an upper room in Jerusalem for the celebration of the Last Supper. Tradition identifies this same room as the place where the disciples received the Holy Spirit on Pentecost.

Read about Jesus' promise to send the Holy Spirit in John 16:12–15.

OUR CATHOLIC TRADITION in Art

Descending Like a Dove   The image of the Holy Spirit as a dove has been used from the earliest times in our Church's history. Matthew 3:16 says, "After Jesus was baptized, he came up from the water and behold, the heavens were opened, and he saw the Spirit of God descending like a dove coming upon him." There are many paintings of the Baptism of Christ which include the descending dove. One of the best is Andrea del Verrocchio's *The Baptism of Christ* (1470). This painting is famous because Leonardo da Vinci is believed to have painted the angel on the far left.

9 The Holy Spirit Guides Us

They were all filled with the Holy Spirit.

Based on Acts 2:4

Share

Signs

There are many signs along the road that guide us to where we want to go. Some signs warn us of danger and help protect us as we travel. Some help us as we travel.

Activities

1. The following are some signs that you may see along the road. In the empty sign, create a sign to direct others. You may use words or pictures.

2. Find your way through the maze. Write the six letters that are along the correct path. Then unscramble them to make a word that completes the sentence. It tells you something important about the Holy Spirit.

   Letters _____

   The Holy Spirit _____ _____ _____ _____ _____ _____
   you on your journey in life.

Why did Jesus promise to send the Holy Spirit?

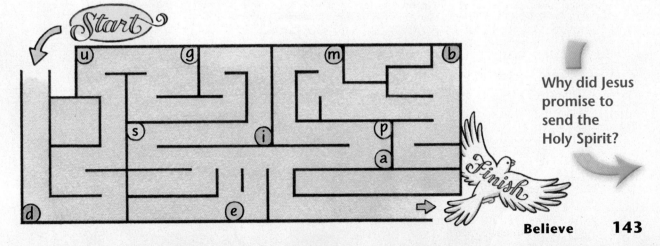

Hear & Believe

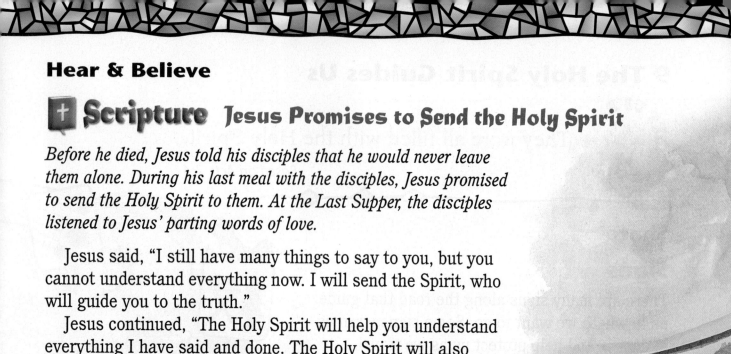

✝ Scripture Jesus Promises to Send the Holy Spirit

Before he died, Jesus told his disciples that he would never leave them alone. During his last meal with the disciples, Jesus promised to send the Holy Spirit to them. At the Last Supper, the disciples listened to Jesus' parting words of love.

Jesus said, "I still have many things to say to you, but you cannot understand everything now. I will send the Spirit, who will guide you to the truth."

Jesus continued, "The Holy Spirit will help you understand everything I have said and done. The Holy Spirit will also help you understand the things that are to come." Jesus reminded his disciples that the Father had sent him to show them how to live in God's love. He pointed out that the Holy Spirit would continue to teach and guide them just as he had done. "The Holy Spirit will speak in my name and glorify me," said Jesus.

Based on John 16:12–15

The Holy Spirit Is with Us

Like most of us, Jesus' disciples were experiencing fear and doubt in life. Jesus reassured them by promising to send the Holy Spirit to guide them. We can be sure that the Holy Spirit continues to guide the Church, bringing us comfort and hope during difficult times.

Activities

1. The Holy Spirit guides us in understanding God's truth in Scripture. Choose an opening Scripture verse from the top of the first page of the chapters you have read. Write what these words mean to you.

_____

_____

_____

_____

2. People of all ages need the Holy Spirit to guide them especially when they have difficult choices to make. On the lines below, write about particular choices that each person might face.

someone your age _____

_____

_____

teenager _____

_____

_____

parent _____

_____

_____

How did the Holy Spirit come to the disciples?

Hear & Believe

 ## The Promise of the Holy Spirit Fulfilled

Before his Ascension into Heaven, Jesus spoke to his disciples. He reminded them of the promise he made at the Last Supper. He told them to remain in Jerusalem to wait for the coming of the Holy Spirit. The Holy Spirit would give them the power to spread Jesus' teachings to the world.

Pentecost

The city was crowded. Many Jewish people had traveled to Jerusalem to celebrate the harvest festival called Pentecost. Jesus' disciples and Mary, his mother, were in a house praying together. Suddenly, from the sky, there was a sound like a strong wind. It filled the house! Then many small flames, like tongues of fire, appeared in the air. These came to rest on each of the people. These were a sign that they were now filled with the Holy Spirit. Right away the disciples left the house and began praising God.

Outside, people heard these joyful voices and they came running to listen. The listeners all spoke different languages, yet each could understand the disciples' praises. They were greatly puzzled and wondered what this might mean.

Based on the Acts of the Apostles 2:1–12

Pentecost, the Beginning of the Church

After Jesus' Ascension, the disciples were lost without Jesus being on earth to guide them. As he promised, Jesus sent the Holy Spirit to be their Helper and Guide. This special event is called **Pentecost** and it marks the beginning of the Church.

The Holy Spirit made the disciples more aware of God's love for them. By the power of the Holy Spirit, Jesus' message of love and forgiveness was ready to be spread to others. The life of the Spirit was alive within the disciples. They knew and loved God as Father, Son, and Holy Spirit.

Our Church Teaches

We pray for the Holy Spirit to be with us each day. The Holy Spirit guides us to do the right thing. If we make bad choices, the Holy Spirit guides us back to God. The Holy Spirit helps us follow Christ, who shows us how to love God and others.

We are part of the Church that began on Pentecost. By letting the Holy Spirit guide us, we continue to show others the goodness of God.

Activities

Write a prayer asking the Holy Spirit to guide you.

_____

_____

_____

We Believe

The Holy Spirit guides us in making choices that show God's goodness.

Faith Words

Pentecost
On Pentecost, Jesus sent the gift of the Holy Spirit to his first disciples. This event marks the beginning of the Church.

How does the Holy Spirit help and guide us?

Respond

Making Choices

Every day we make choices. The Holy Spirit can help us make good decisions that show that God's love is within us.

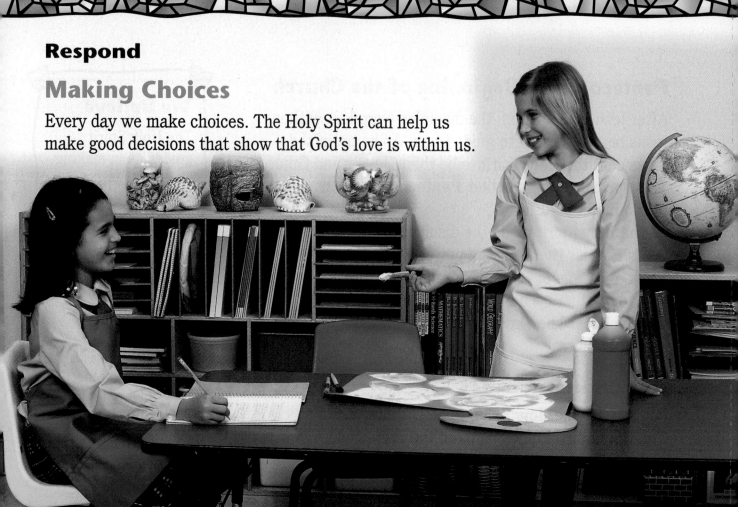

Kayla's Promise

"Let's start working on our science projects," said the teacher, Mrs. Liu. She called the names of partners who would work together on the assignment. Melissa was upset because she could not work with Kayla. They were best friends and did almost everything together.

Kayla was also disappointed. But she liked the idea of working with Marina, the most popular girl in the class. Marina was always telling jokes and making others laugh.

Kayla and Marina began discussing their assignment. They were supposed to make a poster on the different types of clouds. "I'll draw the pictures. Why

don't you write some information about each cloud," said Marina. "OK," agreed Kayla as she opened her book. Kayla enjoyed being with Marina.

While they were working, Marina told Kayla some funny stories about some of their classmates. Kayla laughed so hard she almost fell over. She thought of a funny but embarrassing story about her best friend, Melissa. She had promised Melissa she would never tell anyone. But Kayla was having such a good time with Marina.

She looked over at Melissa, who was busy making a poster with her partner. Then she . . .

Activities

1. Write an ending for the story about Kayla.

_____

_____

_____

_____

2. Discuss with a partner the following questions.

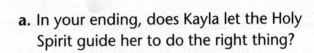

a. In your ending, does Kayla let the Holy Spirit guide her to do the right thing?

b. Why would Kayla want to tell a story that might embarrass her best friend?

c. How would Melissa feel if Kayla broke her promise?

3. Look at a newspaper or a magazine for an example of a person who is spreading God's goodness. Write about that person on the lines below.

NEWS THAT'S FIT TO PRINT

NEWS

TODAY

How can we celebrate the Holy Spirit's life in us?

Prayer Celebration

A Prayer of Intercession

Leader: Each time we show God's goodness to others, the Holy Spirit renews the life of Christ in us.

(Think about the person you wrote about in activity 3 on page 149.)

Leader: For those who spread God's goodness, we pray,

Side 1: Holy Spirit, show us how to love.

Leader: For those who have made a bad choice, we pray,

Side 2: Holy Spirit, forgive us and guide us back to God.

Leader: Holy Spirit, renew the life of Christ in us,

Side 1: when we are polite to others.

Side 2: when we follow the rules at school.

Leader: Holy Spirit, renew the life of Christ in us when . . .

(Add your own intercessions here.)

All: Holy Spirit, give us the strength to care for one another through our words and deeds each day. Amen.

Chapter Review

9

A **Complete** the sentences with words from the box.

forgive	teachings	Church
disciples	Last Supper	Pentecost

1. The event that marks the beginning of the Church is called

   _____.

2. The life of the Holy Spirit was alive within the

   _____.

3. If we make bad choices, we can pray to the Holy Spirit to

   _____ us.

4. The Holy Spirit gave the disciples the power to spread Jesus'

   _____ to the world.

5. At the _____, Jesus promised to send the
   Holy Spirit to guide us.

B **Complete** the following prayer by writing two ways you
have shown God's goodness to others.

Holy Spirit, guide me in making choices when I _____

_____

_____

_____

_____

_____

_____

C **Draw** or write about one of the signs of the Holy Spirit at Pentecost.

D **Respond** to the following questions.

1. What did Jesus mean when he said, "I will send the Spirit, who will guide you to the truth."? (based on John 16:13)

_____

_____

_____

_____

_____

2. In what ways has the Holy Spirit guided you? _____

_____

_____

_____

_____

Take Home

Confirmed in the Spirit

The Gifts of the Holy Spirit were first defined in the Old Testament in the Book of Isaiah. We believe the Seven Gifts are infused in us at Baptism and strengthened through Confirmation and Eucharist. Wisdom, understanding, right judgment, courage, knowledge, reverence, and wonder and awe are the gifts we receive when the Holy Spirit comes upon us.

ACTIVITY

Spirit Cross Place two paint stirrers or ice cream sticks in the form of a cross. Decorate the cross and on one side, write the names of the Gifts of the Spirit. On the other side, write the names of the members of your family. Each day, pray the prayer for the week together, using this Spirit cross.

WEEKLY PLANNER

On Sunday

Choose one of the Gifts of the Spirit to reflect on during the week. How can this gift help you to be a follower of Jesus Christ?

On the Web

blestarewe.com

 Visit our Web site for the saint of the day and the reflection question of the week.

Saint of the Week

 Saint Paul (first century)

At one time in his life, Saint Paul did not like Christians and he arrested them whenever he could. But after he converted to Christianity, he spent his life teaching others about Jesus. Some of his writings are in the Bible.

Patron Saint of: reporters, lay people
Feast Day: January 25

A Prayer for the Week

We thank you, Lord, for the gifts of your Spirit. Let us learn from the life of Saint Paul. Help us to share your Good News with everyone. Amen.

Take Home

FAMILY TIME

✝ Scripture Background

In the Early Church

Paul Once a persecutor of Christians, Paul later converted and spent over ten years spreading the Gospel throughout the Roman Empire. He is often pictured as an elderly man with a pointed beard, holding a sword and a book. The sword is a reminder of Paul's death in Rome where he was beheaded. The book signifies Paul's years of missionary work and the many churches he established.

Paul stayed in one Christian community for nearly two years, where he baptized many people. Read about his ministry in Ephesus in Acts 19:1–6.

OUR CATHOLIC TRADITION in Liturgy

The Ambry The ambry is the cupboard or chest that contains the oils used for the Sacraments. In the sixth century, the ambry held the Eucharist as well as the sacred oils and was located at the bottom of the altar. Between the thirteenth and sixteenth centuries, only the Eucharist was kept in the ambry, which was then called a tabernacle. The oils were kept in the sacristy in a niche in the wall. This became known as an ambry. Today ambries can be found in the sanctuary or near the baptismal font. Their prominent place reminds us of the special use of sacred oils for initiating, healing, and consecrating.

HOLY OILS

10 Confirmed in the Spirit

Be sealed with the Gift of the Holy Spirit.

Rite of Confirmation

Share

The Spirit Within Us

God's hands created
   a teardrop and a waterfall,
   an opening bud, and a tree so tall.
I stand in wonder and awe.
God's Son, Jesus, showed us
   to treat gently and kindly the sick and the poor;
   to reach out to others, always trying to do more.
I follow with understanding and wisdom.
The Church teaches us
   to make wise choices each day;
   to believe in God who strengthens us along the way.
I live with courage and right judgment.
With the knowledge that God loves me,
and with reverence, I pray
that I respond with joy,
each and every day.

Activity

How is your experience similar to that of the person who wrote this poem?

_____

_____

_____

_____

_____

How can we grow stronger in our faith?

Hear & Believe

 ## Worship The Sacrament of Confirmation

When we receive **Confirmation**, the Holy Spirit increases the **grace** of our Baptism. We become more fully united with Christ. Our membership in his Body, the Church, is strengthened. We can become more dedicated to the mission of the Church. We can become true witnesses to the teachings of Christ and the Church.

On Pentecost the disciples accepted the **Gifts of the Holy Spirit** with joy. Made new by the Spirit, they began to share their faith with others.

The Laying on of Hands

The **bishop** celebrates the Sacrament of Confirmation with us. During the Rite of Confirmation, the bishop asks God to send the Holy Spirit to strengthen those about to receive the Sacrament.

My dear friends:
> In baptism God our Father gave the new birth of eternal life
> to his chosen sons and daughters.
> Let us pray to our Father
> that he will pour out the Holy Spirit
> to strengthen his sons and daughters with his gifts
> and anoint them to be more like
> Christ, the Son of God.

Rite of Confirmation

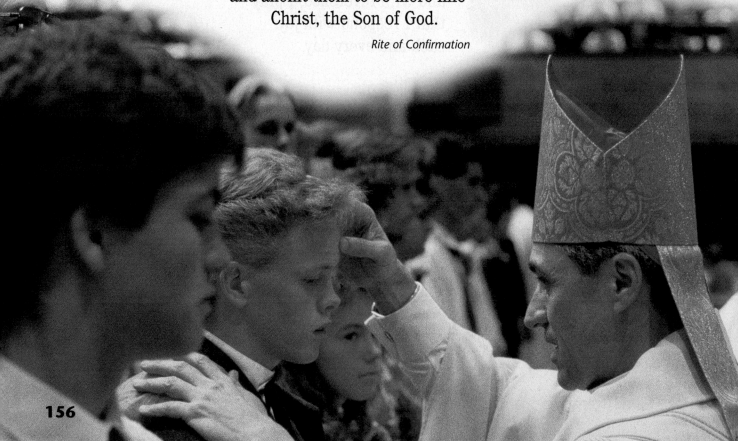

The bishop then prays with the community for the coming of the Holy Spirit. He extends his hands over those receiving the Sacrament. This is called the "Laying On of Hands." He prays:

> All-powerful God, Father of our Lord Jesus Christ,
> by water and the Holy Spirit
> you freed your sons and daughters from sin
> and gave them new life.
> Send your Holy Spirit upon them
> to be their Helper and Guide.
> Give them the spirit of wisdom and understanding,
> the spirit of right judgment and courage,
> the spirit of knowledge and reverence.
> Fill them with the spirit of wonder and awe
>   in your presence.
> We ask this through Christ our Lord.
> Amen.

Rite of Confirmation

The Anointing with Chrism

The bishop lays his hand on those being confirmed, one at a time. He calls each of them by name and anoints them by making the Sign of the Cross with Sacred Chrism on their foreheads. He says,

> Be sealed with the Gift of the Holy Spirit.

Rite of Confirmation

Activity

Write the seven gifts that are prayed for in the "laying on of hands" in the Rite of Confirmation.

w _____   u _____

r _____   c _____

k _____   r _____

w _____

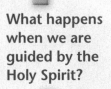

What happens when we are guided by the Holy Spirit?

Hear & Believe

✝ Receiving the Holy Spirit

In the earliest days of the Church, Paul, guided by the Holy Spirit, was a strong witness to the Christian faith. He called upon the Holy Spirit to guide new believers on their Christian journey as followers of Jesus Christ.

Paul went to the city of Ephesus (ef ih suhs), where he met twelve men who said they were followers of Jesus.

Paul asked them, "Did you receive the Holy Spirit?" The men looked puzzled. "We have never even heard that there is a Holy Spirit," they answered.

Paul explained that those who believed in the Risen Christ must be baptized. When they heard this, the twelve men asked Paul to baptize them in the name of Jesus. After he baptized the men, Paul extended his hands over them. The Holy Spirit came upon them, and they began to speak in different languages. Strengthened by the Holy Spirit, they helped teach others the Good News about Jesus.

Based on Acts 19:1–6

Our Church Teaches

Jesus sends us the Holy Spirit in the **Sacraments of Christian Initiation**—Baptism, Confirmation, and Eucharist. In the Sacrament of Baptism, we begin our life as members of the Catholic Church. In the Sacrament of Confirmation, we are strengthened to be Jesus' followers. In the Sacrament of Eucharist, we are united with Christ and strengthened by his Body and Blood.

Holy Spirit

Activities

1. With the help of the Holy Spirit, you can teach others the Good News about Jesus. Write four things you think others should know about Jesus.

_____

_____

_____

_____

2. Think about Pentecost, when the disciples first received the Holy Spirit. How did the men in Ephesus share a similar experience?

_____

_____

_____

_____

_____

_____

_____

_____

How can we use the Gifts of the Holy Spirit?

Respond

The Gifts of the Holy Spirit

At Baptism, we receive the Gifts of the Holy Spirit.
These gifts are strengthened in us at Confirmation
to help us live holy lives.

Wisdom	helps us to know God's will for our lives.
Understanding	enables us to know the teachings of our Catholic faith.
Right Judgment	helps us to know what is right and to make good choices.
Courage	strengthens us to be witnesses of Jesus Christ and to defend our Catholic faith.
Knowledge	helps us to know that God is more important than anything else in life.
Reverence	helps us to love and respect God and all that he has created.
Wonder and Awe	helps us to be filled with reverence for God and thanksgiving for all of creation.

Activities

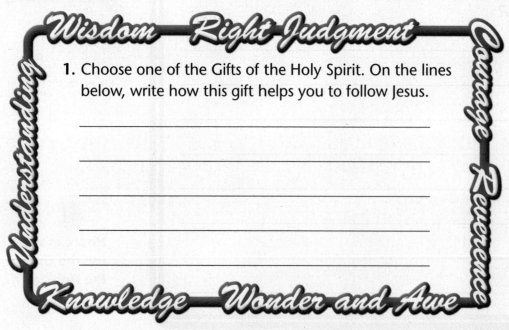

Wisdom   Right Judgment   Courage   Reverence   Understanding   Knowledge   Wonder and Awe

1. Choose one of the Gifts of the Holy Spirit. On the lines below, write how this gift helps you to follow Jesus.

_____

_____

_____

_____

_____

2. The Gifts of the Holy Spirit give us the strength to teach others the Good News about Jesus. With the help of the Holy Spirit, you also can use your gifts and talents to help others.

Imagine that a parish group is planning a visit to the local nursing home. Here are pictures of the children and adults who are going. Below each picture is a description of a talent or personality trait that each person has.

Discuss with your group how each person can use his or her talents to serve the residents of the nursing home. Write your answers on the lines next to each picture.

a. Good listener

b. Knows about sports

c. Likes to read

d. Friendly

Imagine you are part of the parish group. Write what gift or talent you would share with someone at the nursing home.

_____

_____

How can we celebrate receiving the Gifts of the Holy Spirit?

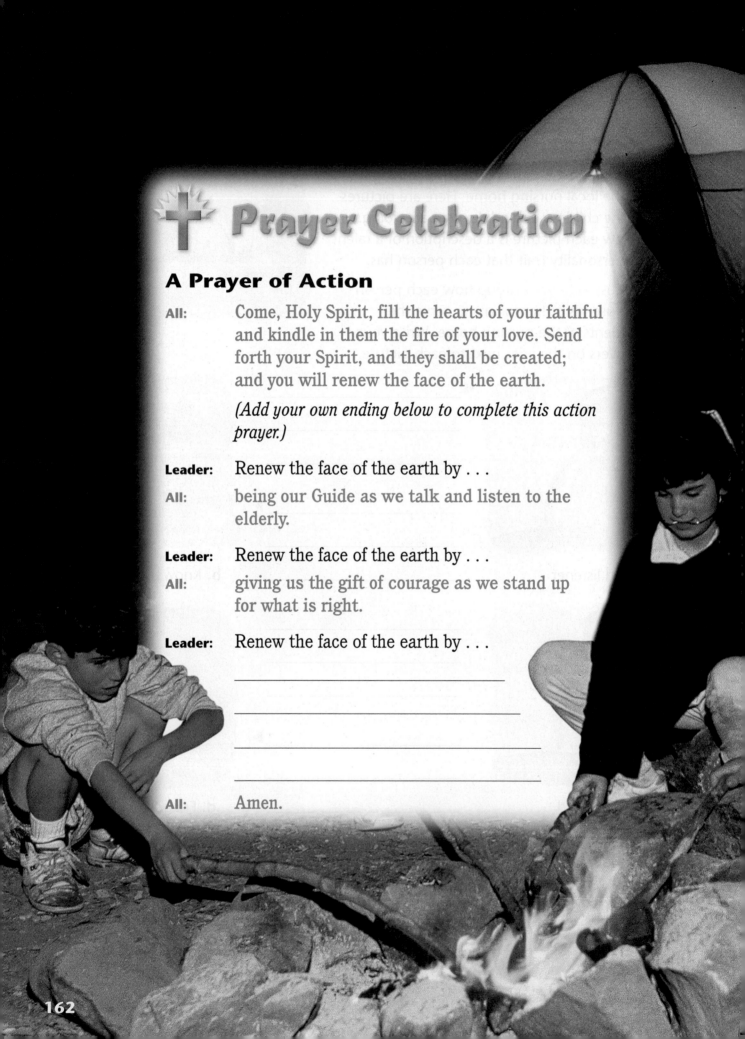

✝ Prayer Celebration

A Prayer of Action

All: Come, Holy Spirit, fill the hearts of your faithful and kindle in them the fire of your love. Send forth your Spirit, and they shall be created; and you will renew the face of the earth.

(Add your own ending below to complete this action prayer.)

Leader: Renew the face of the earth by . . .

All: being our Guide as we talk and listen to the elderly.

Leader: Renew the face of the earth by . . .

All: giving us the gift of courage as we stand up for what is right.

Leader: Renew the face of the earth by . . .

_____

_____

_____

_____

All: Amen.

10 Chapter Review

A **Circle** the letter of the best answer.

1. The Sacraments of Christian Initiation are Baptism, Confirmation, and _____.
   a. Holy Orders
   b. Reconciliation
   c. Matrimony
   d. Eucharist

2. God's life within us is called _____.
   a. grace
   b. mercy
   c. love
   d. power

3. The Holy Spirit strengthens the grace of our Baptism in the Sacrament of _____.
   a. Matrimony
   b. Confirmation
   c. Eucharist
   d. Reconciliation

4. The Seven Gifts of the Holy Spirit are wonder and awe, right judgment, courage, knowledge, reverence, wisdom, and _____.
   a. love
   b. grace
   c. justice
   d. understanding

5. At Confirmation the bishop anoints a candidate and tells the person to _____.
   a. be strong in his or her faith
   b. go and praise the Lord
   c. be sealed with the Holy Spirit
   d. go and follow Jesus

B **Write** the two important actions of the bishop during the Sacrament of Confirmation.

_____

_____

_____

_____

_____

C **Match** column A with column B by writing the correct number in the space provided.

A   **B**

1. wisdom   _____ strengthens us to be witnesses of Jesus Christ and to defend our Catholic faith

2. reverence   _____ enables us to know the teachings of our Catholic faith

3. understanding   _____ helps us to love and respect God and all that he has created

4. knowledge   _____ helps us to know God's will for our lives.

5. courage   _____ helps us to know that God is more important than anything else in life.

D **Complete** this prayer to the Holy Spirit by using the words in the box, then write your own prayer to the Holy Spirit.

Come, Holy Spirit, fill the _____ of your faithful and

kindle in them the _____ of your _____.

Send forth your Spirit, and they shall be created; and you will renew

the face of the earth. Amen.

| love |
| fire |
| hearts |

Prayer to the Holy Spirit

Come, Holy Spirit, _____

_____

_____

_____

_____. Amen.

Take Home

The Commandments and the Law of Love

We all live with rules in our lives, from the formal laws that rule our country and community to the informal rules of our homes. The basis for many of our laws and rules can be found in the Ten Commandments. If we make ourselves familiar with them, it will be easier to live peacefully with those around us.

ACTIVITY

Neighbors Our neighbors are not just the people who live close to us. They can be from countries far away, on the other side of the city, or in the next state. Get the name of a family that lives far away and become pen pals (your parish or a mission organization should be able to help). Getting to know people from another culture is a way of loving our neighbor.

WEEKLY PLANNER

On Sunday

In the homily, the priest or deacon applies the Mass readings to our daily lives. Listen carefully to the homily for words that will help you to live your Catholic faith.

On the Web

blestarewe.com

Visit our Web site for the saint of the day and the reflection question of the week.

Saint of the Week

Saint Margaret of Castello (1287–1320)

Born with several disabilities, Saint Margaret of Castello spent much of her childhood in seclusion. She later became a lay Dominican, and spent her life in prayer. At her funeral, a girl who was disabled was miraculously cured.

Patron Saint of: the physically challenged
Feast Day: April 13

Lord, we thank you for the gift of life. As we remember Saint Margaret of Castello, help us to love others as you love us.
Amen.

Take Home

FAMILY TIME

✝ Scripture Background

In the Time of Jesus

Feasts in Jerusalem   Jews from many countries traveled to Jerusalem to celebrate major festivals. Speaking different languages, they came from places, such as Syria, Asia Minor, Cyprus, Greece, and Egypt. Peasants as well as rich merchants crowded into the Holy City, causing the population to more than double. Many visitors stayed in private homes or in tents they set up in open areas of the city. Passover, celebrated in the spring, was an especially busy holiday. It was during Passover that Jesus taught his disciples the New Commandment.

Read John 13:33–35.

OUR CATHOLIC TRADITION in Religious Life

The Little Sisters of the Poor
The Little Sisters of the Poor are an international congregation of religious sisters who have devoted their lives to serving the elderly. The Little Sisters were founded by Saint Jeanne Jugan in 1839 in Saint-Servan, France. Saint Jeanne began caring for the elderly one day when she came across an old, blind widow who had no one to care for her. Saint Jeanne took the woman into her home and eventually took in more elderly poor. Soon other women accompanied Saint Jeanne in caring for the elderly who were forgotten by society. Saint Jeanne believed that in serving the elderly poor, she was serving Christ himself. Today, the Little Sisters care for the elderly in many countries around the world.

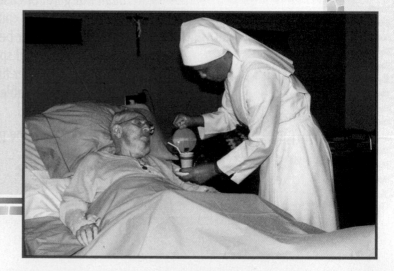

11 The Commandments and the Law of Love

LET US PRAY As I have loved you, so you should love one another.

Based on John 13:34

Share

As Christians we show our love for people by treating them with kindness and respect.

Activity

Play a game of tic-tac-toe. Choose a word in a square. Give an example of how you or someone you know acted in this way. Then mark the square with an *X* or an *O*.

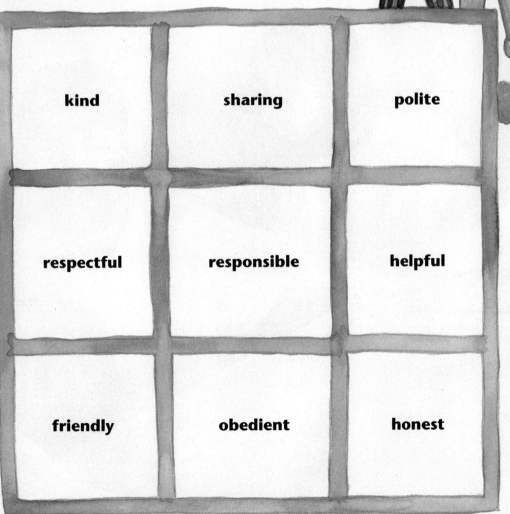

kind	**sharing**	**polite**
respectful	**responsible**	**helpful**
friendly	**obedient**	**honest**

How can we support each other in living the Commandments?

Hear & Believe

 Scripture The New Commandment

*Jesus taught his disciples lessons through examples and words.
Many of these lessons were about loving others. On the night before
he died, Jesus again spoke of love. He said he was giving the disciples
a new commandment about love. In the story below, read how Jesus
explained this commandment to his disciples.*

"My children," Jesus said to his disciples. "I will be with
you only a little while longer. So now I will give you a new
commandment: Love one another. As I have loved you, so you
should love one another. It will be through your love for others
that people will know that you are my followers."

Based on John 13:33–35

Living the New Commandment

Jesus combined the Ten Commandments into one commandment. This commandment is called the **New Commandment**, or the **Law of Love**. We follow the New Commandment when we treat others with love, respect, and kindness. The Holy Trinity works in us helping us to follow the New Commandment so that we can bring God's love to all people.

Sometimes we choose not to follow God's Commandments. We choose instead to sin and turn away from God's love. At these times, we can use the Ten Commandments and the New Commandment to help us examine our conscience. In an **examination of conscience**, we think about how well we have loved God and others. The Church encourages us to follow the Ten Commandments and the New Commandment so that we can stay close to God and please him by making good, moral choices.

> **GO TO** pages 404–405 to review the Ten Commandments and learn more about the New Commandment.

Activity

Create an ad encouraging others to live the New Commandment.

Faith Words

New Commandment
The New Commandment is the loving message in which Jesus united the Ten Commandments and the Beatitudes into one. It is also known as the Law of Love.

examination of conscience
In an examination of conscience, we decide whether our words and actions show love for God and others.

How can we show our love for God?

Hear & Believe

Nicholas Green and the Gift of Life

In September 1994, seven-year-old Nicholas Green was on vacation in Italy with his parents and sister. Without warning, highway robbers shot and killed Nicholas.

Nicholas's parents made a very courageous and loving decision. They donated Nicholas's heart and other organs to people in Italy who needed them to live. Some of the people who received the organs were children who were very sick. They were happy to be given the chance to live a healthy life.

Mr. and Mrs. Green's actions showed people everywhere how something good can come out of evil. Their story inspired people throughout the world.

If you visit Nicholas's hometown in Bodega Bay, California, you will see a magnificent bell tower. Pope John Paul II blessed the largest bell, which hangs from the top of the tower. It has Nicholas's name and the names of the seven people who received his organs. The bell tower stands as a reminder of God's precious gift of life.

Living the 4th, 5th, and 6th Commandments

The story of the Green family reminds us of the importance of respecting life. The Fourth, Fifth, and Sixth Commandments help us to love and respect all people. We keep the Fourth Commandment when we listen to our parents and show that we care about them. When we work together to protect life, we are keeping the Fifth Commandment. The Sixth Commandment helps a husband and wife grow in love and respect for each other. This commandment teaches us that every marriage and family is sacred, or holy.

The Bell Memorial in Bodega Bay, California sculpted by Bruce Hasson

Our Church Teaches

We keep the Covenant God made with Moses and the Hebrew people by following the Ten Commandments. The Fourth through Sixth Commandments guide us to respect all people.

Jesus taught us how to love. He lived by the Commandments, showing us the way to a happy life with God. As Christians, we try to follow the Ten Commandments and the New Commandment. We treat people with kindness, we share in the life of the Trinity—the Father, Son, and Holy Spirit.

We Believe

The Fourth through Sixth Commandments guide us to love and respect all people. We can use the Ten Commandments and the New Commandment to help us examine our conscience.

Activities

1. Read the different endings for the following sentence. Write the number "4" or "5" to tell whether each ending describes the Fourth Commandment or the Fifth Commandment.

   The world is a better place when we . . .

   solve arguments peacefully. _____

   show our parents that we appreciate them _____

   help people who are sick. _____

   use kind words. _____

   obey adults who care for us. _____

2. Mr. and Mrs. Green remember Nicholas as being loyal to his friends and family. Write the number "4," "5," or "6" to tell which Commandment calls for married people to remain loyal to one another.

   _____

How can we apply the Ten Commandments in our lives?

Respond

Activity

Read each journal entry that Peter made this week. Decide which two Commandments are not being followed in each day's entry. In the boxes, write the numbers of the Commandments.

 Page 404 to read more about the Ten Commandments.

Peter's Journal

Monday

Everyone was sharing stories today about what they did during spring vacation. Joan talked about her trip to Florida so much, I felt sick to my stomach. I know she's been there at least five times. I sure wish my parents had more money so I could travel to fun places.

Joan met a famous skater in Florida and showed us an autographed picture of her. My friend Billy decided to play a trick on her. When she wasn't looking, he hid the picture in his desk. I saw Joan get really upset when she couldn't find it. I felt bad about that, so I told Billy to give it back.

Wednesday

Grandma and Grandpa's surprise anniversary party was so much fun. Mom told me they've been married for fifty years! Mom said they had some rough times. Sometimes they even said hurtful things about each other and used the name of God in an angry way. They always apologized and have kept the promises they made to each other on their wedding day.

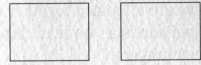

Friday

When I got home from karate lessons today, I was in a good mood. Then Mom said that I had to clean my room before going outside. As I started cleaning, I heard my friend playing in his backyard. I hid the remaining clothes and toys under the bed. Next, I walked by Mom, who was busy talking on the phone. I told her my room was clean and then I rushed outside.

How can we pray to show that we are all connected in the family of God?

Prayer Celebration

A Prayer of the Family of God

Leader: To show that we are all joined together in Christ, let us join hands as we read this Native American prayer.

Reader 1: You must teach your children that the ground beneath their feet is sacred so that they will respect the land.

Reader 2: Tell your children that the earth is rich with the lives of our brothers and sisters.

Reader 3: Teach your children what we have taught our children, that the earth is a gift from God.

Reader 4: Whatever affects the earth, affects the children of earth. This we know.

All: All people are connected, united in the family of God.

Leader: God weaves the web of life. We are a strand in that web. Whatever we do to the web, we do to everyone in God's family.

Based on the Native American Prayer Attributed to Chief Seattle,
Leader of the Duwamish Tribe

Chapter Review

11

A **Complete** the sentences with words from the box.

1. Jesus gave us a new _____ to love one another as he loved us.

2. Jesus lived by the Commandments and taught us how to _____ others.

3. The Fourth through the Sixth _____ guide us to love and respect all people.

4. In an examination of conscience, we decide whether our _____ and actions show love for God and others.

5. If we choose not to follow God's Commandments, we turn away from _____ love.

love	commandment	words
Sacraments	Commandments	God's

B **Write** the number of each Commandment (4, 5, or 6). Then draw a line from the Commandment to the question that can be used in an examination of conscience.

a. _____ You shall not kill.   Do I obey my parents?

b. _____ Honor your father and mother.   Do I respect my body and the body of others?

c. _____ You shall not commit adultery.   Do I respect the life of others?

C **Circle** the letter of the best answer.

1. Deciding whether our actions show love for God and others is called _____.

   a. an examination of conscience

   b. the New Commandment

   c. a Sacrament of Initiation

   d. an examination of sins

2. The Fourth through Sixth Commandments help us to _____.

   a. understand the Trinity

   b. love and respect all people

   c. forgive others

   d. love God.

3. Jesus gave us a new commandment that tells us to _____.

   a. attend Mass

   b. be polite

   c. love one another

   d. tell the truth

4. By treating others with kindness, we share in _____.

   a. the life of the Trinity

   b. how we love God

   c. the life of the Spirit

   d. how good we are

D **Respond** to the following.

1. How did Nicholas Green's parents show their love for others?

   _____

   _____

   _____

   _____

2. How can you show your love for other people?

   _____

   _____

   _____

   _____

Take Home

FAMILY TIME

The Commandments and Doing God's Will

Mary has a special place in our Church as the Mother of Jesus. Over the centuries, mothers have turned to her for support. We also turn to Mary as we would to our own mother. Mary models acceptance and a quiet strength. She is a family person, so it is easy to take the virtues that she models and apply them to our own family life.

ACTIVITY

Mothers Put together a collection of photographs in honor of the mothers in your family. Do you have pictures of grandmothers and great-grandmothers? How about godmothers? Talk about the different qualities of each of these special people.

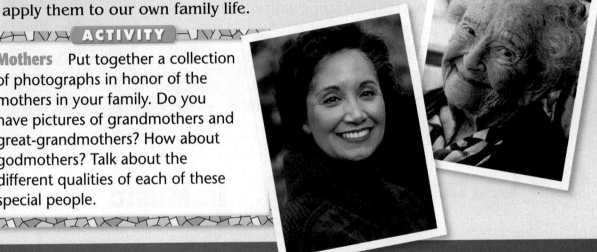

WEEKLY PLANNER

On Sunday

After Mass, look around your church for images of Mary. These images might be in statues, stained-glass windows, and other pieces of art.

On the Web

blestarewe.com

Visit our Web site for the saint of the day and the reflection question of the week.

Saint of the Week

 Mary, Mother of God

The Church celebrates the Solemnity of Mary, Mother of God on January 1. Throughout the Church year we celebrate many events relating to Mary, but on this day we celebrate her motherhood. On this day as well, God's people traditionally have joined together to pray for world peace.

Patron Saint of: many countries, cities, and dioceses; mothers

Feast Day: January 1

A Prayer for the Week

Mary, our Mother, help us to love and honor your Son, Jesus. Help us to model our family life like your Holy Family. Amen.

Getting ready for Chapter 12
Take Home

✚ Scripture Background

In the Time of Jesus

Jesus' Family Tree   Although there are more than twenty genealogies in the Old Testament, only two appear in the New Testament. In tracing Jesus' family, Matthew and Luke both include David, the shepherd boy who became a great king of Israel. Also appearing on both lists is Abraham, a patriarch of the nation of Israel. While Matthew stops with Abraham, Luke traces Jesus' ancestry all the way back to Adam.

In Mark 3:31–35, Jesus talks about who is part of his family.

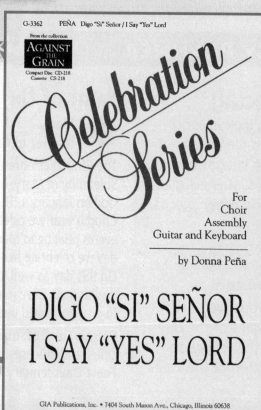

OUR CATHOLIC TRADITION in Music

Marian Songs   Many beautiful songs have been written about Mary. Franz Schubert's "Ave Maria" and the hymn "Immaculate Mary" are, perhaps, the most well known. Contemporary Catholic composers have written Marian songs as well. The bilingual song "I Say 'Yes' Lord," by Donna Peña, speaks of saying yes to the will of God in good times and in bad.

G-3362   PEÑA   Digo "Sí" Señor / I Say "Yes" Lord

From the collection
AGAINST THE GRAIN
Compact Disc CD-218
Cassette CS-218

Celebration Series

For
Choir
Assembly
Guitar and Keyboard

by Donna Peña

DIGO "SI" SEÑOR
I SAY "YES" LORD

GIA Publications, Inc. • 7404 South Mason Ave., Chicago, Illinois 60638

12 The Commandments and Doing God's Will

May this sacrament of new life warm our hearts with your love.

Based on the Prayers from Benediction of the Blessed Sacrament

Share

Living the Commandments

All around, there are people who are sharing the love of God with others. They live according to God's Commandments.

Activity

Look at the pictures. Each one shows people helping one another. Tell how these people are doing the will of God.

How should we live as members of God's family?

Hear & Believe

✝ Scripture Jesus and His Family

Jesus had many ways of showing people the importance of doing God's will.

One day Jesus was teaching a group of people. The crowd told him, "Lord, your mother and family are here. They are waiting outside for you."

Jesus looked around at the people near him. "You are my family, too," Jesus said. "Whoever does what God asks is in my family. They are as close to me as a mother, father, sister, or brother."

Based on Mark 3:31–35

Accepting the Will of God

Jesus showed us how to live according to his Father's will. He followed the Commandments to love others. Jesus treated all people with kindness, justice, and mercy. He always prayed and asked God for strength and courage to bring God's love to everyone.

Mary, Jesus' mother, is a model of Christian faith. When she was asked to be the Mother of God, Mary placed herself in God's loving hands. She responded, "Let it be done unto me according to your word" (based on Luke 1:38).

Like Mary, we are part of Jesus' family when we choose to accept and do the will of God. Above all else, God wants us to love him completely, placing our trust in him. God also wants us to love our neighbor.

Devotion to God

Jesus taught the people that, in order to become close to him, we are asked to accept God's will. We are asked to show that we accept God's will in many ways. We are to keep God's Commandments. We are to live in the spirit of Jesus' command to love others as he loves us.

Jesus often prayed to his Father in Heaven for the strength and courage to do God's will, even when it was difficult. Praying to God is a sign of being faithful to God's will. There are many ways in which we can pray. One special prayer of devotion is to pray quietly before the **Blessed Sacrament**.

In your church, near the altar in the sanctuary, or in a separate chapel, the Consecrated Bread of the Eucharist is kept in a **tabernacle** in order to bring Communion to people who are unable to come to Mass due to old age or illness. The Eucharist when it is reserved in the tabernacle is called the Blessed Sacrament. When we pray silently to Jesus Christ in the Blessed Sacrament, we can ask that we will always accept and do God's will.

Faith Words

Blessed Sacrament
The Blessed Sacrament is another name for the Eucharist kept in the tabernacle.

tabernacle
A tabernacle is a container in the church where the Blessed Sacrament is kept for distribution to those unable to come to Mass due to illness or for personal prayer.

Activity

Write one way you accept and do the will of God in your life.

_____

_____

_____

How can we live according to God's will?

Hear & Believe

Rose Hawthorne and Living the Commandments of Love

Rose Hawthorne was born in Massachusetts in 1851. When she was forty years old, Rose was welcomed into the Catholic Church. As Rose grew in her faith, she discovered God's special plan for her.

Rose went to New York City in 1883. She had a friend named Emma Lazarus who died of cancer. Although Emma received medical treatment, Rose discovered that there were people dying of cancer who couldn't afford such care. Rose was filled with compassion for these suffering people. She asked God to help her to comfort them.

Rose took classes at a hospital to learn more about cancer. Then she rented space in the city and took in cancer patients who had nowhere else to go. In time, other women joined Rose in her efforts. They formed a religious community called the Dominican Sisters of Hawthorne. In February 2003, the Church declared Rose Hawthorne "Servant of God." Receiving this title is one of the first steps before a person is declared a saint.

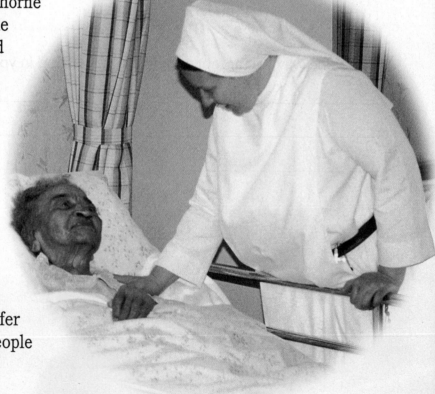

A Dominican Sister of Hawthorne visits a hospital patient.

The Dominican Sisters of Hawthorne are dedicated women who continue Rose's work. Each day, they spend time in **Adoration** of the Blessed Sacrament. They reflect on Jesus' suffering and pray for strength to assist those who are suffering. The Dominican Sisters of Hawthorne also have a special love for Mary. Her life inspires them to trust in God's help as they care for their patients.

Today the Dominican Sisters have six homes for the sick in the United States. They continue to offer Christ's peace and friendship to people in their care.

Our Church Teaches

Like Jesus and Mary, we are called to accept the will of God. When we pray, we can ask for God's help in understanding his plan for each of us. Through prayer our faith grows stronger. We can pray the Lord's Prayer with meaning when we pray, "Thy will be done on earth as it is in heaven."

We Believe

Jesus taught us that through prayer we learn to understand and trust God's plan for each of us.

Activity

Read each situation. Thinking about doing God's will, draw a picture to finish the story. Then pray the prayer beside your drawing, asking for God's help in accepting his will.

A friend is absent from school for two days. He asks you to help him with the work he missed. You would rather play a game outside with the rest of the class.

Lord, help me share my time with those who need me.

You packed your favorite snack to eat at camp. The person next to you forgot to bring something to eat. You would rather eat all the cookies yourself.

Lord, help me share what I have with others.

How can we do more to help others?

Respond

The Fourth Through Sixth Commandments and Our Relationship with God's People

God's Commandments help us respect our own life and the life and health of others. The Fourth Commandment helps us respect members of our families, especially our parents. The Fifth Commandment helps us to keep healthy and respect the life and health of others. The Sixth Commandment helps us respect our bodies and the bodies and privacy of others.

GO TO page 404 to review the meaning of each Commandment.

Activities

1. Even though these laws were given to Moses over three thousand years ago, the Ten Commandments still have meaning for us today. They are based on our relationship with God and all God's children. In the space next to each Commandment below, write a sentence or two about what you think it means and how you can obey it. Obeying the Commandments is one way we follow the will of God.

The Ten Commandments	What this Commandment means to me and how I can obey it
IV Honor your father and mother.	
V You shall not kill.	
VI You shall not commit adultery.	

2. Learn to sign the following phrases from the Lord's Prayer. Review what you learned in Chapters 4 and 8. Then put all the phrases together.

Thy   **will**

be done   **on earth,**   **as it is**

in   **heaven.**

How can I celebrate my faith in God?

✝ Prayer Celebration

A Prayer of Adoration

Leader: People who gather to worship Christ in the Blessed Sacrament may sing songs of praise. They may also listen to God's word and pray together. Let us pray together now.

All: Lord our God, in this Blessed Sacrament, we come into the presence of Jesus Christ, your Son. He was born of the Virgin Mary and crucified for our salvation. May this Blessed Sacrament warm our hearts with your love and make us eager for the eternal joy of your kingdom. We ask this through Christ our Lord. Amen.

Based on the Prayers from the Benediction of the Blessed Sacrament

186

12 Chapter Review

A **Match** column A with column B by writing the correct number in the space provided.

A

1. The _____ is another name for the Eucharist kept in the tabernacle.

2. A tabernacle is a container in church where the Blessed Sacrament is kept for those unable to come to _____ due to illness or for private prayer.

3. Jesus obeyed the Ten _____ by loving others.

4. _____ helps us understand God's plan for each of us.

5. Mary is a _____ of faith.

B

_____ prayer

_____ Blessed Sacrament

_____ model

_____ Mass

_____ Commandments

B **Circle** the letter of the best answer.

1. Who did Jesus say is his family?
   a. the Twelve Apostles
   b. Mary and Joseph
   c. people who do what God asks
   d. people who know the Commandments

2. The _____ Commandment helps us to keep healthy and respect the life and health of others.
   a. First
   b. Fifth
   c. Sixth
   d. Fourth

3. The _____ Commandment helps us respect our parents.
   a. First
   b. Fifth
   c. Sixth
   d. Fourth

4. The _____ Commandment helps us respect our bodies and the bodies and privacy of others.
   a. First
   b. Fifth
   c. Sixth
   d. Fourth

C Circle the letter of the best answer.

1. A special way to pray is in _____ of the Blessed Sacrament.
   a. adoration
   b. prayer
   c. mercy
   d. meditation

2. Rose Hawthorne showed love for others by _____.
   a. visiting people in prison
   b. caring for cancer patients
   c. visiting people in nursing home
   d. caring for the elderly

3. The _____ is a container in which the Blessed Sacrament is kept.
   a. tabernacle
   b. altar
   c. host
   d. chalice

4. The Eucharist is another name for the _____ kept in the tabernacle.
   a. Holy Order
   b. Blessed Trinity
   c. Blessed Sacrament
   d. Holy Spirit

D Respond to the following.

1. Jesus said, "Whoever does what God asks will be in my family" (*based on Mark 3:35*). How can we be part of Jesus' family?

   _____

   _____

   _____

2. How does someone you know live according to God's Commandments?

   _____

   _____

   _____

Faith in Action

Youth Ministers Some of the decisions we make each day are easy, but others are more difficult. As we pray to the Holy Spirit for help, we also look to our parish leaders as role models. Parish and school youth ministers, for example, are leaders who seek the guidance of the Holy Spirit in their own lives. They understand the kinds of decisions young people have to make. They teach us self-respect. They also teach us to take responsibility, both for our own well-being and the well-being of others. Most importantly, they teach us to honor all that is important to Jesus Christ and his Church.

In Everyday Life

Activity Think about who or what most influences the choices you make each day. Describe three ways these people or experiences help you to make good choices.

_____

_____

_____

_____

In Your Parish

Activity Think about the young people in your parish who are your age. What activities or experiences should the parish offer to foster their love for the Catholic Church and their growth in faith?

_____

_____

_____

_____

Faith in Action

The RCIA Team "RCIA" stands for the Rite of Christian Initiation of Adults. Many people work together to prepare adults for Baptism and Confirmation. Along with priests, deacons, and music ministers, catechists and sponsors are very important members of the RCIA team. They support and pray for these adults as they study the teachings of the Catholic Church and talk about the Scriptures proclaimed at Mass each week. They also participate in the various rituals that take place during the time of preparation for the Sacraments.

In Everyday Life

Activity Think about some of the closest friends you have. Write some of the ways a newcomer to your group of friends might get to know each of you better.

_____

_____

_____

_____

In Your Parish

Activity Describe in words or pictures the three most important things about your Catholic faith that you would share with people who want to learn about becoming a Catholic. When you are finished, take time to pray for the adult catechumens (those who will be baptized) and candidates (those already baptized who will be confirmed) as they prepare to receive the Sacraments. Pray that those who become Catholic treasure the same things that you treasure about the Church.

Faith in Action

Respect Life Ministries   Since 1972, Catholics have celebrated Respect Life Sunday on the first Sunday of October each year. Throughout the month of October, we pause to think about the respect for life that our Church teaches. Like our Lord Jesus, we are all called to show a special love and respect for people whom others do not always care enough about. We stand up for people who cannot stand up for themselves. These people include the unborn, the elderly, and people with disabilities.

In Everyday Life

Activity   Write one thing that you (as a group or individually) could say or do to show love and respect for each person in need.

1. Mrs. Johnson's grandchildren moved far away, and nobody visits her anymore.

   _____

2. Your classmate David has a speech problem that other kids often make fun of.

   _____

3. Crystal, the neighbor down the street who just had a baby, always seems tired and sad.

   _____

In Your Parish

Activity   Describe a problem in your community that you believe is caused or made worse by people's lack of respect for life. On the lines below, propose a way for community and parish leaders to respond to the situation.

_____

_____

_____

Faith in Action

Eucharistic Holy Hour Ministry From the time of Christ's birth, people came to worship and adore him. Just before his death, he asked his disciples to stay with him and to watch and pray. Catholics today can spend time with Jesus Christ in a Holy Hour of silent prayer in the Blessed Sacrament. During a Holy Hour, we find peace in our hearts as we pray silently. We also listen during these times of quiet to what Christ wants to say to us. He speaks to us in the silence and through Scripture readings and songs. God knows what is in our hearts, even before we speak.

In Everyday Life

Activity Good friends don't always use words to communicate. Describe a time when you have enjoyed some quiet time, just being with someone you care about.

_____

_____

_____

In Your Parish

Activity A Holy Hour is an opportunity to spend time in the presence of Jesus Christ in the Blessed Sacrament. Place a ✔ next to the things or people you would like to include if you were participating in a Holy Hour.

___ silent prayer time   ___ pray the Rosary

___ prayers to read silently   ___ Scripture readings

___ a basket of written prayer requests   ___ my friends

___ songs   ___ the Blessed Sacrament

___ my parents   ___ the parish staff

Unit Wrap-up

In this unit you have studied the topic of the Holy Spirit and how the gift of the Spirit strengthens us. Match each description with the correct reference.

Rite of Confirmation
_____

John 13:34
_____

1 Jesus commands us to love one another

2 Be sealed with the Gift of the Holy Spirit

3 the coming of the Holy Spirit to guide all those who believe

4 following the will of God

Mark 3:35
_____

Acts 2:1-2
_____

3 Unit Review

Ⓐ Match column A with column B by writing the correct number in the space provided.

A	**B**
1. Pentecost	____ Jesus gave us a New _____ to love one another.
2. Fourth	____ The _____ Commandment teaches us to listen to our parents.
3. Fifth	____ Deciding whether our words and actions show love for God and others is an examination of _____.
4. Sixth	____ At the _____, Jesus promised to send the Holy Spirit.
5. teachings	____ The life of the Holy Spirit was alive within the _____.
6. Commandment	____ We celebrate the beginning of the Church on _____.
7. Last Supper	____ The _____ Commandment helps us to keep healthy and respect the life and health of others.
8. guides	____ If we make bad choices that lead to sin, the Holy Spirit _____ us back to God.
9. conscience	____ At Pentecost, the Holy Spirit gave the disciples the power to spread Jesus' _____ to the world.
10. disciples	____ The _____ Commandment helps us respect our bodies and the privacy of others.

B **Circle** the letter of the best answer.

1. The Gift of the Holy Spirit that strengthens us to be witnesses of Jesus Christ and defend our Catholic faith is _____.
   a. reverence
   b. wonder and awe
   c. courage
   d. knowledge

2. The Gift that helps us to know God's will for our lives is _____.
   a. courage
   b. wonder and awe
   c. wisdom
   d. knowledge

3. The Gift that enables us to know what is right and to make good choices is _____.
   a. right judgment
   b. wisdom
   c. understanding
   d. reverence

4. The Gift that enables us to love and respect God and all that he has created is _____.
   a. courage
   b. wisdom
   c. understanding
   d. reverence

5. The Gift that enables us to know the teachings of our Catholic faith is _____.
   a. knowledge
   b. wonder and awe
   c. understanding
   d. reverence

6. The Gift that enables us to know that God is more important in life than anything else is _____.
   a. knowledge
   b. wisdom
   c. understanding
   d. reverence

7. The Gift that helps us to be filled with reverence for God and thanksgiving for all Creation is _____.
   a. knowledge
   b. wisdom
   c. wonder and awe
   d. courage

8. We first receive the Gifts of the Holy Spirit at _____.
   a. Baptism
   b. birth
   c. Confirmation
   d. First Communion

3 Unit Review

C **Complete** the sentences with words from the box.

Eucharist	grace	Confirmation	Holy Spirit
respect	judge	New Commandment	

1. God's life within us is called _____.

2. The Holy Spirit strengthens the grace of our Baptism in the Sacrament

   of _____.

3. The Fourth through Sixth Commandments help us to _____
   all people.

4. Jesus' teaching that we must love one another as Jesus loves us

   is known as the _____.

5. The Sacraments of Christian Initiation are Baptism, Confirmation,

   and _____.

6. At Confirmation, the bishop anoints us with oil and tells us to be

   sealed with the Gift of the _____.

D **Respond** to the following.

1. Write the Fourth through the Sixth Commandments.

   _____

   _____

   _____

2. What is one positive thing you can do to live one of these commandments?

   _____

   _____

   _____

The Church

The Church spread rapidly in the first century.
Disciples such as Saint Paul preached the Gospel and
established communities around the Mediterranean world.
These churches became centers of a new sense of justice
and worship.

We are all baptized into one body.
Based on 1 Corinthians 12:13

Some of Paul's letters to Christian
communities were sent by
messenger along this ancient
Roman road. Paul wrote his letters
with a reed pen dipped in a pot of
black ink.

Hands of Healing

Words and Music by Marty Haugen

REFRAIN

1.* Let our hands be hands of healing, let our words be

3. clear and true, in our work, God's love re-veal-ing,

just and gen-tle in all we do.

VERSE

Cantor / *All*

1. Safe - ly lead the young ones:
2. Free the ones in bond - age:
3. Touch the ones who sor - row: hands of heal - ing,
4. Com - fort for the dy - ing:
5. May we al - ways be your

Cantor / *All*

bring your joy and laugh - ter:
bring the reign of new hope:
hope be - yond all griev - ing: clear and true;
vi - sion of a new life:
make us in your im - age:

Cantor / *All*

Sing the God of chil - dren:
Sing the God of free - dom:
Sing the God of mer - cy: love re - veal - ing,
Sing the res - ur - rec - tion:
Give us voice to praise you:

D.C.

just and gen - tle in all we do.

*May be sung in canon.

Take Home

FAMILY TIME

Sacraments in the Church

Our Christian vocation begins in the Sacrament of Baptism as we become members of the Church and followers of Christ. In Confirmation we are sealed in that calling. The Eucharist gives us the strength to live in Christ. Reconciliation helps us keep our path clear for living out our vocation. In the Sacrament of Anointing of the Sick, through Jesus Christ, the Church heals our infirmities. Matrimony and Holy Orders are two ways we can live out this vocation. Receiving the Sacraments helps us to be better Christians.

ACTIVITY

Sacramental Signs God uses ordinary things, such as bread, water, and oil in extraordinary ways. They transform our lives and communicate his love for us. Ask family members to share signs that communicate to them that they are loved.

WEEKLY PLANNER

On Sunday

Remember that the Eucharistic celebration makes present the life, Death, and Resurrection of Jesus Christ.

On the Web

blestarewe.com

Visit our Web site for the saint of the day and the reflection question of the week.

Saint of the Week

 Saint Rose Philippine Duchesne (1769–1852)

Born in France, Rose eventually became a Missionary of the Sacred Heart and came to the United States. She opened the first free school for girls and founded six convents along the Mississippi River. Saint Rose died at St. Charles, Missouri, in 1852.

Patron Saint of: Diocese of Springfield-Cape Girardeau, Missouri

Feast Day: November 18

A Prayer for the Week

Dear God, your saving grace surrounds us. We remember Saint Rose's mission of spreading your grace to others. We are thankful for your love and grace that are shared in the Sacraments. Amen.

Take Home

FAMILY TIME

✝ Scripture Background

In the Early Church

Corinth   During the first century, many people passed through the city of Corinth in Greece. Merchants stopped at this busy seaport when traveling between Rome and Asia Minor. The city was well-known throughout the Mediterranean world as a commercial center. Unfortunately, Corinth was also known for its corruption and immorality. Paul took on the challenge of establishing the Church in this prosperous city. After he left the city, Paul continued to guide the Christian community through his writings.

Read his letter in 1 Corinthians 12:12–26.

OUR CATHOLIC TRADITION in Music

One Body In Christ

Receiving the Eucharist reawakens the love of Christ in us and makes us more loving toward others. In 1993, Irish Catholic composer Dana sang the song "We Are One Body" at the World Youth Day ceremonies in Denver, Colorado. She composed this song to remind the thousands of teens and young adults in attendance that we are "one Body in Christ."

Dana singing "We Are One Body" at World Youth Day, 1993

13 Sacraments in the Church

LET US PRAY

We are all baptized into one Body.

Based on 1 Corinthians 12:13

Share

As Christians, we believe that every person is an important member of God's family. We must work together to bring God's goodness to everyone.

Activity

Team Spirit

Choose who will play the following roles and act out the story.

Narrator: At St. Joseph's Parish picnic, a group of girls decide to play volleyball. As they are about to begin a game, Ashleigh comes over to join them.

Ashleigh: "Can I play on a team?"

Narrator: No one answers. Everyone knows Ashleigh does not run very fast. After a while Juanita agrees to let Ashleigh on her team. She tries to help Ashleigh whenever she cannot get to the ball fast enough.

Juanita: "I'll help you, Ashleigh."

Narrator: When it is Ashleigh's turn to serve, she hits the ball really hard and scores a point for her team. Juanita and the others cheer her on. They shout . . .

The Team: "Way to go!"

How do members of the Christian family work together?

Hear & Believe

✝ Scripture   One Body, Many Parts

*Our Church carries out **Christ's mission** in the world. Christ's mission is to bring the Kingdom of God to all people. Every person has talents that help spread God's peace and love to the world. Saint Paul understood that it was necessary that all members of the Church work together. When he wrote to the Christians in the city of Corinth, Paul compared the **Body of Christ** to a human body.*

A body is one, but it has many parts. It needs all its parts: feet, eyes, ears, everything to work. For example, the body has eyes. Is the ear a part of the body even if it is not an eye? Yes! The body needs hearing as well as sight. It is the same with Christ and his Church. Together, we make up the Body of Christ. No matter who we are, we are all baptized into one Body, the Church.

Based on 1 Corinthians 12:12–26

Sharing the Life of Jesus

The Church is a community of people united with God and with each other. Through Jesus Christ, the Church heals the sick and helps those who are poor and hungry. In doing this we carry out Christ's mission in the world. Together we lead all people closer to God's Kingdom.

By the power of the Holy Spirit, Jesus Christ is present when the Church celebrates the **Sacraments**. The Seven Sacraments were instituted by Christ to fill us with grace. Grace strengthens us in carrying out his mission and the mission of the Church. We celebrate the Sacraments in the Catholic Church as a sign that grace comes to us through the Church, united with the Body of Christ.

page 394 to read more about the Sacraments.

> ### Faith Words
>
> **Body of Christ**
> The Body of Christ is the People of God, the Church.
>
> **Sacraments**
> Sacraments are the seven sacred signs that celebrate God's love for us and Christ's presence in our lives and in the Church.

Activity

Through Baptism, we become members of the Body of Christ. Write one way we can show others that Christ is present in us.

_____

_____

_____

_____

How can we carry out Christ's mission in the world?

Lucas Benitez and Bringing Christ's Love to Others

One person who has helped spread God's love to others is a farm worker named Lucas Benitez. When he was a teenager, Lucas left Mexico and came to the United States. He worked on farms picking fruits and vegetables so that he could support his family back home.

Lucas was shocked by the way the farm workers were treated. They worked long hours for very little pay and were often denied clean drinking water.

With the help of God's grace, Lucas began to improve their living and working conditions. He organized the farm workers and encouraged them to work together for change. They held protest marches and spoke in public about their unhealthy and unjust situation.

Lucas wanted the workers to be treated with dignity and respect. Through his efforts, Lucas helped the farm workers earn higher wages. For some, it was their first wage increase in twenty years.

In 1998, the Catholic Campaign for Human Development honored Lucas Benitez with a special award. It recognized him as an outstanding young Catholic leader who helps carry out the mission of the Church. Lucas's actions show us what it means to live as a disciple of Jesus and a member of the Body of Christ.

The Sacraments Strengthen Us

When we celebrate the Sacraments, we experience the love of Christ. Jesus is alive in our hearts, calling us to bring his love to other people. The Sacraments strengthen us to continue Christ's mission in the world.

Our Church Teaches

We celebrate the Sacraments to help us love others as Jesus loved us. Christ's presence in the Church is called a **mystery**. We do not see Jesus in person, yet we know he lives through the Church.

The Church encourages us to receive the Sacraments so that we can be united with Jesus. By leading a Christian life, we move closer to being in God's Kingdom forever.

We Believe

The Church celebrates the Sacraments so that we can fully experience Christ's loving presence. Together with the whole Church, we can carry out Christ's mission in the world.

Activity

Discuss how these people are carrying out Christ's mission. In the box, write or draw one way you can bring Christ's love to others.

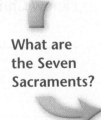

What are the Seven Sacraments?

Respond

We Are Living the Sacraments

When we celebrate the Sacraments, we are united in Christ.

Activities

1. Discover the hidden message by coloring the spaces as marked.
   Diamonds: green. Stars: red. Circles: blue.

2. Complete the following sentence.

   I know Christ lives in me because _____

   _____

   _____

   _____ .

3. Look at the crossword puzzle. Use the clues to fill in the puzzle with the name of the Sacrament being described. Refer to pages 394–397 for help.

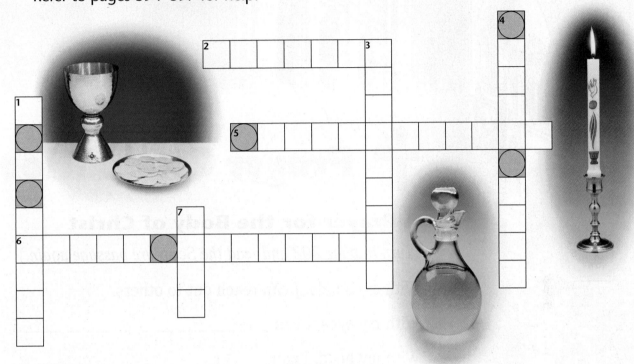

Across

2. We begin our journey of faith.

5. We are sealed with the Gift of the Holy Spirit.

6. God forgives our sins.

Down

1. We receive the Body and Blood of Christ.

3. A baptized man and a baptized woman promise to be faithful to one another.

4. celebrates the ordination of bishops, priests, and deacons

7. celebrates God's love and healing

4. Write the letters that are circled in the crossword puzzle.

Letters _____

Unscramble them to complete this sentence.

The ___ ___ ___ ___ ___ ___ celebrates seven Sacraments.

What can we do as members of the Body of Christ?

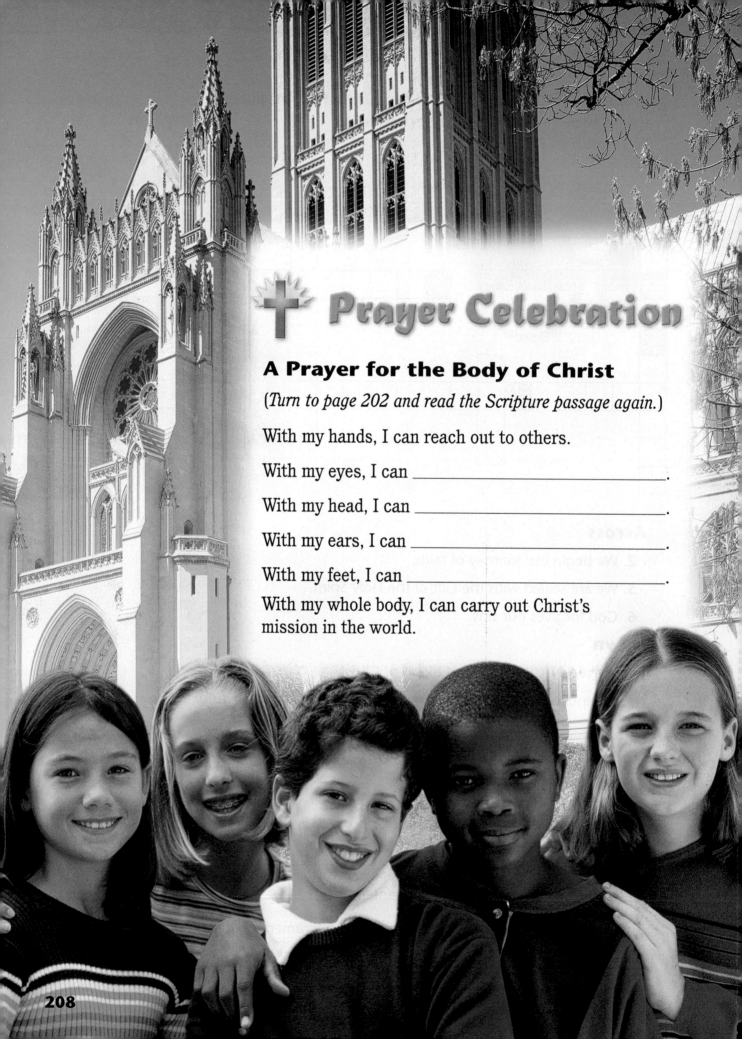

✝ Prayer Celebration

A Prayer for the Body of Christ

(*Turn to page 202 and read the Scripture passage again.*)

With my hands, I can reach out to others.

With my eyes, I can _____.

With my head, I can _____.

With my ears, I can _____.

With my feet, I can _____.

With my whole body, I can carry out Christ's mission in the world.

13 Chapter Review

A **Complete** the sentences with words from the box.

Christ's mission	grace	body
Sacraments	mystery	Church

1. Sacred signs that celebrate Christ's presence in our lives

   are called _____.

2. Saint Paul used the image of a _____ to show that it was
   necessary that all members of the Church work together.

3. The Body of Christ is the People of God or the _____.

4. When we spread God's peace and love to others we are carrying

   out _____.

5. Christ's presence in the Church is called a _____.

B **Match** column A with column B by writing the correct
number in the space provided.

A

1. Baptism
2. Confirmation
3. Eucharist
4. Reconciliation
5. Anointing of the Sick
6. Matrimony
7. Holy Orders

B

___ celebrates God's love and healing

___ become a member of the Body of Christ

___ receive the Body and Blood of Christ

___ promise to do God's work as a priest, bishop,
or deacon

___ sealed with the Gift of the Holy Spirit

___ receive God's forgiveness

___ promise to be faithful to each other

13 Chapter Review

C **Write** or draw how someone can carry out Christ's mission in the world to spread God's peace and love.

D **Respond** to the following questions.

1. How did Lucas Benitez help spread God's love to others?

_____
_____
_____

2. How can you bring Christ's love to others?

_____
_____
_____
_____

Take Home

FAMILY TIME

The Sacrament of Reconciliation

Learning to say "I'm sorry" and learning to say "You're forgiven" are two important lessons that families pass on to their children. Some people find it very difficult to ask for or seek forgiveness. Others find it easy to say the words but don't really understand the meaning behind them. The Church gives us a wonderful opportunity to experience God's forgiveness in the Sacrament of Reconciliation.

ACTIVITY

Forgiveness Chart Write the name of each person in your family on a sheet of paper. Keep a record this week of how many times you have a disagreement with each person by placing a mark next to that person's name. Cross out the mark when you or the person who hurt you says, "I'm sorry."

WEEKLY PLANNER

On Sunday
During the Penitential Rite, reflect on your own need for forgiveness. Make the firm intention to be more forgiving to members of your family.

On the Web
blestarewe.com

Visit our Web site for the saint of the day and the reflection question of the week.

Saint of the Week

Saint John Vianney
(1786–1859)

Saint John Vianney was a French priest. His study for the priesthood was extremely difficult for him and he was eventually ordained because of his good will. He was sent to a poor, remote parish, where he served for forty years.

Patron Saint of: parish clergy
Feast Day: August 4

A Prayer for the Week

Lord, learning can be so demanding at times. Lift us up, Lord, and encourage us. Like Saint John Vianney, may we continue to learn how to forgive others as you have forgiven us.
Amen.

Take Home

✚ Scripture Background

In the Early Church

Confession Early Christians who committed serious crimes such as murder or adultery had to confess their sins and do public penance. Often their act of penance lasted for years. Beginning in the seventh century, confessions became private. Irish missionaries introduced this practice, which allowed for the priest to forgive mortal and venial sins in Christ's name. In the sixteenth century, small rooms called confessionals became a common sight in Catholic churches.

In the Gospels we learn that Jesus often forgave sins. Read Matthew 9:1–8.

OUR CATHOLIC TRADITION in Literature

Confessions Saint Augustine is a saint whose story reveals a sinner who turned to the Lord and turned away from sin. After living a worldly life, he converted to Catholicism at the age of thirty-three. He became one of the most important voices the Church has ever heard. His autobiographical book, entitled *Confessions*, contains the famous quote about searching for God: "You have made us for yourself, and our heart is restless until it rests in you."

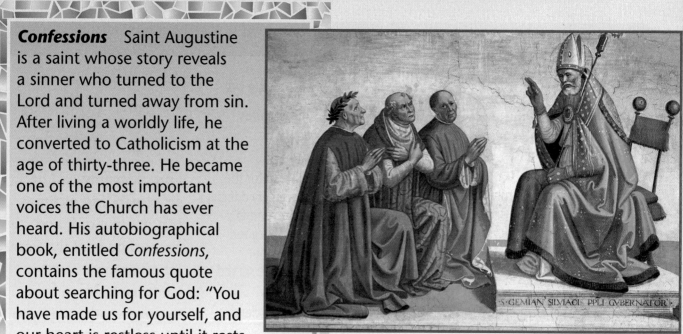

Saint Augustine, 14th–16th century, San Gimignano, Italy

14 The Sacrament of Reconciliation

Give thanks to the Lord for he is good.
His mercy endures forever.

Based on the Rite of Penance

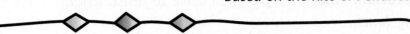

Share

God wants us to be kind and loving. Sometimes we forget that our words and actions affect those around us. If we make selfish choices, then we hurt the people we are with.

Activity

Tell how the entire family is hurt by the actions of the two children.

_____

_____

_____

_____

_____

How did Jesus show us his power to heal and forgive?

Hear & Believe

✝ Scripture Jesus Forgives Sins

In the Gospels, we find many stories of Jesus showing compassion and mercy toward others. People often came to Jesus, asking to receive his healing touch.

One day, Jesus was preaching in the town of Capernaum. Some men came toward Jesus, carrying a paralyzed man on a stretcher. The men carefully set their friend down at Jesus' feet.

Jesus saw the strong faith the men had in him. He said to the paralyzed man, "Take courage, my friend, your sins are forgiven."

Some of the people who heard this became very upset. "How can this man say such a thing? Only God can forgive sins," they said to themselves.

Jesus knew what they were thinking. He asked them, "Which is easier to say, 'Your sins are forgiven,' or 'Rise and walk'?"

Before they could respond, Jesus said to the paralyzed man, "Rise, pick up your stretcher, and go home."

The people were amazed by what happened next. The man stood on his own and walked away praising God.

At that moment, the crowd felt God's presence. They believed that God had given Jesus the power to forgive sins. As they left, they also gave praise and thanks to God.

Based on Matthew 9:1–8

The Sacraments of Healing

God has given us two **Sacraments of Healing**. They are Anointing of the Sick and Reconciliation. In the **Sacrament of Anointing of the Sick**, God comforts the elderly, sick, or dying. In the **Sacrament of Penance and Reconciliation**, God forgives our sins and brings us his peace. In both Sacraments, we are strengthened by Christ's presence.

page 396 to read more about the Sacraments of Healing.

Activity

The men in the story cared deeply for their friend. They brought him to Jesus, who healed and forgave him. We can bring others to Jesus through our prayers. Write a prayer for someone you know who needs Jesus' healing touch.

_____

_____

_____

_____

_____

_____

_____

_____

_____

_____

How does God heal us when we are hurting?

215

Hear & Believe

 ## Jesus Forgives Sins

Through the Sacrament of Penance and Reconciliation, Jesus gave the Church the power to forgive **sin**. When we are sorry for our sins, we can receive this Sacrament. The Sacrament of Penance and Reconciliation heals our relationship with God, the Church, and one another.

Mortal Sin and Venial Sin

When we sin, we turn away from God and the way God wants us to live. A **mortal sin** is a serious sin that separates us from God's grace. To commit a mortal sin, a person must do something that is very wrong, understand that it is wrong, and do it anyway. A **venial sin** is a less serious sin. Our Church teaches us that all sin hurts our relationship with God and one another.

Celebrating God's Love and Forgiveness

We can celebrate the Sacrament of Penance and Reconciliation alone with the priest or as a community with private confession. A communal celebration helps us understand that our individual sins affect the entire Christian community.

 pages 396 and 401 to read more about the Sacrament of Penance and Reconciliation.

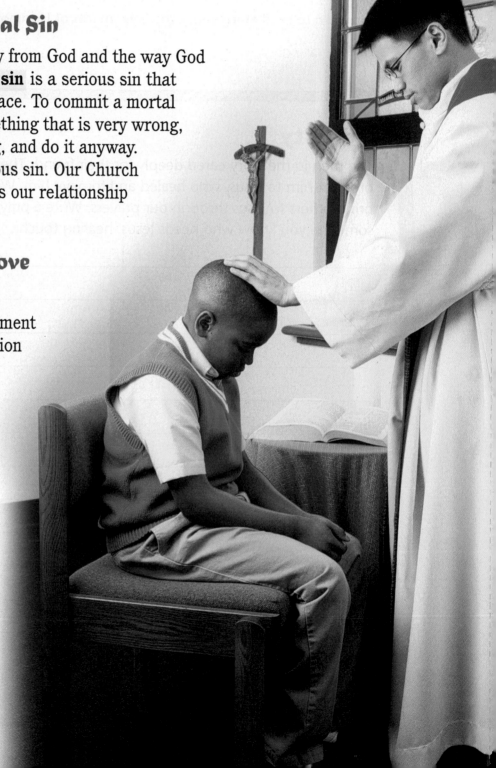

Forgiveness from God

In the special prayer of **absolution**, we are reconciled with God and the Church.

God, the Father of mercies,
through the death and resurrection of his Son
has reconciled the world to himself
and sent the Holy Spirit among us
for the forgiveness of sins;
through the ministry of the Church
may God give you pardon and peace,
and I absolve you from your sins
in the name of the Father, and of the Son,
and of the Holy Spirit.
Amen.

Rite of Penance

Giving Thanks

Before the celebration of this Sacrament is finished, we pray the following prayer of praise of God.

Give thanks to the Lord, for he is good.
His mercy endures for ever.

Rite of Penance

Our Church Teaches

While he was on earth, Jesus showed us his healing power. The Church celebrates the Sacraments of Healing today, bringing us Jesus' strength and peace.

Our sins affect our relationship with God and the entire Christian community. God forgives us through the Sacrament of Penance and Reconciliation. We are reunited with God and the Church and promise to reject sin. We are grateful to God for this special gift.

Activity

Write in your own words what Jesus Christ does for us through the

Sacraments of Healing. _____

_____

Faith Words

mortal sin
A mortal sin is a serious violation of God's Law. It separates us from God's grace until we ask for forgiveness in the Sacrament of Penance and Reconciliation.

venial sin
A venial sin is a sin less serious than a mortal sin. It weakens our love for God and others and can lead to mortal sin.

absolution
Through the prayer of absolution, the priest forgives our sins in the name of God in the Sacrament of Penance and Reconciliation.

How do we bring God's forgiveness to others?

Respond

Saint John Vianney Brought God's Forgiveness to Others

Saint John Vianney hoped to be a priest so he could bring Christ's love and forgiveness to others. He was born near Lyons, France, in 1786. As a boy, he worked on his father's farm. With the help of the local pastor, John studied to become a priest. It was difficult for him to learn. He was ordained a priest at the age of twenty-nine.

It was as a priest that John's gifts and talents became clear. He worked in a small town with only about 200 people living in it. The people loved to hear John preach, and he soon became known throughout Europe.

Crowds started lining up early in the morning to celebrate the Sacrament of Reconciliation with John. People said that John Vianney knew things that they didn't even tell him. With a few simple words, he comforted them and brought them closer to God.

We remember Saint John Vianney's life as a priest and the way he brought God's forgiveness to others. The Church celebrates his feast day on August 4.

Activity

Imagine that you are teaching someone the steps for receiving the Sacrament of Reconciliation. Look at the chart below. Complete the directions for the steps of the Sacrament of Reconciliation.

1. Preparation

   Write one question that could be used to help you examine your conscience.

   _____

2. Priest's Welcome

3. Reading from Scripture

   Write the name of a reading from the Bible that could be used.

   _____

4. Confession

   Give an example of a kind act or a prayer that the priest might give as penance.

   _____

5. Prayer of Sorrow

   Write your own prayer of sorrow.

   _____

   _____

6. Absolution

7. Prayer of Praise and Dismissal

   Write your own prayer of praise. Thank God for the gift of Reconciliation.

   _____

   _____

How do we know if we are living according to God's will?

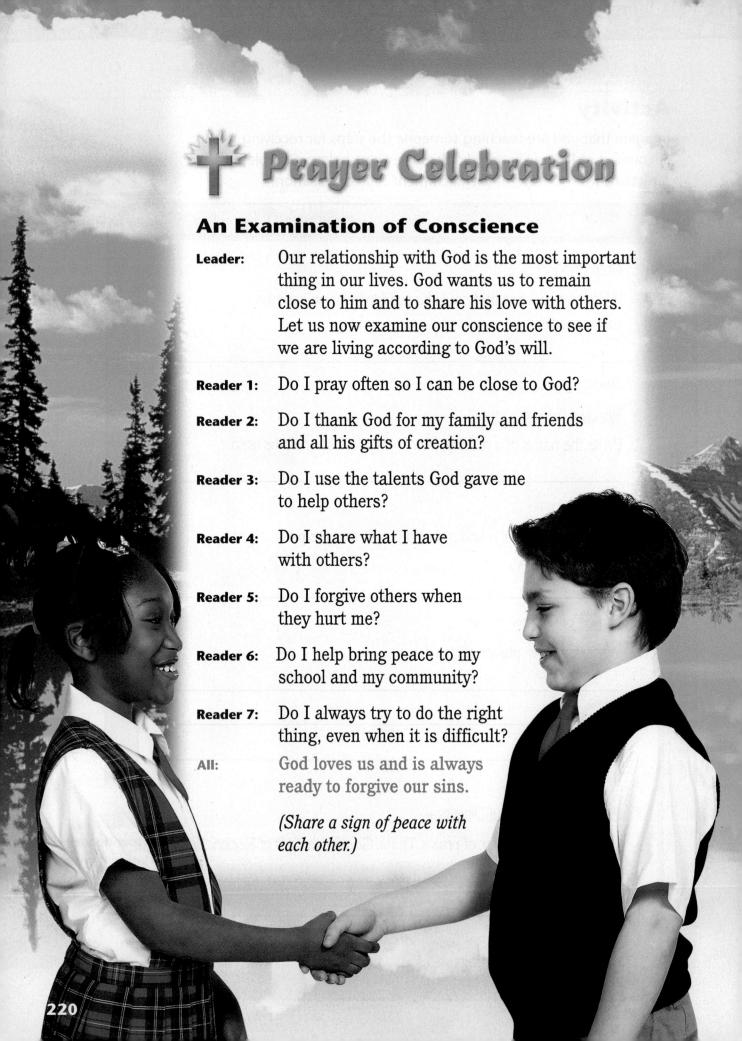

✟ Prayer Celebration

An Examination of Conscience

Leader: Our relationship with God is the most important thing in our lives. God wants us to remain close to him and to share his love with others. Let us now examine our conscience to see if we are living according to God's will.

Reader 1: Do I pray often so I can be close to God?

Reader 2: Do I thank God for my family and friends and all his gifts of creation?

Reader 3: Do I use the talents God gave me to help others?

Reader 4: Do I share what I have with others?

Reader 5: Do I forgive others when they hurt me?

Reader 6: Do I help bring peace to my school and my community?

Reader 7: Do I always try to do the right thing, even when it is difficult?

All: God loves us and is always ready to forgive our sins.

(Share a sign of peace with each other.)

A Circle the letter of the best answer.

1. A _____ sin is a serious sin that separates us from God's grace.
   a. venial
   b. minor
   c. mortal
   d. strong

2. A sin that weakens a person's love for others is called a _____.
   a. venial sin
   b. small sin
   c. serious sin
   d. mortal sin

3. When a priest prays the prayer of _____, we are reconciled with God and the Church.
   a. thanksgiving
   b. praise
   c. absolution
   d. petition

4. The Sacrament of Reconciliation _____ our relationship with God, the Church, and one another.
   a. heals
   b. hurts
   c. loves
   d. weakens

B Number the steps for the Sacrament of Reconciliation in the correct order.

_____ I confess my sins to the priest.

_____ The priest welcomes me in the name of Jesus and the Church.

_____ The priest gives me absolution in the name of the Father, Son, and Holy Spirit.

_____ I examine my conscience.

_____ After I confess my sins, I pray aloud a prayer of sorrow.

_____ Before I leave, the priest and I pray a prayer of praise.

_____ The priest may then read to me from Scripture.

14 Chapter Review

C **Match** column A with column B by writing the correct number in the space provided.

A

1. Anointing of the Sick

2. sin

3. community

4. conscience

5. peace

B

_____ We can celebrate the Sacrament of Reconciliation alone or as a _____.

_____ We examine our _____ to see if we are living according to God's will.

_____ The two Sacraments of Healing are Reconciliation and _____.

_____ In Reconciliation, God forgives our sins and brings us his _____.

_____ When we turn away from God's love, we _____.

D **Respond** to the following questions.

1. How did Saint John Vianney bring God's forgiveness to others?

_____

_____

_____

_____

2. How do you feel after you receive Jesus' forgiveness?

_____

_____

_____

_____

Take Home

FAMILY TIME

The Commandments and Forgiveness

Sin is a concern for the Church because it not only separates us from God's grace, it also affects all of our relationships. When we sin, we choose our wishes over what God asks of us. Reconciliation restores a sense of peace with God and with others, especially with those close to us.

ACTIVITY

How Was Your Day? During this week, spend a few minutes with your child each night to review his or her day. Ask your child to list all the things that he or she liked about the day and then ask if there were any disappointments. It is a good time for each of you to express sorrow for the things that went wrong. Together you can ask for God's forgiveness and help to make tomorrow better.

WEEKLY PLANNER

On Sunday

Listen to the Scripture readings and homily at Mass to discover guidance for leading a moral life.

On the Web

blestarewe.com

 Visit our Web site for the saint of the day and the reflection question of the week.

Saint of the Week

 Saint Matilda
(c. 895–968)

Saint Matilda was a German queen during the tenth century. Her sons fought among themselves and were jealous when Matilda was generous to the poor and the Church. She died with a great reputation for kindness and generosity among people.

Patron Saint of: large families, the falsely accused

Feast Day: March 14

A Prayer for the Week

Dear Lord, forgive us for the times we have failed to love you and for the times we have hurt others. Help us to be like Saint Matilda by being kind and generous towards those we meet. Amen.

Take Home

FAMILY TIME

✚ Scripture Background

Before the Time of Jesus

Inheritance In ancient times, the Israelites considered the land of Canaan as their inheritance from God. They valued the land and passed it on from generation to generation. Sons were first in line to inherit land as well as other property, such as household goods and cattle. The oldest son usually received a greater share, since he was responsible for his mother and unmarried sisters.

In Luke 15:11–20, a son seeks forgiveness for wasting his inheritance.

OUR CATHOLIC TRADITION in Art

Icons Icons are colorful paintings of Jesus, Mary, and the saints that help us pray. They are usually painted directly on flat surfaces such as the wall of a church or on wood panels or screens that are often placed at the front of a church. In the Eastern Catholic Church, icons serve the same function as statues do in the Western Catholic Church. Icons enhance the beauty of a church, instruct the faithful, provide a way to worship God, and nourish growth in holiness.

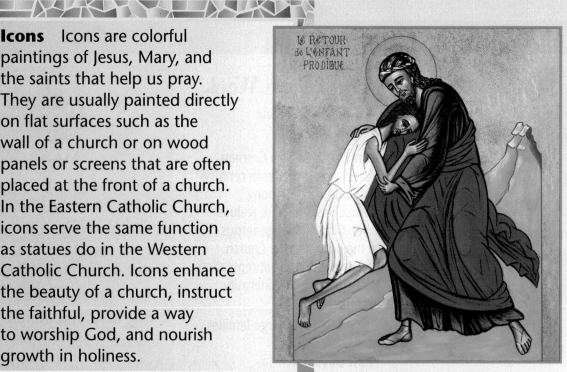

The Return of the Prodigal Son by Sister Marie-Paul Farran, O.S.B.

15 The Commandments and Forgiveness

For we have sinned against you.

Penitential Act of the Mass

Share

Sometimes people may disappoint or hurt us. God calls us to forgive them so that we can continue to grow in God's love.

Activity

Circle the set of pictures that shows hurt and then forgiveness.

How do we react to sin in our lives?

Hear & Believe

✝ Scripture   The Forgiving Father (Part 1)

Jesus understood that sometimes we make selfish choices. He told this story to encourage us to ask for God's forgiveness when we sin.

There was a man who lived on a large estate with his two sons. One day, the younger son came to his father and told him that he was leaving. He asked for the money his father would leave him in his will.

The father was sad that his son wanted to leave, but he gave the son his share of the money. The son quickly packed his belongings. Without looking back, he left home to begin a new life.

He traveled to another country, far away from his father's house. Without his father to guide him, the son made many mistakes. He was very selfish and interested only in having a good time. He spent his money foolishly and did not lead a healthy life.

Soon he had no money left and was always hungry. "I would be living better if I were working for my father!" the son thought. "I will go home, ask my father for forgiveness, and tell him how sorry I am."

Based on Luke 15:11–20

Our Conscience

God calls us always to choose what is good. We are responsible for the choices we make. Our **conscience** helps us to know what is good. It is guided by what the Church teaches about God's laws, especially the Ten Commandments.

Our conscience tells us how our actions will affect our relationship with God and others. To make good **moral decisions**, we must pray, learn the teachings of the Church, and follow our conscience.

Even when we sin, God continues to speak to each of us through our conscience. When we are sorry, God is ready to forgive us, especially in the Sacrament of Reconciliation. As the story of the forgiving father reminds us, we can always come back to God's love.

Activity

Realizing that he acted selfishly, the younger son decided to ask his father for forgiveness. Put a ✓ in front of the selfish actions in which a person should ask for forgiveness.

_____ Helping someone understand how to do a math problem

_____ Spreading gossip about another person

_____ Copying test answers from someone else's paper

_____ Being jealous of a friend's talent in sports

How does God show us forgiveness?

Hear & Believe

✝ The Forgiving Father (Part 2)

In the second part of the story, Jesus explains that God always loves us. He is always ready to forgive our sins and welcome us home.

While the son was still a long way off, his father saw him coming. The father ran to his son and hugged him. The son said, "Father, I have sinned against God and you. I do not deserve to be called your son." But his father was not angry. He told his servants to give the son beautiful clothes and sandals and prepare a special meal.

While they were celebrating, the older brother was returning from his work in the field. As he got closer to the house, he heard the sound of music and dancing. He asked a servant why they were celebrating.

Hearing the party was for his brother, the older brother became angry and refused to enter the house. His father begged him to join in the celebration. "Father, I have always done what you asked, and yet you never had a celebration for me. But my brother, who wasted your money, gets a wonderful feast like this?" the older son complained.

The father said, "You are with me always. All that I have is yours. But we have to celebrate because your brother was dead to us and has come back to life. He was lost and has now been found."

Based on Luke 15:20–32

Understanding the 7th, 8th, 9th, and 10th Commandments

The Seventh through Tenth Commandments teach us to treat others in loving and unselfish ways. The Seventh Commandment teaches us that we must respect the property of others and that we should never take what does not belong to us. The Eighth Commandment teaches us to be honest and truthful.

In the Scripture story of the forgiving father, the younger son was very selfish. The Ninth and Tenth Commandments teach us not to be selfish, envious, or jealous. Instead we should be thankful to God for all the gifts he has given us.

Our Church Teaches

Sin hurts our relationship with God and others as well as ourselves. God helps us avoid sin by speaking to our conscience. Our conscience is our inner self, guided by God. Our conscience also directs us to heal our relationships with God and with each other.

Activity

Find the right path! Start at a dot and follow the line through the map. Unscramble the letters and write each word on the line to show what it means to be reunited with God.

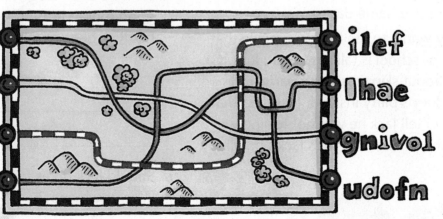

lost
selfish
death
hurt

ilef
lhae
gnivol
udofn

How can we make good moral decisions?

_____

Respond

Three Steps to Making a Good Moral Decision

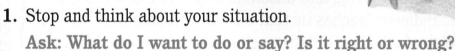

1. Stop and think about your situation.

   Ask: What do I want to do or say? Is it right or wrong?

2. Consider what you have learned about Jesus and the Church.

   Ask: How will my choice affect others? Will my words or actions help or hurt someone?

3. Use your conscience to do the right thing.

   Ask: Am I being pressured by my friends to do this? Am I afraid to do the right thing?

Activities

1. Read the story below. Then answer the questions, using the three steps above as a guide.

   Rick told his friend Jack he would go to his bowling party. Later, he received an invitation from Joey to attend his party at the movie theater. It is the same day as Jack's party.

   Rick really wants to see the new movie that everyone at school is talking about. Rick is thinking about skipping Jack's party and going to Joey's party instead. Joey said that Rick should tell Jack he was not feeling well and that he will have to miss Jack's bowling party.

a. Would it be right or wrong for Rick to miss Jack's party?

   Wrong
   _____

b. Rick has been taught how to make a good moral decision. What three steps has Rick been taught?

   _____
   _____
   _____

c. Should Rick do as Joey says? Why or why not?

   _____
   _____
   _____

2. As the forgiving father did in the story, God will always love us. He wants us to mend our relationships with others. Think about how your conscience would guide you in the following situations. Write or draw an ending to each story.

Have faith and a good conscience.

Based on 1 Timothy 1:19

Your friend starts using your video game without asking permission. Your conscience tells you to…

I would say next time can you please ask.

You have an argument with your parents when they don't give you permission to go out with your friends. Your conscience tells you to…

Say ok maybe next time they'll let me go.

How do we pray for God's forgiveness?

 # Prayer Celebration

A Prayer for Forgiveness

Leader: At Mass and other special times, we ask God to forgive our sins. We pray for his mercy. Let us pause and reflect on the things we are not happy we did. Also, think about the good things we failed to do.

Leader: Lord, we have sinned against you: Lord, have mercy.

All: Lord, have mercy.

Leader: Show us, O Lord, your mercy.

All: And grant us your salvation.

All: May God bless us, protect us, and bring us to everlasting life. Amen.

Leader: Let us now offer each other a sign of peace.

Based on the Penitential Act of the Mass and the Liturgy of the Hours

Take Home

FAMILY TIME

The Commandments and Praying for Forgiveness

The Bible is the account of God's great love for us. The writers of the Bible, inspired by the Holy Spirit, tell stories about God's Creation of the world. One story is about Adam and Eve. God gave them the gift of free will. Adam and Eve used that gift to reject God's love. In God's plan, Jesus was sent to redeem their descendants from sin and death.

ACTIVITY

A Place of Honor If your family has a Bible, put it where you and your child can see it each day. The Bible will be read more often if it is readily seen. Try to read a verse or two every day and discuss its meaning.

WEEKLY PLANNER

On Sunday

During the Lord's Prayer, recall the times you have failed to live according to God's will. Ask for forgiveness.

On the Web
blestarewe.com

 Visit our Web site for the saint of the day and the reflection question of the week.

Saint of the Week

 Blessed Mariana of Jesus (1565–1624)

At age 23, Blessed Mariana of Jesus became a discalced (without shoes) Mercedarian nun in Madrid. She is remembered for her life of penance, devotion to the Eucharist, and intense prayer life. She is also known as the "Lily of Madrid."
Feast Day: April 27

A Prayer for the Week

Lord, we are thankful for your unending love. Help us to follow the example of Blessed Mariana by remembering the need to forgive as we have been forgiven. Amen.

Take Home

FAMILY TIME

✝ Scripture Background

Before the Time of Jesus

Loans In Bible times, it was considered a good deed to lend to people in need. To secure a loan, the borrower had to pledge something such as his land or animals. Sometimes a borrower might even pledge a family member. If the loan was not repaid, the promised relative became a slave to the lender. Every seventh year, all debts were cancelled and these slaves were freed.

In Matthew 18:21–35, Jesus teaches forgiveness through the parable of the king who cancels the debt of his servant.

OUR CATHOLIC TRADITION in Architecture

Church of the Beatitudes
In the place where Jesus spoke the Beatitudes to his followers, there is a church that is named after them. The Church of the Beatitudes is located along the northern shore of the Sea of Galilee on the mount near Capernaum, home to five of Jesus' Twelve Apostles. Built in 1937, the church is octagonal to represent the eight Beatitudes that Matthew describes in his Gospel (Matthew 5:3–10). Inscribed on each window are the beginning words of one of the Beatitudes. A dome of gold mosaic covers the altar and rests on top of the building. Surrounding the outside of the church are columned cloisters. These provide a panoramic view of the Sea of Galilee.

16 The Commandments and Praying for Forgiveness

 Forgive your brothers and sisters from your heart.

Based on Matthew 18:35

Share

Lorraine and Angela had a fight. Angela was telling untrue stories about Lorraine to their friend Dominick. She told Lorraine that she was sorry and promised not to do it again. Although Lorraine was upset, she forgave Angela. A little while later, Angela's brother, Frank, told her that he broke her favorite CD and was very sorry. Angela got angry and yelled at Frank. She said she couldn't forgive him.

Activity

Was Angela wrong? Write a different ending that shows Angela following Jesus' example of forgiveness.

She should forgive him she does in my story.

What are we called to forgive?

Hear & Believe

✝ Scripture The Unforgiving Servant

Peter asked Jesus, "Lord, if my friend sins against me, how often must I forgive him? Seven times?"

"Not seven times, but seventy-seven times," Jesus said. "God's Kingdom is like a king who lent his servant a large sum of money. When the king asked for his money back, the servant begged for more time to pay. Feeling sorry for his servant, the king forgave him and said that he didn't owe him anything."

"Later, the servant saw a man who owed him a little money. The servant demanded to be paid. The other man pleaded for more time, but the servant had him put in prison. When the king heard this, he was angry. 'You wicked servant! I forgave you that large debt. You should have forgiven the small one! You are going to jail,' the king said." Then Jesus said, "My children, your heavenly Father wants you to forgive everyone from your heart."

Based on Matthew 18:21–35

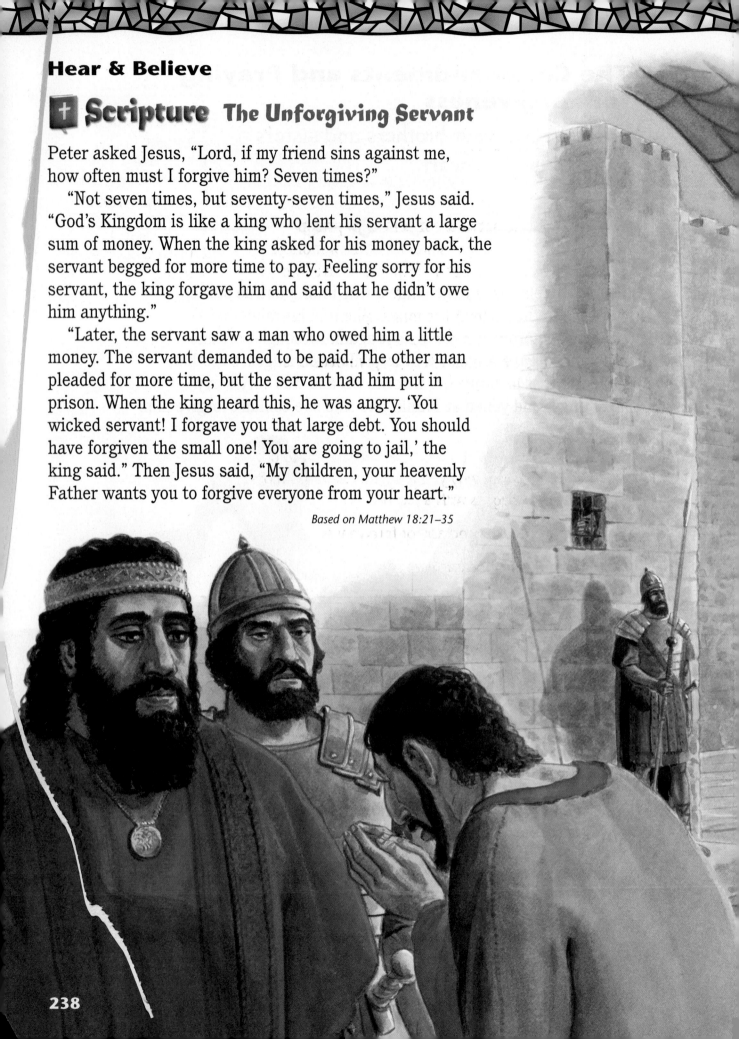

Prayer and Forgiveness

Jesus instructs Peter about forgiveness by telling a **parable**, a story. In the story, the king represents God who is ready to forgive debts that were so great that they could never be repaid. Instead of learning the lesson about forgiveness, the servant condemns to prison another man who owes him a small amount of money.

In teaching us the Lord's Prayer, Jesus calls attention to this lesson on forgiveness with the words, "Forgive us our trespasses as we forgive those who trespass against us." The prayer reminds us that, just as God is ready to forgive us, we are called to forgive even the greatest wrongs.

Activity

Place a ✓ next to the action you think is more difficult to do. On the lines below, explain why you think that action is more difficult. Share your thoughts with a partner.

_____ Admit your mistakes and ask for forgiveness

___✓___ Forgive someone who has hurt you

It is harder to forgive someone who hurt you.

How can we experience God's peace?

239

Hear & Believe

Pope John Paul II and Sharing God's Forgiveness

"Pray for the brother who shot me, whom I have sincerely forgiven." Pope John Paul II spoke these words from his hospital room. It was May 17, 1981.

Just a few days before, Mehmet Ali Agca, a Turkish man, tried to kill the Pope in St. Peter's Square. Doctors operated on the Pope for six hours. Though he was seriously hurt, the Pope responded with love and mercy. He publicly forgave the man who shot him.

The Pope believed that his prayers to Mary, the Mother of God, helped save him. When he recovered, he visited his attacker in prison. He embraced him and prayed with him. Again, the Pope spoke words of forgiveness.

Mehmet Ali Agca was sentenced to life in prison. The Pope, however, spoke on his behalf. In June of 2000, the president of Italy pardoned Mehmet Ali Agca for the shooting. It is still unknown why he tried to kill the Pope.

In his message for the World Day of Peace 2002, John Paul II spoke about forgiveness. He said that when we forgive, we choose to "go against the natural instinct to pay back evil with evil." In 1997, he ended his World Day of Peace message by saying, "Offer forgiveness and receive peace!"

Our Church Teaches

The Seventh through Tenth Commandments tell us to avoid being selfish. When we are unwilling to forgive, it is a sign of our selfishness. This is the same selfishness that leads people to want what is not theirs. It is the same selfishness that leads people to tell lies to avoid their responsibilities to others. Jesus teaches us to be as generous as God our Father. We are to share all the wonderful gifts God has given us, including his **peace** and forgiveness.

Activity

Write how a Christian would respond to each situation.

a. Your older brother promises to take you to the movies. He decides to go with his friends instead.

I would forgive him and ask him to take me next time

b. You discover that your best friend has been spending more time with someone else in your class.

It would be fine and be cool

How can we respect and care for others?

241

Respond

Living the Seventh Through Tenth Commandments

The Seventh through Tenth Commandments require us to give proper respect to and care for the rights of others. Everyone has the right to the things he or she needs to live. We should not be envious of things that belong to others. We should respect our families and the families of others. If we fail, we must do what we can to make up for our actions and ask for forgiveness.

Activities

1. The chart below lists the Seventh, Eighth, Ninth, and Tenth Commandments. In the space next to each Commandment, write a sentence or two about what you think it means and how you can obey it.

The Ten Commandments	What this Commandment means to me and how I can obey it
VII You shall not steal.	To not steal
VIII You shall not bear false witness against your neighbor.	do not akuse him
IX You shall not covet your neighbor's wife.	don't cheat
X You shall not covet anything that belongs to your neighbor.	don't take things.

2. Look up the following Scripture passage in the Bible. Then, in your own words, write what God is telling us about forgiveness.

Luke 15:8–10

To forgive people who are wrong.

GO TO page 19 to review how to look up a Scripture passage.

3. Learn to sign the following phrases from the Lord's Prayer. Review what you learned in Chapters 4, 8, and 12.

| Give | us | this | day |

| our daily | bread, | and forgive | us our |

| trespasses, | as we | forgive | those who |

| trespass | against | us; |

How does God want me to forgive others?

Prayer Celebration

A Prayer for Peace

Reader: A reading from the letter of Paul to the Colossians.

Holy and beloved, God has chosen you as his special people. Be compassionate, kind, humble, and gentle. Be patient with one another and forgive anyone who has hurt you. If one person is upset with another, forgive as the Lord has forgiven you.

Over all these things, put on love. It ties everything together perfectly. Each one of you is part of the Body of Christ. Let the peace of Christ guide your hearts.

Based on Colossians 3:12–16

Reader: The word of the Lord.

All: Thanks be to God.

Leader: Pause and think about the above reading. Complete the following sentences that speak of forgiveness.

It is sometimes hard for me to forgive someone when

_____

_____ .

A quality that I could use to help me forgive others is

_____ .

Leader: Together, let us pray the Lord's Prayer by using sign language.

All: Our Father. . .

A **Complete** the sentences with names from the box.

Jesus	Pope John Paul II	Zacchaeus
Peter	unforgiving servant	king

1. I did not show mercy toward a man who owed me money.

    _____

2. I forgave the man who tried to kill me and I visited him in prison.

    _____

3. I lent my servant a large sum of money.

    _____

4. I said that you should forgive your neighbor seventy-seven times

    _____

5. I asked Jesus how often I must forgive my friend if he sinned against me.

    _____

B **Write** the word from the Lord's Prayer that is being signed in each picture.

_____   _____   _____   _____

C **Circle** the letter of the best answer.

1. The calm, good feeling of being together with God is called _____.

   a. peace

   b. wisdom

   c. love

   d. help

2. Parables use everyday events and objects to _____.

   a. tell a story

   b. explain important truths

   c. describe a scene

   d. solve a problem

3. Jesus teaches us about forgiveness in the _____.

   a. Beatitudes

   b. Ten Commandments

   c. Lord's Prayer

   d. Gifts of the Holy Spirit

4. When we are unwilling to forgive, it is a sign of our _____.

   a. age

   b. disbelief

   c. intelligence

   d. selfishness

D **Respond** to the following.

1. Explain what a parable is. _____

   _____

   _____

   _____

2. Explain how obeying the Seventh through Tenth Commandments helps us in our relationships with others.

   _____

   _____

   _____

   _____

   _____

Faith in Action

The Parish Liturgy Committee Another word for the Mass is "Liturgy," which means "the work of the Church." People work behind the scenes to help us pray when we come together as a faith community. They help us celebrate the seasons of the Church year, such as Advent and Lent, by decorating the church and by working with school and parish music ministers. They may also write the General Intercessions, or Prayer of the Faithful. They help us love and understand Scripture. They teach people to share in the many sacramental ministries and give us opportunities to take part in celebrating the Sacraments.

In Your Parish

Activity Either alone or as a group, write your own General Intercessions. Decide how you want everyone to respond after each petition.

Prayer response: _____.

For our parish leaders, especially, _____

_____. (Response)

For those in our parish and families, who are sick or dying, especially

_____. (Response)

In Everyday Life

TO DO
what   who

Activity Think about the next special event on your family's celebration calendar, such as a birthday. List the jobs that will need to be done before or at the celebration and who will complete each task. More than one person can be named for each task.

Faith in Action

Ministry to the Infirm For many years, Catholics received the Sacrament of Anointing of the Sick only when they were very old or so ill that they might soon die. Today, we can experience the strengthening of this Sacrament any time we need healing. The celebration of this Sacrament can include prayers for healing, anointing of our bodies with the Oil of the Sick, and the laying on of hands. We can all share in the ministry of healing by praying for the sick and for their families. When people are afraid or discouraged, we can encourage them with prayers for strength and peace.

In Everyday Life

Activity Think about a time when you were sick. Place a ✔ next to the things that people did for you during for this time. Which of these can you do for someone else who is sick? Share your answers with a partner.

___ Prayed for me   ___ Visited me   ___ Brought me homework

___ Held my hand   ___ Cheered me up   ___ Made my favorite meal

___ Sent get well cards   ___ Helped me stop worrying   ___ Other (describe)

In Your Parish

Activity Identify two people in your parish or family who need healing. Suggest one way that you and your friends could offer comfort to each person.

Name	How we can help
1. _____	_____
	_____
2. _____	_____
	_____

Faith in Action

Advisory Committees   Catholic schools usually invite parents of students to participate in various advisory committees. These groups help the principal and teachers decide what is taught each year, what activities to schedule for fundraising, and the goals for the school. Sometimes an advisory committee will interview people who wish to teach in the school. All these people share their time and talent to make the school a place where learning takes place and faith grows.

In Everyday Life

Activity   Name some committees in your school. How did each committee contribute to the good of your school?

_____

_____

_____

_____

_____

In Your Parish

Activity   Make a list of the qualities or talents you believe people should have in order to serve on advisory committees. Pray for all those who serve on the committees.

_____

_____

_____

_____

Faith in Action

Lectors Lectors proclaim the Word of God at Mass, usually the First Reading and Second Reading during the Liturgy of the Word. If the Psalm is not sung, they might also read the Psalm and lead the people in the response. A priest or deacon reads the Gospel. To do the best job possible, lectors prepare by prayerfully reading the Scriptures they will proclaim. And they make sure they can pronounce correctly any difficult names of people or places.

In Everyday Life

Activity Fill in the blanks and take turns making each announcement with expression.

1. Ladies and gentlemen, please welcome _____!

2. Let's all join in wishing _____ the best birthday ever!

3. Please join us after school today to support the best soccer team in

   _____!

In Your Parish

Activity Look back at the Scripture reading from the letter of Paul on page 244. Underline the words you do not understand the meaning of. Circle the words you are not sure how to pronounce. Then write one sentence to summarize the reading. Share your work with a partner.

Summary: _____

_____

_____

_____

_____

Find the letters in the stained glass to make the word that is discussed in this unit. Write the word below the stained glass.

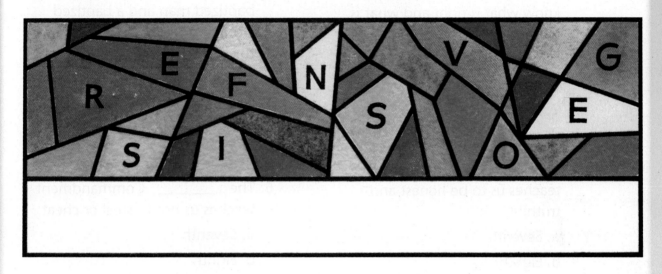

List the Seven Sacraments then circle the two Sacraments of Healing.

_____   _____

_____   _____

_____   _____

_____

Complete the banner below with the words we pray at Mass to ask for God's mercy.

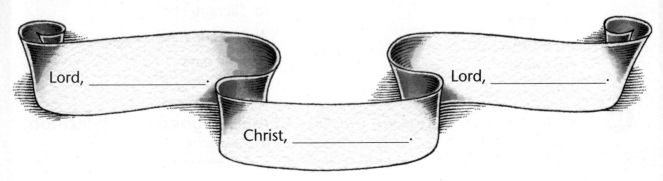

Lord, _____.

Lord, _____.

Christ, _____.

4 Unit Review

A **Circle** the letter of the best answer.

1. Our _____ is our ability to know what is right and what is wrong.
   a. conscience
   b. heart
   c. mind
   d. spirit

2. The _____ Commandment teaches us to be honest and truthful.
   a. Seventh
   b. Eighth
   c. Ninth
   d. Tenth

3. The Sacraments of Healing are Reconciliation and _____.
   a. Baptism
   b. Confirmation
   c. Anointing of the Sick
   d. Eucharist

4. The _____ Commandment teaches us to respect the property of others.
   a. Seventh
   b. Eighth
   c. Ninth
   d. Tenth

5. The Sacrament in which a baptized man and a baptized woman promise to be faithful to each other is _____.
   a. Holy Orders
   b. Matrimony
   c. Confirmation
   d. Anointing of the Sick

6. The _____ Commandment teaches us not to steal or cheat.
   a. Seventh
   b. Eighth
   c. Ninth
   d. Tenth

7. The Sacrament in which we receive God's forgiveness is _____.
   a. Confirmation
   b. Matrimony
   c. Holy Orders
   d. Reconciliation

8. Sacred signs that celebrate Christ's presence in our lives are called _____.
   a. Sacraments
   b. blessings
   c. holy days
   d. relics

B **Write** the three things we must do to make a good moral decision.

_____

_____

C **Complete** the sentences with words from the box.

mortal	absolution	venial	sin
peace	community	pardon	

1. When we turn away from God, we _____.

2. A _____ sin is a serious sin that separates us from God's grace.

3. We can celebrate the Sacrament of Reconciliation alone or

   as a _____.

4. A sin that weakens a person's love for God and others is called

   a _____ sin.

5. In Reconciliation, God forgives our sins and brings us

   his _____.

6. When the priest prays the prayer of _____, we are reconciled with God and the Church.

D **Write** about how Pope John Paul II showed forgiveness.

_____

_____

_____

_____

_____

_____

_____

_____

E **Match** column A with column B by writing the correct number in the space provided.

A	B
1. selfishness	____ Our Church carries out Christ's _____ in the world.
2. mystery	____ A _____ uses everyday events and objects to explain important truths.
3. parable	____ Through the prayer of _____, the priest forgives our sins in the name of God.
4. absolution	____ In Reconciliation, we pray a prayer of _____ after confessing our sins.
5. Lord's Prayer	____ The choices we make between what is right and what is wrong are _____.
6. sorrow	____ When we are unwilling to forgive, it is a sign of our _____.
7. mission	____ We bring God's _____ to others.
8. Church	____ Christ's presence in the Church is called a _____.
9. moral decisions	____ Jesus teaches us about God's forgiveness in the _____.
10. forgiveness	____ The Body of Christ is the People of God or the _____.

F **Respond** to the following.

1. Write what the Seventh and Eighth Commandments teach us.

_____

_____

2. How does obeying these Commandments help your relationships

with other people? _____

_____

_____

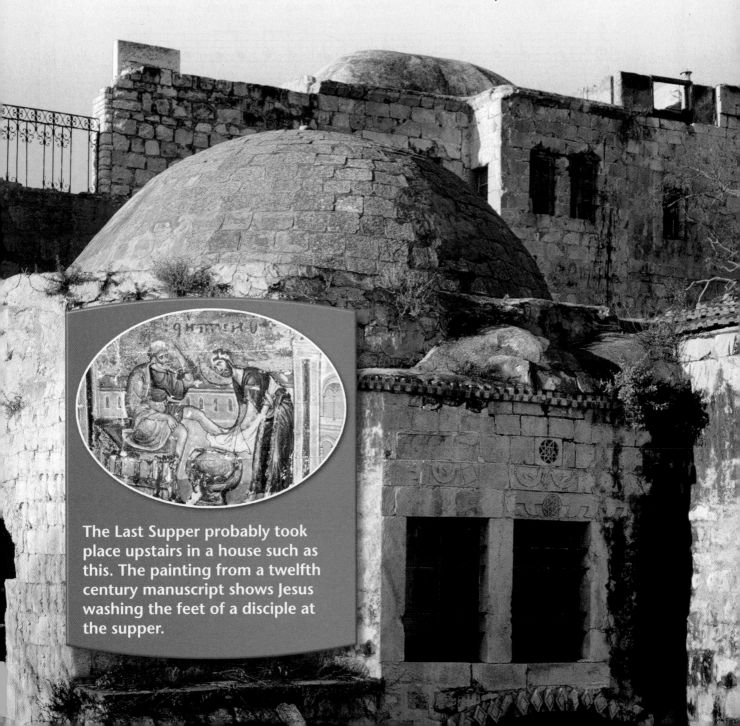

Social Justice

Jesus taught that the way to holiness is to serve others. Today the Church is dedicated to serving the poor and disadvantaged throughout the world.

As I have done, so you must do.
Based on John 13:15

The Last Supper probably took place upstairs in a house such as this. The painting from a twelfth century manuscript shows Jesus washing the feet of a disciple at the supper.

Song of the Body of Christ/ Cancíon del Cuerpo de Cristo

Words by David Haas
Spanish translation by Donna Peña

NO KE AND'AH AHI, Hawaiian traditional
Arranged by David Haas

REFRAIN

We___ come___ to share our sto - ry, we
Ve - ni - mos a de - cir del mis - te - rio, y par -

come to break the bread,___ We___ come___ to know our
tir el pan de vi - da. Ve - ni - mos a sa - ber de

ris - ing from the___ dead.___
nuew - tra e - ter - ni - dad.

VERSE

1. We___ come___ as your peo - ple, we
2. We are called to heal the bro - ken, to be
3. Bread of life and cup of prom - ise, in this
4. You will lead and we shall fol - low, you will
5. We will live and sing: "A - lo - ha," "Al - le -
   (live and sing your prais - es,)

come___ as your own, u - nit - ed with each
hope___ for the poor, we are called to feed the
meal we all are one. In our dy - ing and our
be the breath of life; liv - ing wa - ter, we are
lu - ia" is our song. May we live in love and

D.C.

oth - er, love___ finds a home.___
hun - gry at___ our door.___
ris - ing, may your king - dom dome.___
thirst - ing for___ your light.___
peace our whole life long.___

© 1989, GIA Publications, Inc.

Take Home

FAMILY TIME

Our Vocation to the World

At Baptism we become a sign of God's love for the world. Jesus said, "This is how all will know that you are my disciples, if you have love for one another" (John 13:35). The work we do should reflect our vocation of Christian love.

ACTIVITY

Who Am I? Describe the qualities of an occupation. Tell what the person does and what he or she needs to do his or her job. See if others in your family can guess who that person is!

WEEKLY PLANNER

On Sunday

As a family, identify the different ministries people take part in at Mass. Don't forget the assembly!

On the Web

blestarewe.com

Visit our Web site for the saint of the day and the reflection question of the week.

Saint of the Week

 Saint Louis IX (1214–1270)

Saint Louis IX of France became King of France at age twelve and married seven years later. He had eleven children. Louis, a man of great integrity, was religious, just, respectful of all people, trustworthy, and a man of peace.

Patron Saint of: Archdiocese of St. Louis, Missouri; parenthood
Feast Day: August 25

A Prayer for the Week

Help us today, God, to search for goodness and, like Saint Louis, do everything we can to make your world better. Give us the wisdom to see how we can best do your work. Amen.

Take Home

✝ Scripture Background

In the Time of Jesus

Lamps   A simple oil lamp was the main source of light in a Palestinian home. Originally made of clay, it was decorated with geometric or floral designs. A basic lamp had at least one wick and burned constantly, possibly to help light other household fires when needed. Olive oil was usually used as fuel since it gave off less smoke than animal fat. Typically, the lamp was kept on a wooden or ceramic lampstand.

In Matthew 5:14–16, Jesus uses the image of a lamp on a stand to show how we are to be a light of the world.

Our Catholic Tradition in Art

Pietro Perugino   On the side walls of the Sistine Chapel in the Vatican, one painting stands out among the rest. It is *Christ Handing the Keys to Saint Peter* by Pietro Perugino. The painting is based on Jesus' calling of Saint Peter to be the head of the Church.

Perugino was one of the greatest fresco, or wall, artists of his time. In this painting the figures of Christ and Saint Peter (kneeling) are surrounded by the other Apostles and some people of the artist's day. Perugino included himself in the group of onlookers (fifth figure from the right.)

Christ Handing the Keys to Saint Peter (1482) by Pietro Perugino

17 Our Vocation to the World

Share

God calls all Catholics to do the work of the Church. We continue Christ's mission in the world by serving those who are in need. Our light is Christ living in us. It shines as we share God's love with others.

Activity

Read the headlines about ways people do Christ's work. Then write your own headlines about a person or group you know who serves others.

> Children Sign Up for
> Walk-a-Thon to Help Poor

> Rescue Teams Sent to Help
> Earthquake Victims

> Neighbors Help Rebuild
> House After Fire

How do we show others the goodness of God?

 **Scripture** **The Light of the World**

In Jesus' time there were no electric lights, so nights were very dark. An oil lamp was the only light in a house. It was placed on a stand so that everyone would be able to see. Jesus told his followers that they were to be the light of the world. They were to be an example to help all see the goodness of God. Jesus called himself the Light of the World. He calls each of us to be like him.

Jesus said, "You are the light of the world. You are like a city on a mountain. Everyone can easily see you. People do not put their lamp under a basket. Instead they put it on a stand for everyone to see. Like that lamp, your light must shine for others. People will see your good deeds and glorify your heavenly Father."

Based on Matthew 5:14–16

Serving Others

As Christians, we are called to use our special talents to serve those in our community and the world. The type of work we do to serve God and others is called a **vocation**. Some people carry on Christ's mission as members of a religious community. Men who are called to serve God as priests, deacons, or bishops celebrate the Sacrament of **Holy Orders**. Every person who is baptized has a vocation to serve God and other people.

All vocations are important. Each of us has different talents, but we share in the work of Christ.

 page 406 to read more about vocations.

Priest, Prophet, and King

Through Baptism and Confirmation, we join all Christians in bringing peace and justice to the world. Like Jesus we are anointed as priest, prophet, and king. When people ask us to pray for them or if we do a kind act for someone, we are fulfilling our role as priest. As a prophet we spread God's message of goodness and love to others. Leading and serving others with justice and mercy helps us to live out our role as king.

Activity

Complete the following sentence.

I am a light for people in my community, family or school when I

_____

_____

How can we show others the light of Christ?

Hear & Believe

Being a Light to Others

You can begin now to share in the work of Christ. You are a light to others each time you perform a simple act of kindness. Your caring words and actions help others to experience Christ's love. The following story tells how one girl reached out to help a friend.

Karin was celebrating her tenth birthday with friends. After playing miniature golf, they gathered at a picnic table for cake and ice cream. Everyone seemed to be having a great time except for Patty. Karin noticed that she was unusually quiet.

When Karin had the chance, she took Patty aside and asked her if anything was wrong. Patty hesitated for a moment. She was embarrassed to talk about her problems. "Besides," she thought to herself, "I don't want to spoil Karin's birthday."

Karin, wanting to help her friend, gently encouraged Patty to talk. "I'm sorry I haven't been much fun to be with lately," Patty finally said. "My mom lost her job a few weeks ago. She's worried and upset."

Karin listened as Patty shared her concerns. Patty said, "I probably won't be able to go on the class trip to the zoo. Mom says we have to be careful about spending money."

Patty seemed relieved to be able to share her problems with someone. After their conversation, Karin thought about how she could help her friend. She decided that she would talk with her mom after the party.

Our Church Teaches

In Holy Orders, men are chosen for the special ministry of the priesthood. God wants each of us to serve others. Through our vocations, we help people to understand his Kingdom. God will judge us on how well we love our neighbor, especially those who are poor or suffering.

To help us in our vocation, we pray in union with the **Communion of Saints**. We ask the followers of Jesus, including those who have died, to help us to live God's message of peace and love.

We Believe

We share Christ's role as priest, prophet, and king with those who are baptized. Through our vocations we carry on Christ's mission in the world.

Faith Words

Communion of Saints
All people living and dead who believe in Jesus Christ make up the Communion of Saints.

Activities

1. What are some ways people use their talents to do the work of Christ? _____

   _____

   _____

   _____

2. Think about a problem that a friend, relative or neighbor has. What could you do to help?

   _____

   _____

3. Saints are holy men and women who lived the Gospel by serving God and others. We can ask the saints to help us be a light of hope for others. Think of a saint you admire and tell how that person continued Christ's mission in the world.

   _____

   _____

   _____

How do people use their individual talents to do the work of Christ?

Respond

Saint Louis IX Let His Light Shine

King Louis IX of France is a light for us to follow. Throughout his life, Louis praised God, fulfilling his baptismal role as priest. He also served God as the husband of Margaret and the father of eleven children. In 1235, Louis followed his vocation to be the ruler of France.

He shared in Christ's role as prophet when he spread God's message of peace and justice to the people of France. He was well-known for his fairness and honest treatment of the people under his rule.

King Louis IX shared in Christ's role as king when he served all the people of France, especially those in need. He reached out to the poor and established hospitals for the sick. He also worked to provide a good education for his people.

We admire King Louis IX because he ruled with justice and helped bring God's peace to the people of France. We celebrate the feast day of Saint Louis IX, King of France, on August 25.

Following Others

We can talk to adults for help in understanding what our vocation may be. We can join adults who are doing God's work. This will help us learn about the many ways we can serve God and others.

Activities

1. Look at the pictures. Discuss how each person is being a light to others.

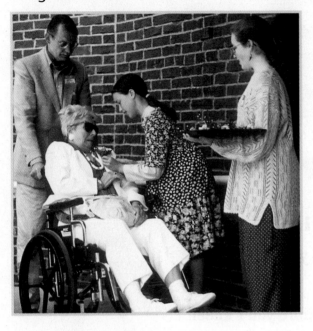 

2. Write about how you might like to serve others when you are older.

_____

_____

_____

_____

_____

_____

_____

_____

3. Rearrange the four words to write a sentence that tells what all Christians should do.

     others   love   with   serve

_____

How does Jesus help us serve others?

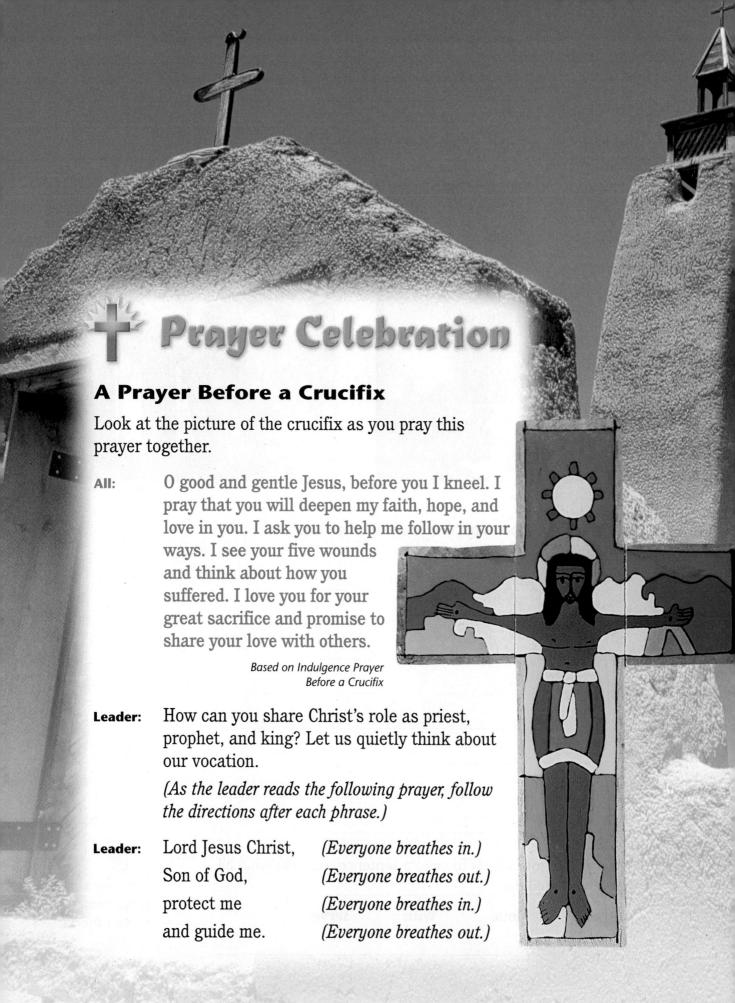

✝ Prayer Celebration

A Prayer Before a Crucifix

Look at the picture of the crucifix as you pray this prayer together.

All: O good and gentle Jesus, before you I kneel. I pray that you will deepen my faith, hope, and love in you. I ask you to help me follow in your ways. I see your five wounds and think about how you suffered. I love you for your great sacrifice and promise to share your love with others.

Based on Indulgence Prayer Before a Crucifix

Leader: How can you share Christ's role as priest, prophet, and king? Let us quietly think about our vocation.

(As the leader reads the following prayer, follow the directions after each phrase.)

Leader: Lord Jesus Christ,   *(Everyone breathes in.)*
Son of God,   *(Everyone breathes out.)*
protect me   *(Everyone breathes in.)*
and guide me.   *(Everyone breathes out.)*

17 Chapter Review

A **Circle** the letter of the best answer.

1. All people living and dead who believe in Jesus Christ make up the _____.

   a. Apostles

   b. Prophets

   c. religious community

   d. Communion of Saints

2. The work we do as members of the Church is called our _____.

   a. vocation

   b. devotion

   c. prayer

   d. job

3. Men called to serve God as priests, deacons, or bishops celebrate the Sacrament of _____.

   a. Reconciliation

   b. Baptism

   c. Holy Orders

   d. Confirmation

4. Through Baptism, Jesus anoints us as priest, _____, and king.

   a. friend

   b. Apostle

   c. prophet

   d. angel

5. In "A Prayer Before a Crucifix", we think of Jesus' five _____ and how he suffered for us.

   a. miracles

   b. gifts

   c. wounds

   d. parables

B **Write** two ways Saint Louis IX was a light to the world.

_____

_____

_____

_____

_____

_____

_____

C **Complete** the sentences with words from the box.

prophet	king	kindness
Light	ruler	priest

1. Jesus said, "I am the _____ of the World."

2. We fulfill our role as _____ when we spread God's message of love to others.

3. Saint Louis IX shared in Christ's role as _____ when he served the people of France, especially those in need.

4. We are a light to others each time we perform an act of _____ .

5. We fulfill our role as _____ when we pray for others.

D **Respond** to the following.

1. What did Jesus mean when he told his followers to be the light of the world? _____

_____

_____

_____

2. Write about how a person you know uses his or her talents to light the world. _____

_____

_____

_____

Take Home

The Eucharist

The Eucharist, Bread of Life, is the gift Christ gave us. How to make it central to our life is the challenge that faces all Catholics. We often think that we must be self-reliant, but God invites us to come to the Eucharist for help.

ACTIVITY

Grains of Wheat What are the ingredients needed to make bread? Look in a recipe book to see. Talk with your child about how important each ingredient is for the recipe to work properly. Relate this to how each person is important in making up the Body of Christ.

WEEKLY PLANNER

On Sunday

Remind your child that the Eucharist is kept in the tabernacle. The sanctuary lamp is kept alight near it to honor the presence of Christ.

On the Web

blestarewe.com

Visit our Web site for the saint of the day and the reflection question of the week.

Saint of the Week

 Saint Alphonsus Liguori (1696–1787)

Saint Alphonsus Liguori was a bishop and Doctor of the Church. Alphonsus began a career as a lawyer, and later decided to become a missionary. He organized a group of priest missionaries, now known as the Redemptorists.

Patron Saint of: vocations
Feast Day: August 1

A Prayer for the Week

Your Body gives us life, dear Lord. Keep us strong and faithful. Like Saint Alphonsus Ligouri may we never tire of your care for us. Amen.

Take Home

FAMILY TIME

✝ Scripture Background

In the Time of Jesus

Bread Every morning women worked for hours to make bread for their families. They began by using a hand mill to grind the kernels of barley or wheat into flour. After mixing it with other ingredients, the women shaped the dough into round thin disks, about seven inches in diameter. They baked the bread on hot stones or in ovens located outside the home. Typically, a person ate three loaves of bread at every meal. Besides being a staple food, bread is also associated with religious rites.

Read about the bread Jesus shared with his disciples in Mark 14:12–16; 22–26.

OUR CATHOLIC TRADITION in Church Teachings

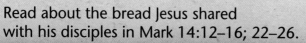

The Year of the Eucharist In what turned out to be the final year of his pontificate, Pope John Paul II proclaimed 2005 as the Year of the Eucharist. In his encyclical on the Eucharist, the Holy Father wrote, "The Church draws her life from the Eucharist. This truth does not simply express a daily experience of faith, but recapitulates the heart of the mystery of the Church" *(Ecclesia de Eucharista, 1)*. In October 2005, as this special year came to a close, newly elected Pope Benedict XVI was asked by a child how Jesus Christ can be truly present in the Eucharist. He said, "We do not see him with our eyes, but we see that wherever Jesus is, people change— they improve… We do not see the Lord himself, but we see the effects of the Lord: so we can understand that Jesus is present."

18 The Eucharist

... through their merits and prayers, grant that in all things we may be defended by your protecting help.

Eucharistic Prayer I

Share

The people we love help us learn about God and the world around us. Even when they are not with us, we think of them when we do certain things. What they teach is a part of us.

Activity

Role-Play

Choose who will play the following roles and act out the story.

Narrator: The Salerno family gathered in the park for a special reunion. Everyone was there except Grandpa. He had died a few months earlier.

David: "I miss Grandpa. I sure wish he was here to help us catch a fish."

James: "He always knew just when to pull in the line."

Narrator: The two boys stood on the dock and cast their lines. Suddenly David noticed something different about James's line.

David: "Reel it in!"

Narrator: James pulled in his line and was surprised to see a large fish dangling from the hook.

James: "That's just like Grandpa always did it! It feels like he is here with us."

What did Jesus ask us to do to remember his life, Death, and Resurrection?

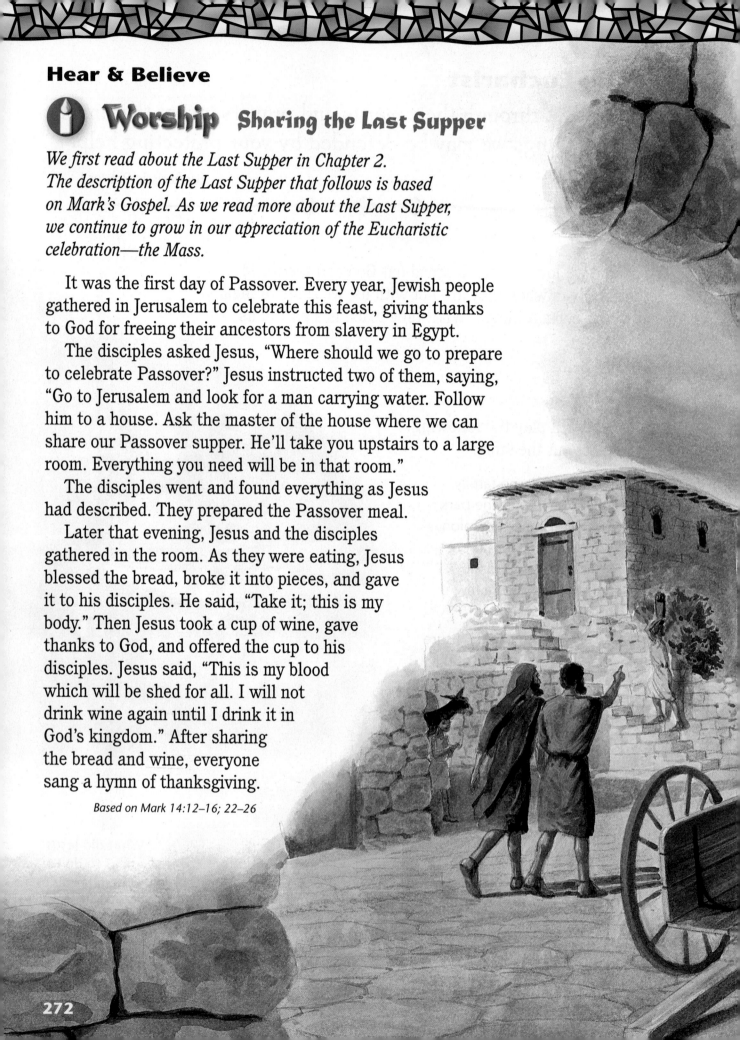

Hear & Believe

🕯 Worship Sharing the Last Supper

We first read about the Last Supper in Chapter 2.
The description of the Last Supper that follows is based
on Mark's Gospel. As we read more about the Last Supper,
we continue to grow in our appreciation of the Eucharistic
celebration—the Mass.

It was the first day of Passover. Every year, Jewish people gathered in Jerusalem to celebrate this feast, giving thanks to God for freeing their ancestors from slavery in Egypt.

The disciples asked Jesus, "Where should we go to prepare to celebrate Passover?" Jesus instructed two of them, saying, "Go to Jerusalem and look for a man carrying water. Follow him to a house. Ask the master of the house where we can share our Passover supper. He'll take you upstairs to a large room. Everything you need will be in that room."

The disciples went and found everything as Jesus had described. They prepared the Passover meal.

Later that evening, Jesus and the disciples gathered in the room. As they were eating, Jesus blessed the bread, broke it into pieces, and gave it to his disciples. He said, "Take it; this is my body." Then Jesus took a cup of wine, gave thanks to God, and offered the cup to his disciples. Jesus said, "This is my blood which will be shed for all. I will not drink wine again until I drink it in God's kingdom." After sharing the bread and wine, everyone sang a hymn of thanksgiving.

Based on Mark 14:12–16; 22–26

The First Eucharist

At the Last Supper, Jesus shared a meal with his disciples that is also known as the first Eucharist. At this supper, Jesus offered his Body and Blood as a sacrifice for us. Today during the Liturgy of the Eucharist, we celebrate Jesus' words and actions from the Last Supper long ago.

Activity

The sentences below tell about the Last Supper. Complete each sentence with a word from the box.

Blood	hymn	God	sacrifice
Body	Eucharist	bread	

1. Jesus thanked _____ for the bread and wine.

2. Jesus broke the _____ and gave it to his disciples to eat.

3. Jesus said the bread was his _____.

4. Jesus said the cup of wine was his _____.

5. After the meal, everyone sang a _____ of thanksgiving.

6. Jesus offered his Body and Blood as a _____ for us.

7. The Last Supper was the very first _____.

How do we become one in Christ?

Hear & Believe

Gathered as One in Christ

On Sunday, God's family gathers at Mass to celebrate the Eucharist. The Eucharist unites us with God and the Church. The Church includes all those living on earth and all those who have died as followers of Christ. Like Mary and all the saints, we are together in Christ. During the celebration of the Eucharist, the **assembly** honors the saints by praying the following prayer.

> In communion with those whose memory we venerate, especially the glorious ever-Virgin Mary, Mother of our God and Lord, Jesus Christ, and blessed Joseph, her Spouse, your blessed Apostles and Martyrs, . . . and all your Saints; we ask that through their merits and prayers, in all things we may be defended by your protecting help.
>
> *Eucharistic Prayer I*

The Eucharist

The Eucharist is the center of Catholic life and the memorial of Christ's Passover. We express our faith in Jesus, who died on the cross for our sins, and joyfully celebrate his Resurrection. Through his Son, Jesus, God shows us his kingdom of justice, mercy, and love.

The Eucharist unites us to all members of the Church.

The Role of the Priest

In the name of Christ, the priest celebrates the Eucharist with the assembly at Mass. He leads the assembly in the celebration of the Sacrifice of our Salvation—the life, Death, and Resurrection of Jesus Christ. The priest brings Jesus' message of love each time he proclaims the **Gospel** and preaches the **homily**.

At Mass the priest leads the assembly in prayer. He asks the Holy Spirit to make Christ present for us. Through the Holy Spirit and the words of the priest, the gifts of bread and wine are changed into the Body and Blood of Christ.

The priest also presides over the other Sacraments. He guides members of a parish in their journey of faith. United with the priest through the Eucharist, together we help bring God's love and mercy to the world.

Our Church Teaches

The priest has the important role of leading the Church in the Liturgy. At Mass we celebrate the Eucharist with the Communion of Saints. Christ brings all Christians together—those who are living and those who have died. Each time we celebrate the Eucharist, we grow stronger in our faith. In the Eucharist we are reconciled with God and with one another.

Activity

Why is the Eucharist important to our Catholic faith?

_____

_____

_____

_____

We Believe

The Eucharist is central to our Catholic faith. We remember how Jesus freed us from sin by his Death and Resurrection.

Faith Words

assembly
Catholics gathered to celebrate the Eucharist and other Sacraments are called the assembly.

Gospel
The word *Gospel* means "Good News." At Mass, we listen to readings about the life and teachings of Jesus Christ from the four Gospels in the New Testament.

How can we describe the Eucharist?

Papal Mass, Central Park, New York, 1995

Respond

When we receive the Eucharist, we realize that we are one Body of Christ.

Activities

1. Draw a box around the words or phrases in the word bank below that refer to the celebration of the Eucharist. In the blank boxes, write your own words or phrases that describe the Eucharist. Use the word bank to help you.

war   leads us to peace   a special gift   separates people

leads us to sin

a sign of God's Kingdom

unites us with Jesus

hate

love

unites us with all Christians

2. The priest has a special vocation to lead the Catholic community in prayer. Draw a picture of a priest celebrating a Sacrament. Below your picture, write how the priest leads members of the Catholic community in that Sacrament.

GO TO pages 394–397 to review the seven sacraments.

_____

_____

_____

_____

3. In addition to celebrating the Liturgy, the priest ministers within the parish. Think about a priest you know and then complete the sentence.

Father _____ helps people in

the parish by _____

_____

_____

_____

_____

_____.

How can we ask the saints to pray for us?

277

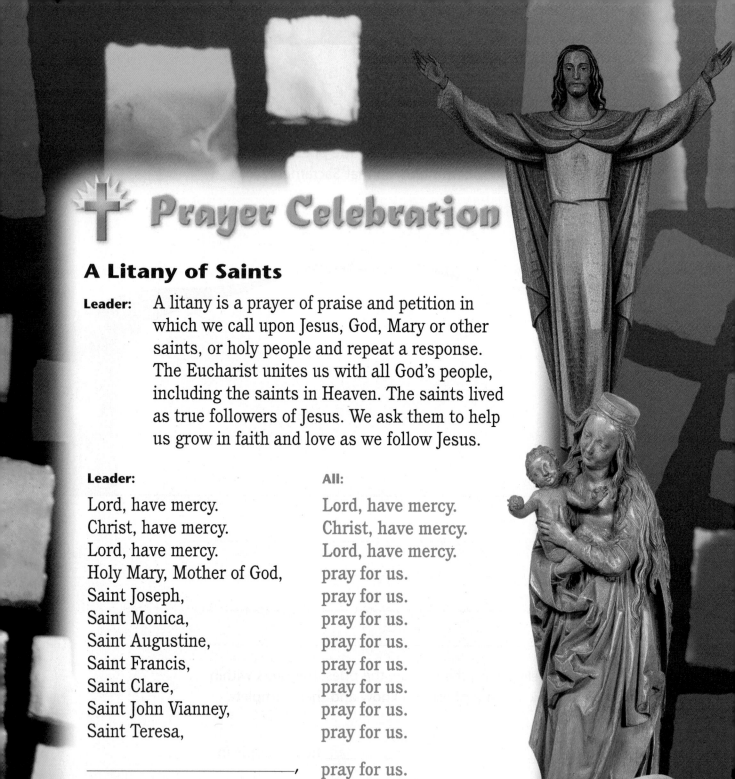

✟ Prayer Celebration

A Litany of Saints

Leader: A litany is a prayer of praise and petition in which we call upon Jesus, God, Mary or other saints, or holy people and repeat a response. The Eucharist unites us with all God's people, including the saints in Heaven. The saints lived as true followers of Jesus. We ask them to help us grow in faith and love as we follow Jesus.

Leader:	All:
Lord, have mercy.	Lord, have mercy.
Christ, have mercy.	Christ, have mercy.
Lord, have mercy.	Lord, have mercy.
Holy Mary, Mother of God,	pray for us.
Saint Joseph,	pray for us.
Saint Monica,	pray for us.
Saint Augustine,	pray for us.
Saint Francis,	pray for us.
Saint Clare,	pray for us.
Saint John Vianney,	pray for us.
Saint Teresa,	pray for us.
_____,	pray for us.
All holy men and women,	pray for us.
Lord, be merciful,	Lord, save your people.
From every sin,	Lord, save your people.
By your death and rising to new life,	Lord, save your people.
Lord Jesus, hear our prayer.	Lord Jesus, hear our prayer.

Based on the Litany of Saints from the Rite of Baptism

A **Match** column A with column B by writing the correct number in the space provided.

A

1. Litany of Saints
2. assembly
3. Gospels
4. homily
5. Eucharist
6. priest

B

_____ Catholics gathered to celebrate the Sacraments

_____ special talk the priest gives after reading the Gospel

_____ guides members of the parish in their journey of faith

_____ special prayer to God, Jesus, or the saints

_____ unites us with God and one another

_____ a section of the New Testament about the life and teachings of Jesus Christ

B **Circle** the letter of the best answer.

1. The Eucharist is the memorial of _____.
   a. Christ's Passover
   b. the feast of the Annunciation
   c. the saints
   d. Christ's birth

2. The _____ leads the Church in the Liturgy.
   a. assembly
   b. Eucharistic minister
   c. priest
   d. choir

3. Through the _____ the bread and wine are changed into the Body and Blood of Christ.
   a. assembly
   b. Holy Spirit
   c. deacon
   d. Communion of Saints

4. The _____ is central to our Catholic faith.
   a. assembly
   b. Eucharist
   c. litany
   d. homily

C **Draw or write** about Jesus' celebration of the Eucharist.

[blank box for drawing or writing]

D **Respond** to the following questions.

1. Why is the Eucharist important to the faith of a Catholic?

_____

_____

_____

2. What would you say about the meaning of the Eucharist to a second-grader who is receiving Holy Communion for the first time?

_____

_____

_____

Take Home

FAMILY TIME

The New Commandment and the Works of Mercy

There are people who are so afraid of breaking rules that they can become paralyzed when they have to make a decision. Jesus often challenged the rules that governed civil and religious practice. He had respect for the law but taught that the law was made for people, not the other way around. The law Christ teaches is simple but demanding. It requires us to use love as the standard by which we judge our actions.

ACTIVITY

Loose Change   Make a donation box and put it in a special place. Ask your whole family to collect loose change and place it in the box. Take the money collected and give it to a charity, such as Catholic Relief Services, or to a parish ministry for the poor.

WEEKLY PLANNER

On Sunday

Look in your parish bulletin for ways people offer service to the community. Is there something in which your family could participate?

On the Web

blestarewe.com

Visit our Web site for the saint of the day and the reflection question of the week.

Saint of the Week

Saint Louise de Marillac (1591–1660)

Saint Louise de Marillac founded the Daughters of Charity community in 1633. She was a friend of Saint Vincent de Paul, who depended on her assistance. She was an intelligent and generous woman who had great stamina and determination.

Patron Saint of: social workers
Feast Day: March 15

A Prayer for the Week

Lord, help us be good stewards of all the good things you have given us. As we remember the good works and deeds of Saint Louise, give us the strength to spread your love. Amen.

Getting ready for Chapter 19

Take Home

✚ Scripture Background

In the Time of Jesus

Beggars In New Testament times, beggars were commonly seen outside the temple gates or along the roads. Making up about fifteen percent of the population, they were forced to live outside the cities and villages. With little or no support from their families, they begged for food or alms. Beggars were often blind or suffered from other disabilities or illnesses. Jesus embraced the begging poor and taught his followers to treat them with compassion.

In Matthew 25:31–41 Jesus invites us to ease the sufferings of others by caring for their physical needs.

OUR CATHOLIC TRADITION in Film

Monsieur Vincent In 1948 a popular film was made about Saint Vincent de Paul, called *Monsieur Vincent*. It tells the story about the sixteenth-century saint growing up in a poor family. He was a bright, charming, ambitious boy who was drawn to the priesthood. He became wealthy and was even chaplain to the queen. Then in midlife he discovered his vocation to serve the poor. He devoted his talents to serving the underprivileged, especially prisoners and slaves, and used his association with the rich to fund his charitable projects. He founded the Vincentian Order of priests and helped Saint Louise de Marillac to establish the Sisters of Charity.

Pierre Fresnay as Saint Vincent de Paul in *Monsieur Vincent*

282 blestarewe.com

19 The New Commandment and the Works of Mercy

This is my commandment:
love one another as I love you.

John 15:12

Share

Jesus knew the needs of others. He asks us to follow his example and help spread God's love to the world. We can love others in simple ways every day.

Activity

In the blank hearts, use words or pictures to show how you share God's love with others.

Listen to someone with a problem

smile

What did Jesus teach us about love?

Hear & Believe

✠ Scripture The Washing of the Feet

On the night before he died, Jesus taught his disciples an important lesson. They must care for others by serving one another. In the story below, read how Jesus taught his disciples this lesson, when he did something even slaves were not expected to do.

Jesus was having dinner with his disciples. He got up from the table. After tying a towel around his waist, Jesus poured water into a bowl. Then he began washing the disciples' feet! Peter was embarrassed and cried, "Do not wash my feet, Master!"

"You do not understand now, but you will later," Jesus said, still washing. He dried Peter's feet with the towel. When he was done, Jesus spoke again, "You call me Teacher and Master, and I am both. So if I have washed your feet, you should wash each other's feet. I have given you a model to follow. As I have done, you should also do."

Based on John 13:1–15

Called to Serve

In the Scripture story "The Washing of the Feet," Jesus calls all of us to serve one another. At the Last Supper, Jesus gave his disciples a New Commandment. The New Commandment combines the Ten Commandments and the Beatitudes into one law of love. We can follow this law of love by doing daily acts of kindness. By treating others as God would want, we can love as Christ loves.

 page 405 to read more about the New Commandment.

Faith Words

Corporal Works of Mercy

The Corporal Works of Mercy are ways the Church takes care of the basic physical needs of others.

The Corporal Works of Mercy

Jesus cared for the poor and the sick. We follow Christ's example of love by respecting people and taking care of their basic physical needs. We can use the **Corporal Works of Mercy** as our guide.

The Corporal Works of Mercy

Feed the hungry.

Give drink to the thirsty.

Give clothing to the poor.

Visit those in prison.

Shelter the homeless.

Visit the sick.

Bury the dead.

Activity

Write two ways people in your parish or community take care of the physical needs of others.

1. _____

_____

_____

2. _____

_____

_____

What does Jesus promise for those who fellow the law of love?

Hear & Believe

✝ Seeing Christ in Others

In Chapter 11 we learned that at the Last Supper, Jesus gave his disciples a New Commandment to love one another. When we follow this law of love, we see Christ in others and treat them with kindness and mercy. How do we see Christ in others? Read what Jesus says.

"When the Son of Man returns in glory with angels all around him, he will sit on a glorious throne. Everyone will gather before him, and he will separate them, like a shepherd separates his sheep from goats.

"He will place the sheep on his right and the goats on his left. Then he will say to those on his right, 'Come, you are blessed by my Father and shall inherit the Kingdom of God. You are blessed because when I needed food and drink, you nourished me. When I needed a friend, you welcomed me. When I needed something to wear, you gave me clothes. When I was sick and needed attention, you cared for me. When I needed a friend in prison, you visited me.'

"Then the blessed will ask, 'When did we give you food and drink? When did we welcome you? When did we give you clothes? We don't remember seeing you sick or visiting you in prison. When did we do these things?'

"The Son of God will reply, 'Whenever you helped someone in need, you helped me.'"

Based on Matthew 25:31–41

Loving Acts

The loving acts described in this passage from Scripture (Matthew 25:31–41) are the Corporal Works of Mercy. As you have learned, the Corporal Works of Mercy are ways of caring for the basic physical needs of all people. Jesus teaches us to love others as he loves us.

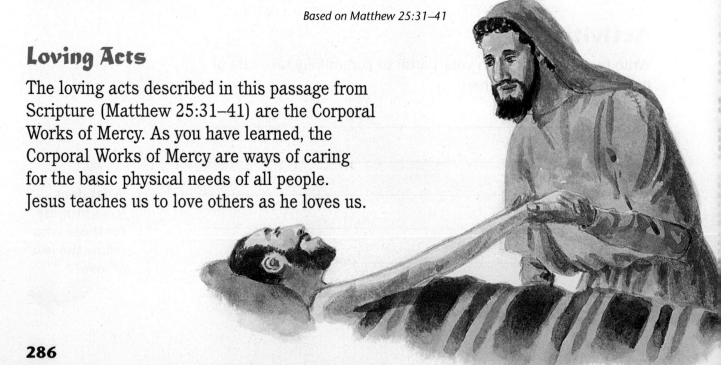

The Spiritual Works of Mercy

Jesus also wants us to listen and respond to people as they express their thoughts and emotions. He asks us to reach out lovingly to people who are lonely, discouraged, or struggling in life. Jesus wants us to pray for their needs. To encourage and support others in these ways, we use the **Spiritual Works of Mercy** as our guide.

Spiritual Works of Mercy

Help others do what is right.

Teach the ignorant.

Give advice to the doubtful.

Comfort those who suffer.

Be patient with others.

Forgive injuries.

Pray for the living and the dead.

We Believe

Jesus combined the Ten Commandments and the Beatitudes into one law of love. Jesus said that if we love others as he loves us, we will have eternal happiness with God.

Faith Words

Spiritual Works of Mercy
The Spiritual Works of Mercy are loving actions that describe how to respond to people's basic spiritual needs.

Our Church Teaches

Jesus said that we should love others as he loves us. Jesus showed God's love to others by taking care of their basic needs. The Corporal Works of Mercy are ways we can care for the physical needs of others. The Spiritual Works of Mercy show us ways to encourage, guide, and give emotional support in response to people's spiritual needs.

Activity

Write two ways people in your parish or community take care of the spiritual needs of others.

1. _____

   _____

2. _____

   _____

How can we take care of the basic needs of others?

Dr. Albert Schweitzer and Caring for Others

Albert Schweitzer was born in Germany in 1875. He was aware of the needs of others even as a child. One way Albert learned about caring for others was by reading the Bible.

At school he noticed that some of the children were poorly dressed or had less food than he did. Albert was uncomfortable with this difference.

When he got older, he enrolled in medical school and became a doctor. On a trip to Africa, Alfred saw people who were poor and sick. He decided to help those who were suffering there. He and his wife, Helene, became famous for practicing the Corporal Works of Mercy. They built a hospital at Lambaréné in Africa. There they took care of the sick, and shared all they had with others.

Albert won the 1952 Nobel Peace Prize for the care he gave to the sick people in Africa. Dr. Albert Schweitzer died in 1965 and is buried at Lambaréné.

Activity

Begin at Start on the game board. Roll one dice and move the correct number of spaces following the direction of the arrows. If you land on a picture, tell which work of mercy is being shown. If you land on an action that describes a work of mercy, give an example of someone doing this work of mercy. It can be someone at school, in your family, in your community, or in the world.

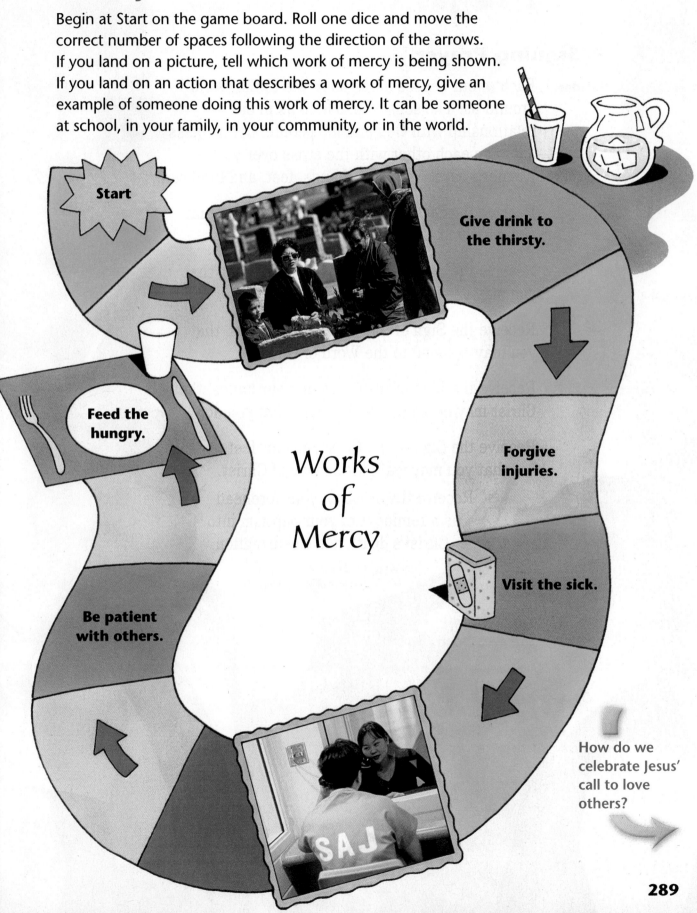

Start

Give drink to the thirsty.

Feed the hungry.

Works of Mercy

Forgive injuries.

Visit the sick.

Be patient with others.

How do we celebrate Jesus' call to love others?

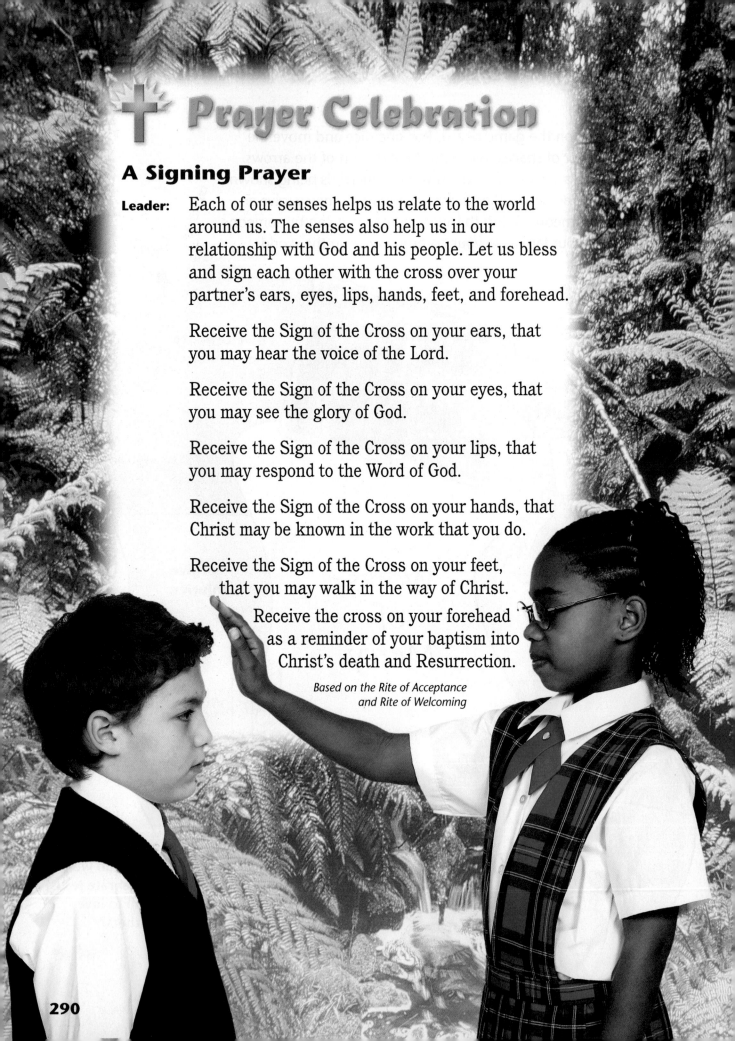

✝ Prayer Celebration

A Signing Prayer

Leader: Each of our senses helps us relate to the world around us. The senses also help us in our relationship with God and his people. Let us bless and sign each other with the cross over your partner's ears, eyes, lips, hands, feet, and forehead.

Receive the Sign of the Cross on your ears, that you may hear the voice of the Lord.

Receive the Sign of the Cross on your eyes, that you may see the glory of God.

Receive the Sign of the Cross on your lips, that you may respond to the Word of God.

Receive the Sign of the Cross on your hands, that Christ may be known in the work that you do.

Receive the Sign of the Cross on your feet, that you may walk in the way of Christ.

Receive the cross on your forehead as a reminder of your baptism into Christ's death and Resurrection.

Based on the Rite of Acceptance and Rite of Welcoming

A **Write** the letter "C" for one of the Corporal Works of Mercy or "S" for one of the Spiritual Works of Mercy.

1. _____ Visit those in prison.

2. _____ Comfort those who suffer.

3. _____ Be patient with others.

4. _____ Shelter the homeless.

5. _____ Help others do what is right.

6. _____ Visit the sick.

7. _____ Give drink to the thirsty.

8. _____ Teach the ignorant.

9. _____ Bury the dead.

10. _____ Forgive injuries.

11. _____ Pray for the living and the dead.

12. _____ Give clothing to the poor.

13. _____ Feed the hungry.

14. _____ Give advice to the doubtful.

B **Draw or write** one way you have shared God's love with others.

C **Circle** the letter of the best answer.

1. Jesus combined the Commandments and the _____ into one law of love.
   a. Beatitudes
   b. Scriptures
   c. Bible
   d. Gospel

2. The law of love is also known as the _____.
   a. Gospel
   b. Beatitudes
   c. New Commandment
   d. Act of Love

3. In the Scripture story of the washing of the feet, Jesus calls us to _____.
   a. be more clean
   b. forgive others
   c. heal others
   d. serve others

4. Jesus said that if we love others as he loves us, we will have eternal _____.
   a. peace
   b. happiness
   c. intelligence
   d. love

5. Ways of encouraging, guiding, and supporting others are known as the _____.
   a. Prophets
   b. gifts of faith
   c. Corporal Works of Mercy
   d. Spiritual Works of Mercy

6. Ways of taking care of the physical needs of others are known as the _____.
   a. Prophets
   b. gifts of faith
   c. Corporal Works of Mercy
   d. Spiritual Works of Mercy

D **Respond** to the following questions.

1. How did Dr. Albert Schweitzer share God's love with others?

   _____

   _____

2. What can someone your age do to practice the Works of Mercy?

   _____

   _____

Take Home

The Commandments and Bringing God's Message to the World

No matter how closely a parent watches a child, he or she cannot be present all the time to protect or guide in difficult situations. Catholic parents know that God's assistance is available through prayer.

ACTIVITY

Prayer Table Locate a place in your home where your family can pray this week. If you have a favorite prayer card or statue, consider displaying it there. In addition to religious articles, you can place a family picture at your prayer table. Each person in the family can put a prayer request on the table as well.

WEEKLY PLANNER

On Sunday

Before the Sign of Peace at Mass, listen to the words of Jesus regarding peace and unity.

On the Web

blestarewe.com

 Visit our Web site for the saint of the day and the reflection question of the week.

Saint of the Week

 Blessed Junípero Serra (1713–1784)

Blessed Junipero Serra was a Spanish Franciscan priest who founded nine Catholic missions in California in the 1700s. He preached and evangelized throughout the region. The Serra Club, an organization dedicated to the promotion of vocations to the Catholic priesthood and religious life, is named after Blessed Junipero.

Feast Day: July 1

A Prayer for the Week

Lord, Junipero Serra brought the Gospel and education to the Native Americans of California. Help us follow you in our own lives and to always know your peace. Amen.

Take Home

FAMILY TIME

✝ Scripture Background

In the Time of Jesus

Galilee   Most of Jesus' ministry was centered in Galilee, the northern section of Palestine. It was fertile land with olives, grapes, and wheat growing throughout the countryside. A main feature of the region was the Sea of Galilee where fishermen could be seen casting their nets. Just west of the lake is the village of Cana where Jesus performed a miracle. While attending a wedding there, Jesus changed water into wine. After his Resurrection, Jesus returned to Galilee with a special message for his disciples.

Read about the commissioning of the disciples in Matthew 28:16–20.

OUR CATHOLIC TRADITION in Art

The _Angelus_   The _Angelus_ is a prayer that people have prayed since the Middle Ages. The prayer consists of the dialogue between Mary and the Angel Gabriel, interspersed with a series of Hail Marys, followed by a closing prayer. By the fourteenth century, church bells were tolled at six in the morning, noontime, and six in the evening, reminding people to pray the prayer. The painting _L'Angélus_ by Jean-Francois Millet (1814–1875) shows that wherever people are, they can pause to pray this special prayer. This devotion is still popular today in many churches.

L'Angélus, (1857–1859) by Jean-Francois Millet

20 The Commandments and Bringing God's Message to the World

LET US PRAY Go and make disciples of all nations.

Based on Matthew 28:19

Share

Through prayer we can grow as Christians. We can pray for God's help as we try to bring God's peace and justice to the world.

Activity

Complete the prayer below. You may use the words that are shown or your own ideas.

sad   sick   poor   fighting

I see people who are lonely;

   help me extend my hand in friendship.

I see people who are suffering;

   help me ease their pain.

I see people who are _____;

   help me _____.

I see people who are _____;

   help me _____.

Lord, forgive me when I fail to do something I should for people.

How do we bring peace and justice to the world?

Hear & Believe

✝ Scripture The Commissioning of the Disciples

After Jesus' Resurrection, he came to the disciples in Galilee. He told them what God wanted them to do, saying: "Go and travel to all nations. Teach the people there what I have commanded. Baptize them in the name of the Father, the Son, and the Holy Spirit. You also will show them how to become disciples of mine. And remember, I will always be with you."

Based on Matthew 28:16–20

The Power of Prayer

God is always with us, especially when we pray. He touches our hearts with his love and strengthens us to live his Law of Love.

As Catholics, we have a responsibility to show God's goodness to one another. Prayer helps us feel the power of God's love and then share it with others. Through prayer, we listen to God's call to do what is good. We can ask God to help us do better.

Prayer helps us work against the sin and evil in the world. We can pray a prayer of **petition** to ask for God's help for others and ourselves. We can also ask for God's help in bringing his love to the world.

When we need God's help to live as he asks, we can pray, "Dear God, help me to love others as you love me."

GO TO pages 407–410 to read more about prayer.
pages 9–16 to read more traditional Catholic prayers and devotions.

Faith Words
petition
A petition is a prayer in which we ask for God's help for others and ourselves.

Activities

Prayer is powerful. What can prayer help you do?

_____

_____

_____

_____

_____

What are we called to do as Christians?

Hear & Believe

Saint Josephine Bakhita

Josephine Bakhita was born in Sudan, Africa, in 1869. When she was nine years old, she was kidnapped and sold into slavery. She had several owners who treated her cruelly, even beating her.

Eventually, Josephine was sold to a man who took her to Italy to be a nanny. Her new family sent their daughter, escorted by Josephine as her caretaker, to a school run by the Canossian Daughters of Charity.

At the school, Josephine learned about the Catholic faith. She learned that there was a gentle God who loved her. Through prayer, she came to experience God's goodness and love. "What a great grace it is to know God!" she said. Josephine prayed for those who did not know about God's love.

Since slavery was illegal in Italy, Josephine now was free. When she was twenty-one years old, she was baptized into the Catholic Church. After much prayer and thought, Josephine decided to remain with the sisters and devote her life to helping others. In 1896 she joined the order as a religious sister where Josephine did everything with great love.

Her daily chores included cooking, sewing, and welcoming visitors. Josephine greeted those who came for help with a warm and friendly smile. During World War II, she prayed for peace and comforted those who were suffering.

Josephine's kind and loving nature helped others experience God's love. She even forgave those who earlier had kidnapped and tortured her. Josephine spent fifty years as a religious sister working for peace and justice. "The Lord has loved me so much," she said. "We must love everyone . . . we must be compassionate!" On October 1, 2000, Pope John Paul II canonized Josephine Bakhita. She is the patron saint of Sudan.

Our Church Teaches

As Christians, we are called to bring God's love, peace, and justice to the world. We lift our hearts in prayer, asking for God's help to ease the suffering of others. Our prayers of petition are heard by God, who is always with us. Through praying, following the Ten Commandments, and living the Law of Love, we help to bring God's love, peace, and justice to the world.

We Must Love Everyone

We Must Be Compassionate

Activities

1. Look up the words *peace* and *justice* in the Glossary located in the back of your book. Review the meaning of these words. Write how Saint Josephine Bakhita helped bring peace and justice to others.

_____

_____

_____

_____

_____

2. What is one way your parish brings peace and justice to others?

_____

_____

_____

_____

_____

We Must Be Compassionate

We Must Love Everyone

How does prayer help us grow in understanding our faith?

Respond

We need God's help to follow the Commandments and live the Law of Love.

 Activities

1. On the lines below, write a prayer of petition for the Fourth and Fifth Commandments. Then select and write a prayer of petition for another Commandment. Commandments one and two have been done for you. Refer to the Ten Commandments chart on page 404 for help.

I   Dear God, help me to keep you first in my life.

II   Dear God, help me to always use your name respectfully.

IV   Dear God, _____

_____

_____

V   Dear God, _____

_____

_____

Dear God, _____

_____

_____

We Must Love Everyone

2. Write ways that you can bring peace and justice to others.

_____

_____

_____

_____

We Must Love Everyone

3. Learn to sign the following phrases from the Lord's Prayer. Review what you learned in Chapters 4, 8, 12, and 16. You can now sign all of the Lord's Prayer!

and lead

us not into

temptation,

but deliver

us

from evil.

Amen.

How do we pray for justice and peace?

✝ Prayer Celebration

A Prayer of Commitment

Leader: Be an instrument of peace in our world today. Where you find hateful words, be a model of acceptance and love. Where you find prejudice and ignorance, be a source of knowledge and truth. Where you find fear and doubt, be a sign of faith and confidence. Where you find darkness and poverty, be committed to the basic dignity of every person. Where you find violence, be compassion and peace. You are children of the light; be a sign of the living Gospel!

All: Amen.

Based on the Prayer of Saint Francis, adapted by the Capuchin Youth and Family Ministries Center, Garrison, NY

Leader: Together, let us pray the Lord's Prayer, using sign language.

All: Our Father . . .

A **Complete** the sentences with words from the box.

peace	petition	grace
love	pray	goodness

1. When we pray, God touches our hearts with

   his _____.

2. A _____ is a prayer in which we ask
   for God's forgiveness and help.

3. God is always with us, especially when we _____.

4. Following the Commandments and the Law of Love, we help bring

   God's love, _____, and justice to the world.

5. As Catholics, we have a responsibility to show

   God's _____ to one another.

B **Circle** the letter of the best answer.

1. The prayer of commitment on
   page 302 is based on a prayer
   of Saint ___.
   a. Joseph
   b. Martin de Porres
   c. Francis
   d. Patrick

2. Jesus told his disciples
   to ___ what he had commanded.
   a. write Psalms about
   b. sing Psalms about
   c. write a book about
   d. teach others

3. Jesus promised his disciples
   that he would ___.
   a. think about them often
   b. always be with them
   c. perform many miracles
   d. build a church for them

4. Prayer helps us work against
   sin and ___ in the world.
   a. evil
   b. justice
   c. sacrifice
   d. helplessness

C **Write** two ways Josephine Bakhita showed God's goodness to others.

_____

_____

_____

_____

D **Write** a prayer for peace and justice in the world.

_____

_____

_____

_____

E **Respond** to the following questions.

1. What instructions did Jesus give his disciples after his Resurrection?

_____

_____

_____

_____

2. How can you spread Jesus' message of love, peace, and justice to

the world? _____

_____

_____

_____

Faith in Action

Ministries to the Unemployed   In many parishes, there are people who have lost their jobs and are unable to find work. Like families, parish communities support and encourage its members in difficult times. The unemployed have many different needs that the parish can help meet. A parish can help provide food and money as a family tries to get back on its feet. We can bring people together to talk about the many ways unemployment affects their lives. We can bring people together who can help one another find jobs. And we can help know that brighter days lie ahead.

In Everyday Life

Activity   Think of some jobs people do for us that we tend to take for granted. Think how much harder our life would be without them.

List three of these jobs here.

1. _____

2. _____

3. _____

In Your Parish

Activity   The phrase *"in the same boat"* means that a group of people are in a similar situation. They understand one another and can help one another. Choose one or more of the words below to use in a sentence that describes one way people who are "in the same boat" of unemployment can help one another. Then pray for the unemployed of your parish.

pray	babysit	share	invite	respect
talent	write	hug	newspaper	meet

_____

_____

Faith in Action

Extraordinary Ministers of Holy Communion Extraordinary ministers of Holy Communion help the parish priest distribute Holy Communion to the people who wish to receive it. After special training, they bring the Sacrament to people who are sick at home, in nursing homes, and hospitals. To emphasize that these volunteers bring with them the love and prayers of the parish community, the celebrant at the parish Mass often gives a special blessing to the volunteers who will visit the sick during the coming week.

In Everyday Life

Activity On the line below, write the name of someone you feel especially close to. Then draw two images that would help others understand why you feel this way about the person you named.

MY FAMILY AND FRIENDS

_____

In Your Parish

Activity Create a greeting card that an extraordinary minister of Holy Communion could give to someone they will bring the Eucharist to this week.

Faith in Action

Ministries to the Poor While some poor people live on the streets of our nation's biggest cities, some may live in the house or apartment right next to us. Others are barely surviving on their farms. Many volunteer organizations in the United States and throughout the world help poor people seeking shelter, food, and clothing. Volunteers also reach out to find people in need who may be too afraid or embarrassed to ask for help. Volunteers also work with local communities and governments to try to improve the conditions that cause poverty. The Corporal and Spiritual Works of Mercy taught by Jesus inspire their work.

In Everyday Life

Activity Write an article for your local newspaper suggesting some of your ideas on ways to help the poor in your community.

_____

_____

_____

_____

In Your Parish

Activity Write or draw one way people in your parish can take care of the physical needs of others.

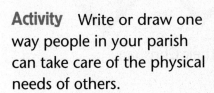

Faith in Action

Sports Ministry Many Catholic schools have sports programs that draw young people from the school, from the parish and sometimes from the local community. These programs have coaches who volunteer their time to make the programs a positive experience for all involved. Coaches have a powerful influence over the attitudes and behavior of the young people on their teams. They serve not just as teachers, but as role models for the young athletes.

In Everyday Life

Activity Write and decorate an ad for a volunteer who will coach a team at your school. What qualities does he or she need to have?

In Your Parish

Activity Write a list of rules coaches should follow that show their Christian love for their players.

_____

_____

_____

_____.

Add some of your own words to this poster about the Catholic Church.

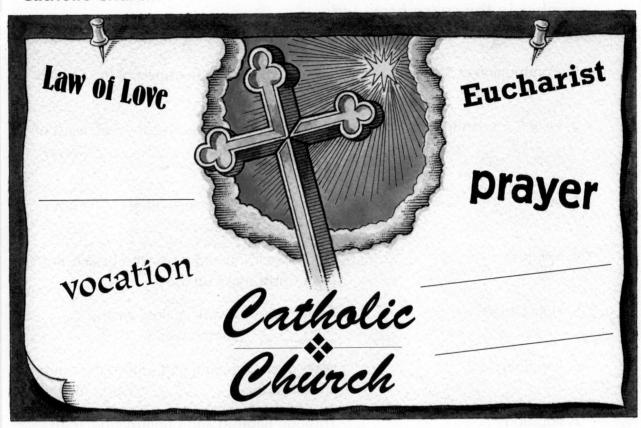

Law of Love

Eucharist

prayer

vocation

Catholic Church

Write a word or phrase from the poster associated with each sentence or phrase shown below.

1 God calls all Christians to do the work of the Church.

_____

2 The center of the Christian life

_____

3 Love one another as I have loved you (based on John 15:12).

_____

4 One way we communicate with God

_____

A **Match** column A with column B by writing the correct number in the space provided.

A

1. Communion of Saints

2. New Commandment

3. evil

4. Spiritual

5. Holy Orders

6. happiness

7. vocation

8. Beatitudes

9. Corporal

10. prophet

B

_____ The work we do as members of the Church is called our _____.

_____ Ways of taking care of the physical needs of others are called the _____ Works of Mercy.

_____ Jesus said that if we love others as he loves us, we will have eternal _____.

_____ All people living and dead who believe in Jesus Christ make up the _____.

_____ Prayer helps us work against sin and _____ in the world

_____ Ways of encouraging and supporting others are called the _____ Works of Mercy.

_____ Through Baptism and Confirmation, Jesus anoints us as priest, _____, and king.

_____ Baptized men called to serve God as priests, deacons, or bishops receive the Sacrament of _____.

_____ The Law of Love is also known as the _____.

_____ Jesus combined the Commandments and the _____ into one Law of Love.

B **Write** what someone your age can do to practice one of the Corporal Works of Mercy.

_____

_____

C **Circle** the letter of the best answer.

1. Jesus called himself the
   _____ of the World.
   a. Power
   b. Ruler
   c. Light
   d. Teacher

2. Just like Jesus, we are _____
   as priest, prophet, and king.
   a. anointed
   b. blessed
   c. named
   d. called to work

3. We fulfill our role as _____
   when we pray for others
   a. minister
   b. priest
   c. prophet
   d. king

4. A _____ is a prayer in
   which we ask for God's help.
   a. petition
   b. indulgence
   c. litany
   d. meditation

5. We fulfill our role as _____
   when we spread God's message
   of love to others.
   a. saint
   b. priest
   c. prophet
   d. king

6. As Christians, we are called to
   bring God's love, _____, and
   justice to the world.
   a. peace
   b. temperance
   c. courage
   d. patience

7. God is always with us, especially
   when we _____.
   a. kneel
   b. sing
   c. pray
   d. walk

8. As Catholics, we have
   a responsibility to show God's
   _____ to one another.
   a. qualities
   b. goodness
   c. words
   d. patience

D **Complete** the sentences with words from the box.

Eucharist	Passover	assembly	audience
Spiritual	Corporal	Holy Spirit	priest

1. The Eucharist is a memorial of Christ's _____.

2. The _____ is the gathering of Catholics to celebrate the Sacraments.

3. Feeding those who hunger is one of the _____ Works of Mercy.

4. The _____ leads the Church in the Liturgy.

5. Through the _____ the bread and wine are changed into the Body and Blood of Christ.

6. Comforting those who suffer is one of the _____ Works of Mercy.

7. The _____ is the center of our Catholic life.

E **Respond** to the following.

1. What did Jesus tell his disciples to do after his Ressurection?

_____

_____

_____

_____

2. How can you spread Jesus' message of love, peace, and justice to the world?

_____

_____

_____

FEASTS AND SEASONS

The Liturgical Year

The Church Year is called the Liturgical Year. During the Liturgical Year, we celebrate special seasons and feasts that help us remember important times in the life of Jesus. We also celebrate special feasts that honor the Blessed Virgin Mary and the saints.

ORDINARY TIME

Holy Week begins on Palm Sunday. It ends with the three holiest days of the Liturgical Year. We call these three days "the Triduum."

The Liturgical Year begins with the **Advent** season. For four weeks, we prepare for the birth of Jesus. We count the four weeks by lighting the candles on the Advent wreath.

ADVENT

The Liturgical Year begins.

The **Triduum** begins on Holy Thursday evening and ends on Easter Sunday evening. During these three days, we remember the Last Supper, Jesus' Death on the cross to save us from sin, and his Resurrection from the dead.

During the **Easter** season, we celebrate the Resurrection of our Lord Jesus Christ. This season lasts for fifty days. It is a time of great joy.

EASTER

The season of **Lent** begins on Ash Wednesday and lasts for forty days. During Lent, we prepare for Easter, which is the greatest feast of the Liturgical Year. We get ready for Easter by praying and doing good acts.

Ordinary Time has two parts. The first part is between Christmas and Lent. The second part is between Easter and Advent. During Ordinary Time, we learn about the life and teachings of Jesus.

LENT

ORDINARY TIME

The **Christmas** season begins with the Feast of Christmas. On Christmas Day, we celebrate the birth of Jesus. We thank God the Father for sending his only Son to be our Savior.

CHRISTMAS

The Liturgical Year

The Church guides us in celebrating the great events and people of our faith through the seasons and feasts of the Liturgical Year. The special feasts of the Liturgical Year include Sundays and the Holy Days of Obligation.

Sunday

Sunday is the Lord's Day. On Sunday, we celebrate the Resurrection of our Lord Jesus Christ. Sunday is so important that the Church requires us to celebrate Mass. We gather with our family and parish to give thanks to God the Father for sending his Son to save us.

Holy Days of Obligation

The Holy Days of Obligation are special days when we honor Jesus, the Blessed Virgin Mary, and the saints. Like Sundays, these holy days are so important that the Church requires us to celebrate Mass. In the United States, the Church celebrates the following Holy Days of Obligation.

The Immaculate Conception of the Blessed Virgin Mary December 8	We celebrate that Mary, the Mother of Jesus, was conceived without Original Sin.
Christmas Day December 25	We celebrate the birth of Jesus, our Savior.
Mary, the Mother of God January 1	We celebrate that Mary is the Mother of God's Son, Jesus Christ.
Ascension of the Lord forty days after Easter Sunday	We celebrate the moment when Jesus, in his resurrected body, returned to his Father in Heaven.
Assumption of the Blessed Virgin Mary August 15	We celebrate that Mary was taken body and soul into the glory of Heaven. She fully shares in the Resurrection of Jesus.
All Saints Day November 1	We celebrate all the people who lived holy lives on earth and who now live with God in Heaven.

The Sunday Mass Readings

At Sunday Mass, we listen to three readings from Sacred Scripture. The first reading is usually from the Old Testament, the second reading is from the New Testament, and the third reading is always from the Gospels.

There are two cycles of readings: the Sunday Cycle and the Weekday Cycle. The Sunday Cycle contains readings for Year A, Year B, and Year C. The Gospel readings for Year A are from the Gospel of Matthew, Year B from the Gospel of Mark, and Year C from the Gospel of Luke. The Gospel of John is read on certain Sundays and feast days during each year.

Activity

2008 A   Which year is the Church currently in?

2009 B   Year _____
2010 C
2011 A   Which Gospel is being read at Sunday Mass?

2012 B   Gospel of _____
2013 C

First Sunday in Advent			
	Year A	Year B	Year C
First Reading	Isaiah 2:15	Isaiah 63:16b–17, 19b; 64: 2–7	Jeremiah 33: 14–16
Second Reading	Romans 13: 11–14	1 Corinthians 1: 3–9	1 Thessalonians 3: 12–4:2
Gospel	Matthew 24: 37–44	Mark 13:33–37	Luke 21:25–28, 34–36

Read the Gospel reading for this Liturgical Year for the First Sunday in Advent. In your own words, write the message of the Gospel reading.

_____

_____

_____

Advent

Look! There is the Lamb of God, who has come to take away our sins.

Based on John 1:29

Jesus, the Light of the World

Many centuries ago, God promised his people that he would send them a savior. Life then was often hard. People had problems and sometimes there was pain and suffering. Sin, fear, anger, violence, and pain were a part of life. God's people looked forward to the time when he would send the promised savior. They waited and hoped for this savior, whom they called the Messiah. People trusted that God would keep his promise. When the Messiah came, their lives would be filled with hope. The Messiah would bring peace, justice, joy, and love to their lives.

Jesus Christ is the Messiah. Just as God promised, Jesus fills our lives with hope and brings peace, justice, joy, and love into our hearts. Our world has begun to change because Jesus lived, died, and rose from the dead. Jesus began God's saving plan for our lives.

The writers of the Gospels share this Good News of hope and love with us. They tell us that Jesus explained who he was to his followers. "I am the Light of the World," Jesus told them. "Whoever follows me will not walk in darkness" (based on John 8:12). Jesus was proclaiming that he came to deliver us from the sin, pain, and suffering of the world. Just as a light makes it easy to see and move around at night, Jesus makes our lives easier. He makes it easy for us to live with love and joy in a world sometimes filled with sin and suffering.

During the season of Advent, we celebrate Jesus' coming anew into our lives. We also wait for the rest of God's promise to be fulfilled. We look forward to the time when Jesus Christ will bring God's Kingdom into the world once and for all.

Sharing with Others

Jesus Christ is the Light of the World. He told us that when we live the way he asks, we show others the way to him. Every day we have many chances to remind people that Jesus Christ is the promised Messiah.

Activities

1. Use the letters in the word *Messiah* to give examples of how you share joy, peace, and hope with others. One has been done for you.

M _____

E _____

S   end a get-well card to a sick person _____

S _____

I _____

A _____

H _____

2. Unscramble the words below to discover a sentence about who we are.

ew   rea   drlenhic   fo   het   ghtil

Based on 1 Thessalonians 5:5

_____

_____

Jesus, you are the Light of the World. Thank you for coming into our lives. Help us to share with one another the joy, peace, and hope you bring. Amen.

The Three Comings of Jesus

Advent is the time the Church uses to help us prepare to meet Jesus in three ways. We know that on Christmas we remember and celebrate Jesus' coming in Bethlehem more than 2,000 years ago. We call this coming into our lives Jesus' coming in *history*.

Jesus continues to come to us each day. He no longer comes as a baby born to Mary and Joseph. Jesus' coming into our lives each day is called a *mystery* because it cannot be completely understood. We can meet Jesus in our families, in our friends, or in other people who show that they care about us. We can recognize him when we see those who are poor, hurting, ill, or without hope.

Before Jesus returned to his Father in Heaven, he promised to one day return to earth as our King. We call that coming of Jesus at the end of time *majesty*. On that day, Jesus will reign over God's Kingdom on earth. God's Kingdom will be a kingdom of love, peace, justice, and joy.

During the four weeks of Advent, we prepare to remember, celebrate, and look forward to Jesus' comings in history, mystery, and majesty.

Getting to Know Jesus

Christ, our Lord, comes into our lives every day. Sometimes we grow closer to him through the people in our lives. When we help them or they share their talents with us, Christ is present.

Activity

Tell how Jesus Christ might be with you in each example.

When your best
friend is having a bad day, you

_____

_____ .

When you visit someone who is sick, you

_____

_____ .

When someone on the playground bumps into you, you

_____

_____ .

When an older relative asks you to do
something with him or her, you

_____

_____ .

Jesus, come to us each day.
Help us prepare to welcome
you as our King in the
fullness of God's Kingdom.
Help us to recognize you in
one another. Amen.

Advent Customs

We spend the four weeks of Advent getting ready to celebrate Jesus' coming anew. There are many ways to prepare for this great event. As we prepare, our hearts fill with hope. We look forward to the time when we will be with Jesus Christ forever in his kingdom.

The tradition of the Advent wreath began in Germany. An Advent wreath is made up of a wreath of evergreen branches and four candles. The four candles stand for the four weeks of Advent. One candle is lit for the first week. Two candles are lit for the second week. On the Third Sunday of Advent, three candles are lit to celebrate what is known as Gaudete (gow DAY tay) Sunday. On the fourth week, all of the candles are lit. Every time the candles are lit, a prayer is prayed, and a song may be sung. The Advent wreath reminds us of the coming of Jesus, who is the Light of the World.

Advent wreath

Other people use Advent calendars or Advent houses to prepare for Christmas. They contain little doors or windows, one of which is opened each day of Advent. Inside there is a picture or words that help us prepare to celebrate Jesus' coming anew. The last door or window is opened on Christmas Eve, December 24, and usually shows the Nativity scene.

Some people prepare for Advent by setting up a Nativity scene without any of the figures in it. Then on each day of Advent, they do a good deed or say a prayer for others, and they place a piece of straw in the manger to prepare for Christmas.

Advent calendar

Some people use the Jesse tree to help them prepare to better understand Jesus' coming at Christmas. The Jesse tree is a good way to remember all of Jesus' ancestors. A Jesse tree can be made from a bare branch and symbols of Jesus' ancestors can be hung on the tree. Some people use a banner or collage to make a Jesse tree. Others arrange boxes or baskets in different sizes to hold the symbols.

Activity

How will you prepare to celebrate Jesus' coming anew at Christmas?
Choose three things you can do during Advent.

_____ Pray for my family every day

_____ Do my chores without being told

_____ Help someone in my class with his or her homework

_____ Take better care of my pets

_____ Tell the truth every day

_____ Stop complaining about things I don't want to do

_____ Be more patient

_____ Share my toys without being told

Nativity scene

Jesse Tree

Jesus, set us free! Fill our hearts with hope and love. This Advent, help us prepare to celebrate your coming. Deepen our understanding of the true meaning of the Christmas spirit. Amen.

Prayer Celebration for Advent

Waiting with Joy

Reader: Rejoice in the Lord always! Rejoice! The Lord is near. Put all worries from your minds. Tell God what you need and be thankful. Then God's own peace will be in your hearts and minds, in Christ Jesus.

Based on Philippians 4:4–7

Reader: I am the Lord and there is no other.
There is no other God besides me, says the Lord.
Let justice come down to the earth from the heavens.
Like dew from above, like gentle rain,
let the skies drop it down.
Let the earth open and salvation bud forth.
Let justice spring up!
I, the Lord, have created this.

Based on Isaiah 45:5–8

All: I shall wait for my Savior. I will point him out when he is near. Alleluia.

Leader: Come and set us free.

All: Come, Lord Jesus.

Leader:	Keep us safe from harm until you come again.
All:	Come, Lord Jesus.
Leader:	Teach us that we belong to you.
All:	Come, Lord Jesus.
Reader:	Lord, our God, help us to prepare for the coming of Christ, your Son. May he find us waiting, with glad hearts. Amen.

Based on the Liturgy of the Hours, First Week of Advent

Activity

What good deeds for others can you do during Advent? On the lines below, write three things you can do to help someone else, such as a family member, a classmate, or a friend.

_____

_____

_____

_____

Christmas

The Word of God became human and made his home among us.

Based on John 1:14

Simeon and Anna Meet the Baby Jesus

Since Mary and Joseph were faithful to God's laws, they took Jesus to the Temple in Jerusalem soon after he was born. Following the Law of Moses, Mary had to sacrifice two pigeons or two turtledoves there. This was a way for Joseph and Mary to offer thanks to God for Jesus' birth.

When they arrived at the Temple with Jesus, Mary and Joseph met Simeon, a very old and wise prophet. Simeon believed that God was sending the Savior to his people. He believed that even though he was old, he would not die before he met the Savior.

Simeon saw Mary and Joseph bringing the baby Jesus onto the Temple grounds. He took Jesus in his arms and praised God, saying, "Now, Lord, I am ready to die in peace. I have seen the Savior you have sent to your people. He is the glory of your people" (based on Luke 2:29–32).

We still remember Simeon's prayer to God. Catholics call Simeon's prayer the Canticle of Simeon or the *Nunc Dimittis* (noonk DIH mih tihs). The words *nunc dimittis* are the first words of Simeon's prayer in Latin. Simeon's prayer showed his thanks for all God would do for us.

After Mary and Joseph met Simeon, they met an old woman at the Temple named Anna. She was a prophet, too. Like Simeon, Anna had been promised by God that she would meet the Savior. Anna was always at the Temple, praying and fasting. When Anna saw the baby Jesus, she gave thanks to God for his Son and for all that Jesus would do for the human race.

Today, we remember Simeon and Anna for their great faith in God. They trusted in God even when they did not know how he could keep his promise to them. Then, when they saw Jesus, they recognized that he was the Savior. Simeon and Anna remind us what being faithful to God means.

Activity

The story of Simeon and Anna teaches us that God keeps his promises. Complete the following sentences to show what else you learned from this story.

Mary and Joseph took Jesus to _____.

At the Temple, Mary offered a _____.

Mary, Joseph, and Jesus met a man called _____.

Simeon took Jesus in his arms and _____.

Then Mary, Joseph, and Jesus met _____. Anna

spent her days at the Temple, fasting and _____.

Today, we remember Simeon and Anna for their

_____. God promised Simeon

and Anna that before they died they would see

_____. One name we call Simeon's

prayer is _____.

> Simeon and Anna, you lived lives of faith in God. Remember us when we need strength to live our faith. Help us to believe in God's promises. Amen.

Christmas: A Time to Remember, Believe, and Celebrate

Christmas is a time to remember. We remember that God kept his promise to send the Savior. We remember that God the Father loved us so much that he sent his own Son to be that Savior! And we remember that Jesus is the Light of the World when we use Christmas candles, lights on our Christmas trees, and window lights.

Christmas is a time to believe. We believe that Jesus is God's Son and the Second Person of the Holy Trinity. We believe that he was born, lived among us, and died on a cross. And we believe that he rose again and shares new life with us.

Christmas is a time to celebrate all that we remember and believe about Jesus. At Mass, our parish community sings of his birth, prays to him at the crèche, and hears about this special child in Scripture. Here is a tiny infant who needs Mary, his mother, and Joseph, his foster father, to care for him. Yet the angel calls this helpless child the Son of the Most High, the shepherds praise God for his birth, and the Magi travel from the East to honor him. Through the Eucharistic celebration, the Church unites in joy. We thank and praise God for sending us Jesus, the Savior of the World.

The Coming of Jesus

Christmas Day and the entire Christmas season is a time of great joy in our Church. It is a time to remember, believe, and celebrate.

Activity

In each ornament, write one thing you remember, believe, and celebrate about Jesus.

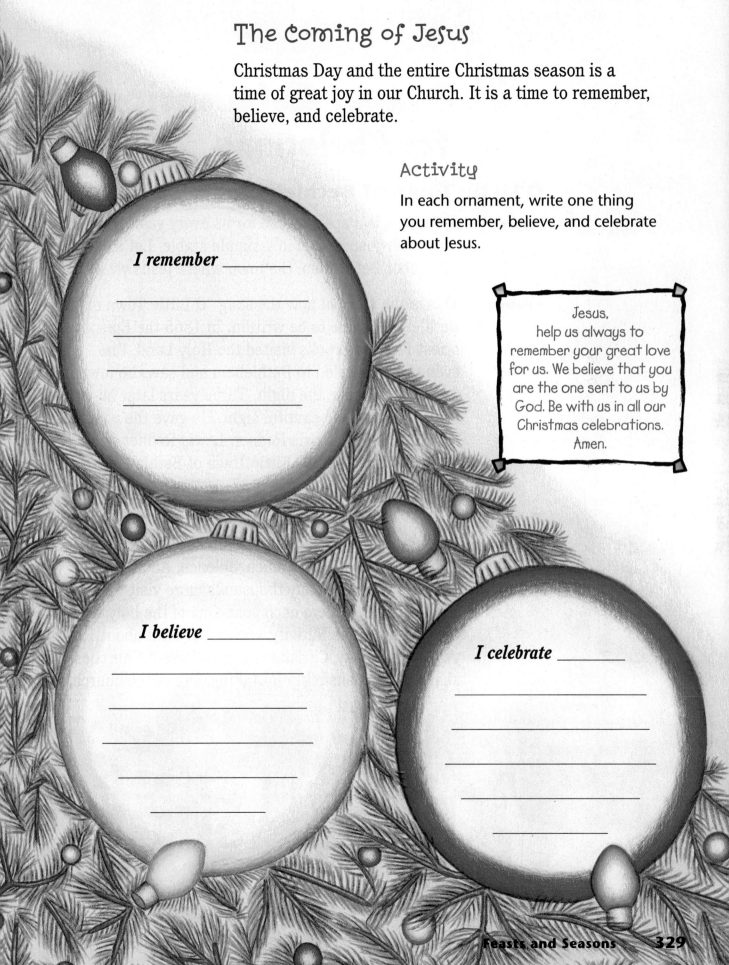

I remember _____

_____

_____

_____

_____

Jesus,
help us always to remember your great love for us. We believe that you are the one sent to us by God. Be with us in all our Christmas celebrations.
Amen.

I believe _____

_____

_____

_____

_____

I celebrate _____

_____

_____

_____

_____

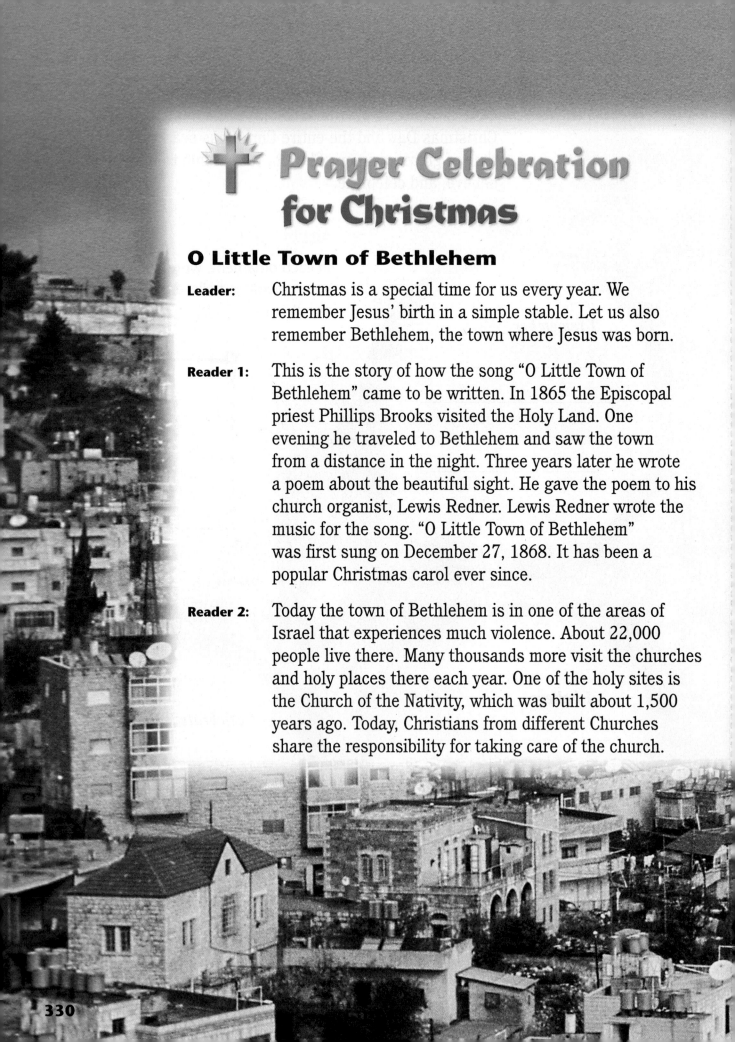

✝ Prayer Celebration for Christmas

O Little Town of Bethlehem

Leader: Christmas is a special time for us every year. We remember Jesus' birth in a simple stable. Let us also remember Bethlehem, the town where Jesus was born.

Reader 1: This is the story of how the song "O Little Town of Bethlehem" came to be written. In 1865 the Episcopal priest Phillips Brooks visited the Holy Land. One evening he traveled to Bethlehem and saw the town from a distance in the night. Three years later he wrote a poem about the beautiful sight. He gave the poem to his church organist, Lewis Redner. Lewis Redner wrote the music for the song. "O Little Town of Bethlehem" was first sung on December 27, 1868. It has been a popular Christmas carol ever since.

Reader 2: Today the town of Bethlehem is in one of the areas of Israel that experiences much violence. About 22,000 people live there. Many thousands more visit the churches and holy places there each year. One of the holy sites is the Church of the Nativity, which was built about 1,500 years ago. Today, Christians from different Churches share the responsibility for taking care of the church.

All: Lord, remember the place where your Son was born.

Leader: In a land torn by war, keep the people who live in Bethlehem safe.

All: Lord, remember the place where your Son was born.

Leader: In a land important to the peoples of many nations, keep the visitors to Bethlehem safe.

All: Lord, remember the place where your Son was born.

Leader: Let us share our thoughts and prayers for the birthplace of Jesus, God's only Son.
(*Share each other's thoughts and prayers here.*)

All: O little town of Bethlehem, how still we see thee lie!
Above thy deep and dreamless sleep the silent stars go by;
Yet in thy dark streets shineth the everlasting light;
The hopes and fears of all the years are met in thee tonight. Amen.

Ordinary Time

 As they were stoning Stephen, he called out, "Lord Jesus, receive my spirit."

Based on Acts 7:59

The Feast of the First Holy Martyrs of the Holy Roman Church

A martyr is someone who is killed because he or she refuses to deny the Christian faith. In the early Church there were many martyrs, including the First Martyrs of the Church of Rome. Today, we celebrate the feast days of many of the martyrs during Ordinary Time.

Nero was the emperor of the Romans between A.D. 54 and A.D. 68. He is remembered as being a bad emperor who treated people unfairly. One day in A.D. 64, a fire broke out in a small store in Rome. In those days, there were no fire departments. The fire quickly raged out of control. It burned for six or seven days, destroying many homes and shops. Finally, it died down, but then it started again and continued for two or three more days. By the time it finally stopped burning, the fire had destroyed much of Rome.

So much had been destroyed and so many lives lost that people called for justice. Nero decided to take the easy way out. He told everyone that Christians had set the fire. He had a number of Christians arrested and sentenced to death. Even though there were many people who did not believe that the Christians had started the fire, Nero had the Christians killed in cruel ways. Worst of all, Nero had this done in his own gardens as part of the entertainment for a party that he was giving. Even though Romans loved gladiators and other violent entertainments, this was too much for them. They were angry with Nero and felt truly sorry for his victims.

In 1923 a feast day was started in Rome to remember this first large group of Christian martyrs. In 1969 everyone in the Church began to celebrate this feast. Today we celebrate this feast day on June 30.

Remembering the Martyrs

The Church never forgets Catholics who die for their faith. The Church keeps a list, or martyrology, of those who have died for Jesus. We also celebrate feast days in their honor. We ask them to pray for us to God, and we share their stories with one another so that they will never be forgotten. Can you recall the story of a martyr?

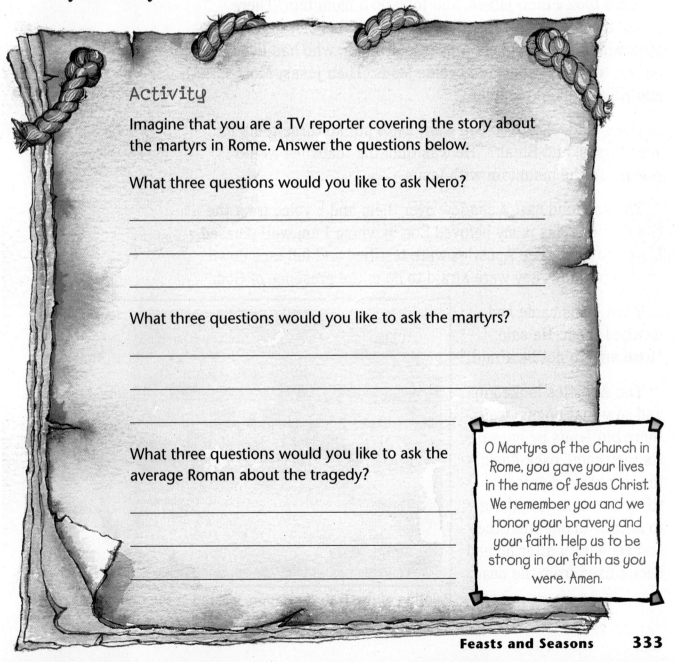

Activity

Imagine that you are a TV reporter covering the story about the martyrs in Rome. Answer the questions below.

What three questions would you like to ask Nero?

_____

_____

_____

What three questions would you like to ask the martyrs?

_____

_____

_____

What three questions would you like to ask the average Roman about the tragedy?

_____

_____

_____

O Martyrs of the Church in Rome, you gave your lives in the name of Jesus Christ. We remember you and we honor your bravery and your faith. Help us to be strong in our faith as you were. Amen.

Lent

 Jesus was led away, and, carrying a heavy cross, sent to the place where he was to be crucified.

Based on John 19:16–17

The Transfiguration

One of the readings of the Second Sunday of Lent is the Gospel story of the Transfiguration.

Jesus took Peter, James, and John up a mountain. There Jesus' face began to shine like the sun and his clothes became pure white. The Prophets Moses and Elijah, who had lived long before, suddenly appeared beside Jesus. Then Jesus, Moses, and Elijah talked together.

Peter said, "Lord, do you want us to put up three tents for you, Moses, and Elijah?" He was thinking that they would remain on the mountain with Jesus.

Then a cloud cast a shadow over them and a voice from the cloud said, "This is my beloved Son in whom I am well pleased. Listen to him." The Apostles were terrified and fell face down on the ground. They were afraid to be in the presence of God.

Then Jesus came and touched them. He said, "Rise and do not be afraid."

The Apostles looked up and saw that no one was there but Jesus by himself. As they came back down the mountain, Jesus told them not to say anything to anyone about what they had seen until after he had been raised from the dead.

Based on Matthew 17:1–9

Painting of the Transfiguration, located in the Church of the Transfiguration in Mount Tabor, Israel

This Gospel story has two points. The first is that three of the Apostles received the special favor of seeing Jesus as he truly is: the Son of God. Second, the Apostles found out that God meant to keep his promises to save his people. The cloud they saw and the voice that they heard was God. Centuries ago, people thought that if they were in the presence of God, they would die. But Jesus showed that the glory of God brings a new and wonderful life to us.

During the season of Lent, we have the chance to think about how we are living and the choices we make. During this time the Church calls us to repent and turn back to God. The word *repent* means "to turn away from sin." When we repent, we can prepare ourselves for the glory of God, which is brought to us by Jesus, the Son of God. This is the new life that we receive at Easter.

Learning How to Repent

The Gospel story of the Transfiguration shows us something of what God has in store for us. Jesus' Resurrection brings new life to all of us. During Lent, will you reflect on your life?

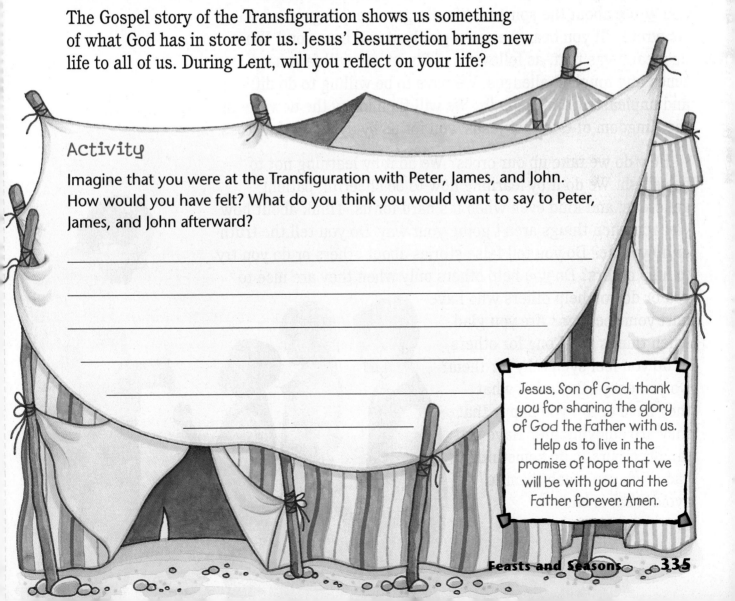

Activity

Imagine that you were at the Transfiguration with Peter, James, and John. How would you have felt? What do you think you would want to say to Peter, James, and John afterward?

_____

_____

_____

_____

_____

Jesus, Son of God, thank you for sharing the glory of God the Father with us. Help us to live in the promise of hope that we will be with you and the Father forever. Amen.

Take Up Your Cross

Christians use the cross as the main sign of who we are. The cross is also the main symbol for Lent. During Lent, we recall how Jesus suffered and died for us. We think about the meaning of what he has done for us. We also think about Jesus' words, "Whoever does not take up his cross and follow me is not worthy of me" (Matthew 10:38).

What does this mean for us? We all have hard times to bear in our lives. These hard times and challenges are our crosses. One person might have trouble controlling his or her temper. Another person might have to put up with a difficult classmate. Someone might have to take care of a family member who is ill. Someone else may be ill and find it difficult to live a happy life.

Thomas à Kempis (1380–1471) was a priest who preached and wrote about the spiritual life. He gave people good advice. He wrote, "If you bear the cross gladly, it will bear you." What he meant was that, as followers of Christ, we will face hard times and tough challenges. We have to be willing to do difficult and unpleasant things gladly. We will then know the new life in the Kingdom of God that Jesus won for us by dying on the cross.

How do we take up our cross? We do it by learning not to be selfish. We do it by learning how to be cheerful, patient, generous, and kind even when it's hard for us. Think about how you act when things aren't going your way. Do you tell the truth or do you lie? Do you tell false stories about others or do you try to help others? Do you help others only when they are nice to you or do you help others who have hurt your feelings? Are you glad when things go wrong for others or do you feel sympathy for them? Do you envy others and what they have or are you happy that they are enjoying life? Have you taught others to do something bad or do you teach them to avoid what is bad?

Taking up our cross means doing the right thing even when it is hard. During the season of Lent, we can try to do this more often in our lives.

Handling Challenges

Every day we are faced with challenges. Every day we get a new chance to do good, avoid sin, and make sacrifices of ourselves, just as Jesus did. It can be helpful to look back, think about our lives, and see how we are doing.

Activity

On the cross, write three or four sacrifices you will make during Lent.

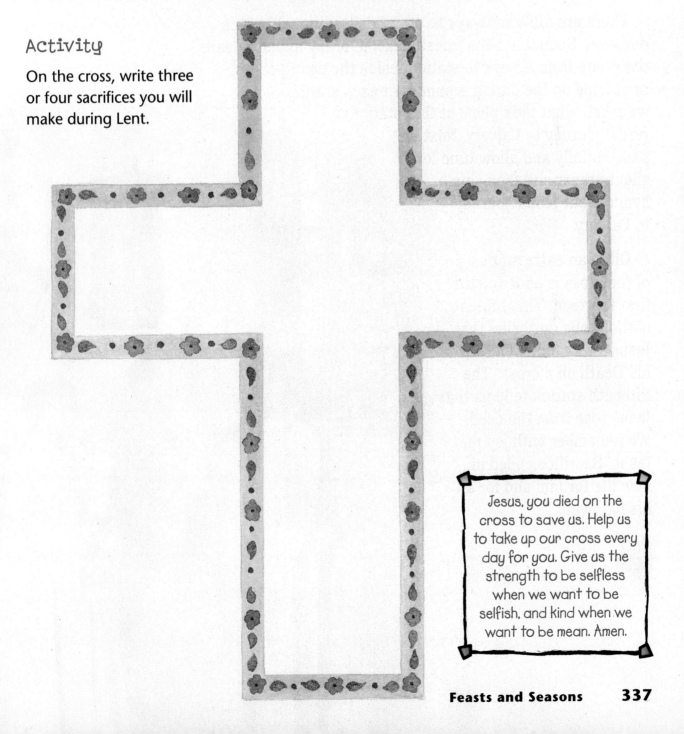

Jesus, you died on the cross to save us. Help us to take up our cross every day for you. Give us the strength to be selfless when we want to be selfish, and kind when we want to be mean. Amen.

The Way of the Cross

Our Church wants to remember always the great Sacrifice that Jesus made for us through his suffering and Death on the cross. One way our Church remembers Jesus' love for us is by recalling his journey to Calvary. Calvary is the hill where Jesus died. We call this special devotion the Way of the Cross, or the Stations of the Cross. Sometimes Christians visit the Holy Land and actually walk the same path as Jesus. Usually we recall Jesus' journey to the cross by reflecting and praying at each station.

There are different ways to pray this traditional Lenten devotion. Sometimes the priest, deacon, or lay minister leads the group from station to station inside the parish church or outside on the parish grounds. At each station, we recall what took place at that station in Jesus' journey to Calvary. Next we pause briefly and allow time for silent prayer and then sing a hymn about Jesus' journey to Calvary.

Often an extra station of the cross is added to the first fourteen. This fifteenth station tells our belief that Jesus' story didn't end with his Death on a cross. The fifteenth station tells us that Jesus rose from the dead. We remember with joy that Jesus' Sacrifice ended in new life for him and for all his followers.

page 16 to read more about the Stations of the Cross.

Activity

At each station of the cross, we pause for prayer. Turn to page 16 and choose one of the Stations of the Cross. Then in the space below, write a prayer that you can pray with your class or family at this station. Your prayer should be at least three or four sentences long.

_____

_____

_____

_____

Christians follow the Way of the Cross on Good Friday in Jerusalem.

Jesus, through your suffering, death, and Resurrection, you won new life for us. Help us always to remember your great love for all people. Amen.

Jesus Raises Lazarus from the Dead

On the Fifth Sunday of Lent, we read the Gospel story of the raising of Lazarus from the dead. The story takes place in the village of Bethany, which was near Jerusalem. Lazarus and his sisters, Martha and Mary, lived there. Lazarus became very ill, and his sisters sent a message to Jesus that Lazarus was dying. But Jesus did not hurry to Bethany. Instead, he said, "This illness is for the glory of God."

When Jesus and his Apostles finally arrived in Bethany, Lazarus was dead and had been buried for four days. Martha and Mary were upset and said to Jesus, "Lord, if you had been here, Lazarus would not have died." Jesus said, "If you believe, you will see the glory of God." Then he asked to see Lazarus' tomb, which was a cave along a hillside. Martha and Mary took Jesus there, and he became upset and wept. A large stone had been placed in front of the entrance to the cave. Jesus commanded, "Take away the stone."

Martha said, "Lord, there will be a bad smell. Lazarus has been dead for several days." But Jesus said, "Didn't I tell you that if you believe you will see the glory of God?"

They took away the stone, and Jesus prayed to his heavenly Father. Then he shouted, "Lazarus, come out!" And the dead man came out of the tomb, still wrapped in the burial cloths. Jesus said to them, "Take these away and let him go."

Based on John 11:1–44

Everyone must have been amazed and shocked when Lazarus walked out of the tomb. This miracle showed Jesus' followers that God the Father had given Jesus power over death. It was a sign that Jesus was the Son of God as he claimed to be. The story of Lazarus tells us that people will gain new life if they believe in Jesus. The Gospel of John

The Raising of Lazarus by Léon Joseph Florentin Bonnat

tells us this story so that we will be prepared for Jesus' own Death and Resurrection. The story also gives us hope that at the end of time Jesus will give us new life just as he brought Lazarus back to life.

The Hope of New Life

When Jesus raised Lazarus from the dead, Jesus showed us the special way he takes care of his friends. When we were baptized, we became one of Jesus' friends. We received the promise of new life. During Lent, we remember what it means to be one of Jesus' friends.

Activity

Unscramble the words in the stones below to complete a message about new life in Christ.

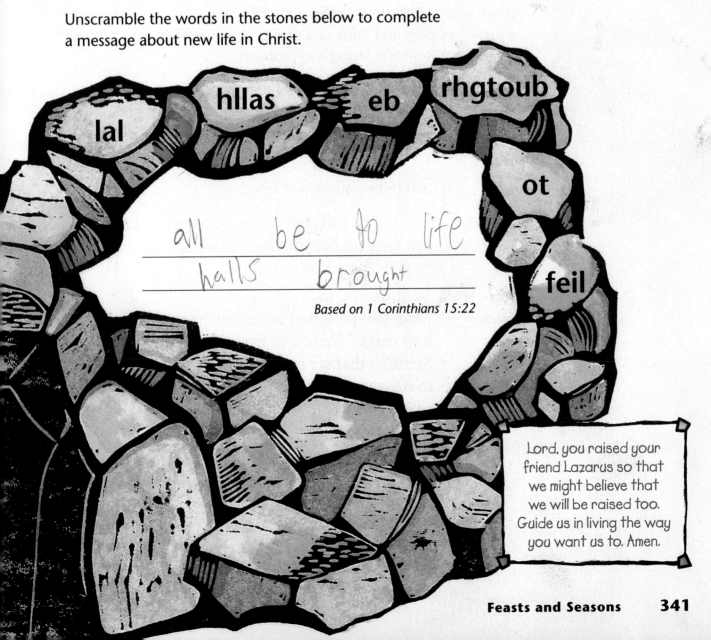

lal   hllas   eb   rhgtoub   ot   feil

all   be   to   life
halls   brought

Based on 1 Corinthians 15:22

Lord, you raised your friend Lazarus so that we might believe that we will be raised too. Guide us in living the way you want us to. Amen.

✝ Prayer Celebration for Lent

A Prayer for Renewal

All: Lord, we are your people. Hear us whenever we call upon you. You have made us your own and set us free.

Activity

Jesus' friends help one another to follow him. Pick one of the situations below and think of a saying or words of advice that you might give someone facing this problem.

_____ You don't want to do your homework or your chores.

_____ Someone is making fun of you.

_____ You feel lonely.

_____ It is hard to be patient and kind.

Leader: Blessed be God, the Giver of Salvation. Lord, you commanded that human beings should be given new life.

All: Lord, renew us.

Leader: Lord, you promised us "a new heaven and a new earth." Renew us every day through your Spirit so that we may be with you forever in Heaven.

All: Lord, renew us.

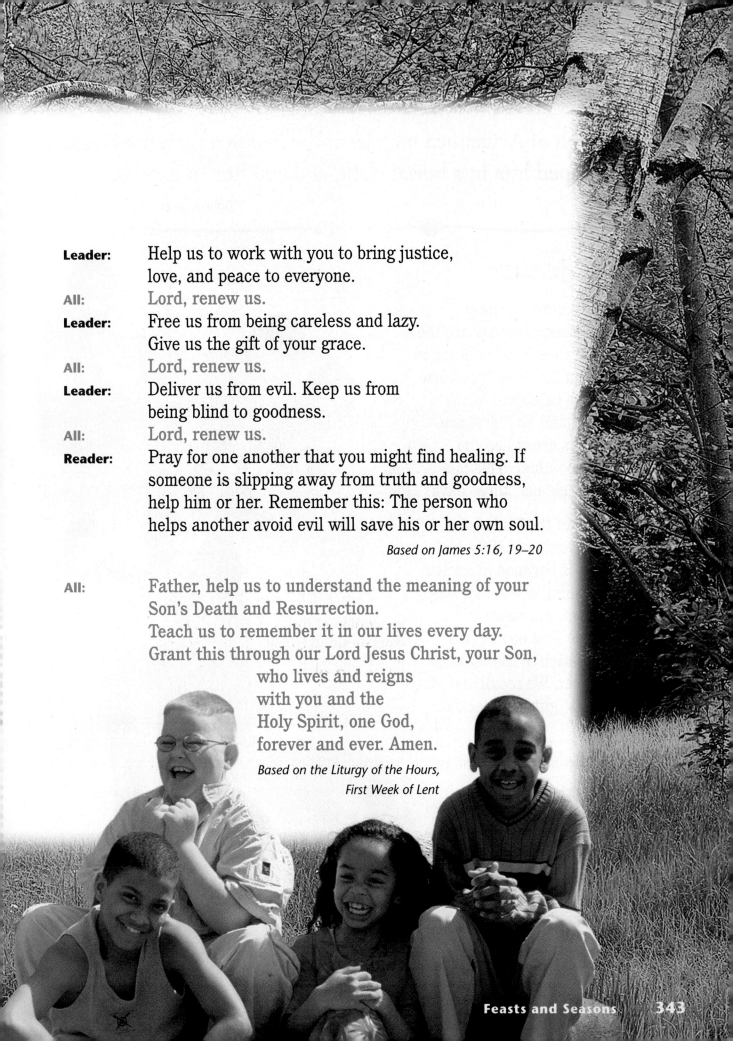

Leader: Help us to work with you to bring justice, love, and peace to everyone.

All: Lord, renew us.

Leader: Free us from being careless and lazy. Give us the gift of your grace.

All: Lord, renew us.

Leader: Deliver us from evil. Keep us from being blind to goodness.

All: Lord, renew us.

Reader: Pray for one another that you might find healing. If someone is slipping away from truth and goodness, help him or her. Remember this: The person who helps another avoid evil will save his or her own soul.

Based on James 5:16, 19–20

All: Father, help us to understand the meaning of your Son's Death and Resurrection.
Teach us to remember it in our lives every day.
Grant this through our Lord Jesus Christ, your Son, who lives and reigns with you and the Holy Spirit, one God, forever and ever. Amen.

Based on the Liturgy of the Hours,
First Week of Lent

Holy Week

 Joseph of Arimathea took Jesus' body down from the cross, wrapped him in a burial cloth, and laid him in a tomb.

Based on Luke 23:53

The Triduum

The three days between Holy Thursday and Easter Sunday are the most important time of celebration in the Catholic Church. This is because these three days celebrate Jesus' Passion, Death, and Resurrection. These three days are called the Triduum (trih doo uhm). This is a Latin word that means "three days."

The first day of the Triduum begins on the evening of Holy Thursday. This is because in ancient times the beginning of the day was when the sun set, not dawn or midnight. So the first day begins with our celebration of the Mass of the Lord's Supper. We recall and give thanks for Jesus' gift of himself in the Eucharist.

On the second day, Good Friday, we remember that Jesus died on the cross. The Eucharist is not consecrated during the Good Friday Service. We receive Holy Communion that was consecrated at Mass on Holy Thursday.

Washing of feet on Holy Thursday

Veneration of the cross on Good Friday

Blessing of the fire and lighting of the candle on Holy Saturday

On the third day, we rejoice that Jesus has been raised from the dead and is no longer in the tomb. We celebrate the Easter Vigil on Holy Saturday evening. On Easter Sunday we remember that Easter began the night before and we continue our celebration of joy. We are glad that our sins have been forgiven and that as Christians we share in the new life won for us by Christ.

Celebrating the Triduum

The Triduum has been celebrated for centuries, since the days of the early Church. How much do you know about the Church's celebration of these special days?

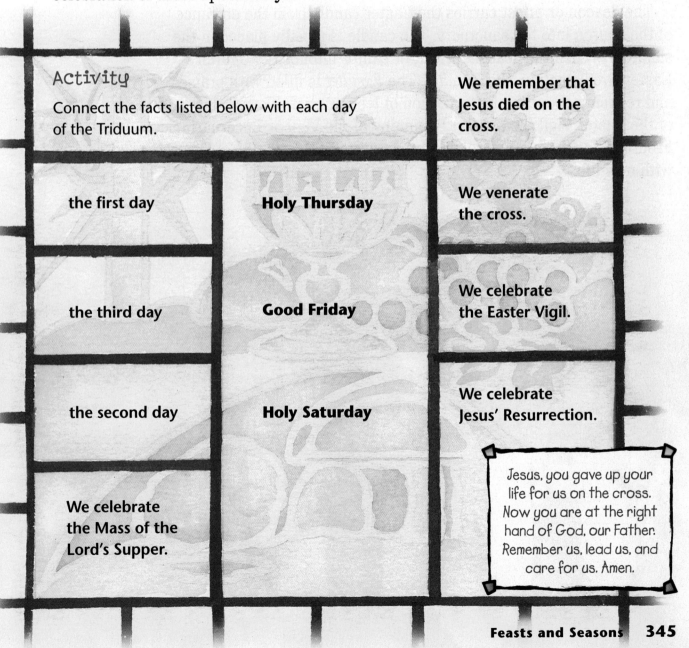

Activity

Connect the facts listed below with each day of the Triduum.

We remember that Jesus died on the cross.

the first day

Holy Thursday

We venerate the cross.

the third day

Good Friday

We celebrate the Easter Vigil.

the second day

Holy Saturday

We celebrate Jesus' Resurrection.

We celebrate the Mass of the Lord's Supper.

Jesus, you gave up your life for us on the cross. Now you are at the right hand of God, our Father. Remember us, lead us, and care for us. Amen.

Our Church Watches and Waits

On Holy Saturday, we remember Jesus in the tomb where Joseph of Arimathea laid his body. The day is spent in quiet prayer, while we watch and wait.

On Holy Saturday night, we can gather with the Church for the Easter Vigil. The first thing we notice is that the church is dark inside. As the service begins, the priest and other ministers gather at the entrance of the church. A fire is lit and glows in the darkness. From this fire a new Paschal, or Easter, candle is lit. The deacon or priest, holding the candle high in the darkness, sings out three times, "The Light of Christ." The community responds, "Thanks be to God."

The deacon or priest carries the Easter candle from the entrance of the church into the sanctuary. The candle is usually placed in the sanctuary. Then the deacon, priest, or cantor intones the Church's Easter Proclamation, the *Exsultet*. The *Exsultet* is filled with praises and rejoicing about the Resurrection of Jesus Christ. We call this part of the Easter Vigil the Solemn Beginning of the Vigil or Lucernarium. From the darkness of the tomb, Christ bursts forth, lighting our world with new life.

A Time of Waiting

Waiting for someone to come home or come to visit can be very difficult. The time just seems to stand still! On Holy Saturday, the Church waits for our celebration of the Resurrection. How will you watch and wait with the Church on Holy Saturday?

Activity

Complete the sentences to describe what waiting for someone feels like.

1. Once, I was waiting for _____.
These are some of the things I did while I waited.

_____

_____

These are some of the feelings I felt while I waited.

_____

_____

2. On Holy Saturday I can watch and wait with the Church. I will

be waiting for _____.
These are some of the things that I can do while I wait.

_____

_____

These are some of the people who will wait with me.

_____

_____

3. Finally, the time for the Easter Vigil will arrive. This is how I will feel when my waiting, and the Church's waiting, is over.

_____

_____

Jesus, help us watch and wait for you on Holy Saturday and every day of our lives. Help us remember that you rose from the dead and are alive in our hearts, sharing your life with us. Amen.

✝ Prayer Celebration for Holy Week

The Blessing of Food

Leader: Throughout Lent we have prepared for Jesus' Resurrection. We hunger and thirst for holiness. Jesus will feed and nourish us by God's Word and the Sacraments. When we gather for our first meal of Easter may our food be a sign of the heavenly banquet Jesus has prepared for us.

Reader: Send forth your light and your faithfulness.

They shall lead me on and bring me to your holy mountain, to your dwelling place.
Then will I go to the altar of God,
the God of my gladness and joy;
then will I give you thanks upon the harp,
O God, my God!

All: Bless the Lord.

Group 1: Jesus invites us to the heavenly banquet.
Let us call upon him.

Group 2: Lord, prepare us for the feast of life.

Group 1: May we be ready to live as good Christians,
we pray to the Lord.

Group 2: Lord, prepare us for the feast of life.

Group 1: May the food we share remind us of the Bread of
Life, the Eucharist, we pray to the Lord.

Group 2: Lord, prepare us for the feast of life.

Group 1: May we be ready to share our table with those
who are hungry and thirsty, we pray to the Lord.

Group 2: Lord, prepare us for the feast of life.

Group 1: May we one day enjoy the banquet of the Lord
in the heavenly kingdom, we pray to the Lord.

Group 2: Lord, prepare us for the feast of life.

Leader: God of glory, all our eyes turn to you
as we celebrate Christ's victory over sin and death.
Bless us and this food.
May we who gather at the Lord's table
continue to celebrate the joy of his Resurrection
and be admitted one day to his heavenly banquet.
Grant this through Christ, our Lord.

All: Amen.

Based on the Blessing of Food for Easter from the Book of Blessings

Easter

Why do you look for him among the dead? He is alive!

Based on Luke 24:5–6

The Church's Greatest Celebration

It is time to put away our sadness. It is time for celebrations of joy and new life. Easter has come!

We know that something wonderful has happened when we walk into our parish church on Easter Sunday. The colors are bright and beautiful. The songs are happy and filled with praise. We have new water for blessing and baptizing and a new fire to remind us of Jesus, the Light of the World. The Paschal candle is new and will remind us of Easter joy as it is lit each Sunday of the Easter Season. It will also be lit at each Baptism that is celebrated, bringing the new life of Jesus to each new Christian.

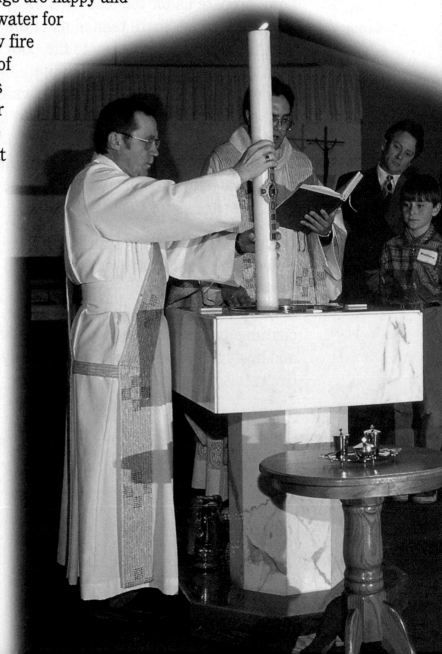

At Mass on Easter Sunday, we are sprinkled with the water that was blessed the night before at the Easter Vigil. The blest water reminds us that we are each a new creation—our old lives have passed away and we are new in Christ, our Savior. We use again the Church's word of praise and thanks—*Alleluia!* We pray and sing, "Alleluia! Jesus is risen! We will live forever!"

350

Jesus Is Risen!

The joy of Easter fills us with a sense of new life, of beginning again in Christ. We sing aloud our praise and thanks.

Activity

What do you like about Easter? Use markers to create Easter egg designs on the egg shapes below. Use two of the following words in your designs: *Easter, Jesus, New Life, Alleluia.*

Risen Jesus, come into our hearts this Easter season. You are the reason we celebrate all the blessings in our lives, especially the gift of new life we received at Baptism. Amen.

Jesus and Mary Magdalene

Early in the morning on the first day of the week, Mary Magdalene came to Jesus' tomb. Mary saw that the stone had been removed from the tomb. She ran and told Simon Peter and the other Apostles. Simon Peter and John came back to the tomb with her to investigate. The tomb was empty! Simon Peter and John could not believe their eyes. They went home, but Mary stayed at the tomb and wept.

As Mary was weeping, she looked into the tomb and saw two angels sitting there. They asked her why she was crying. She replied, "They have taken my Lord. I don't know where they put him."

Then Mary turned around and saw a man standing there, watching her. It was Jesus, but Mary did not recognize him. He asked her why she was crying and whom she was looking for. Mary thought he was the gardener and said to him, "If you took Jesus away, please tell me where you put him. I will take him." Then Jesus said, "Mary!"

Mary suddenly recognized that the man was Jesus. "Rabbi!" she said and fell at his feet, clinging to him.

"Do not hold on to me." Jesus said, "I have not yet gone home to my Father. But, tell my followers I am going home to my Father, who is their Father, too."

So Mary went to the Apostles and other followers and said, "I have seen the Lord." Then she told them all that Jesus had said to her.

Based on John 20:1–18

In the Gospel story we read that Mary Magdalene received the great privilege of seeing Jesus after his Resurrection. As far as we know, she was the first person to do so. Today we remember her as a saint because of her strong faith in Jesus Christ. Her feast day is July 22.

Recognizing Jesus

Mary Magdalene did not recognize Jesus at first. He had to call her by name before she knew who he was. Jesus is always calling to us, too. He wants us to recognize him as well. How do you think we can recognize Jesus in our lives?

Activity

Imagine the conversation between Mary Magdalene and the Apostles on the first Easter Sunday. Write what you think they talked about.

Mary Magdalene _____

_____

Apostles _____

_____

Mary Magdalene _____

_____

Apostles _____

_____

Mary Magdalene _____

_____

Apostles _____

_____

Mary Magdalene, you were given the great gift of seeing Jesus after his Resurrection. Teach us how to repent of our sins. Guide us in living good and holy lives. Amen.

Jesus and the Apostles on the Shore

Simon Peter and several of Jesus' disciples went fishing. They went out in a boat onto the Sea of Galilee. They fished all night, but caught nothing. At dawn, they saw someone standing on the shore. They did not recognize that it was Jesus.

Jesus called to them, "Have you caught anything?"

They shouted back, "No."

Jesus told them to throw their net over the right side of the boat. So they did and there were so many fish they could not pull the net back in. Then one of the disciples recognized that the man on the shore must be Jesus. He told this to Simon Peter.

Simon Peter was so happy to see Jesus that he jumped into the water right away and headed toward land. The rest of the disciples were also very happy and could not wait to see Jesus again. They came in the boat, dragging the heavy, full net behind them.

On the shore, the disciples saw a fire with fish cooking on it. Alongside the fire was a basket of bread. Jesus said, "Come, have breakfast." The disciples didn't have to ask who he was. They knew that this was Jesus, and they were so glad to be with him again. Jesus then took the bread and gave it to them. And he gave them some fish to eat as well.

Based on John 21:1–14

The Sea of Galilee, Israel

The Gospel story is about one of Jesus' appearances after the Resurrection. This is why Simon Peter and the rest of the disciples were so glad to see Jesus. They thought they were never going to see him again. They loved Jesus, and had missed him. His appearance was exciting and made them happy. The disciples' happiness at being with Jesus again reminds us of Easter. We celebrate Easter with great joy because we remember that we will be with Jesus again, too.

Breakfast on the Shore

Jesus knew his friends had been hard at work all night long. He knew that they would be hungry and tired. So he prepared a meal for them. He cared about their needs and was willing to serve them. How do we care for our friends and their needs?

Activity

Look at the fish and figure out the word that all the letters spell. Write it on the line below.

Simon Peter, you became the first leader of the Church. Help us to be joyful as you were joyful when you saw Jesus standing on the shore. Amen.

_____

 # Prayer Celebration for Easter

A Prayer from the Byzantine Church

Leader: At Easter, Christians in Russia and other countries in Eastern Europe greet each other by saying "Christ is risen" and by answering "He is truly risen." This reminds them of the importance of the Easter celebration. Let us begin our prayer today by greeting one another in this way.

Activity

Write a petition that you would like to pray with the rest of your class.

_____

_____

_____

Leader: Glory be to the Father, and to the Son, and to the Holy Spirit. As it was in the beginning, is now, and will be forever.

All: Amen.

Leader: This is the day that the Lord has made. Let us be glad and rejoice in it. As each student prays his or her petition, please respond, "Christ is risen."

(*Invite students to share their petitions.*)

All: Christ is risen.

Reader: While the disciples were gathered together, they talked about Jesus. Then suddenly, he was there with them. "Peace be with you," he said. But they were terrified and thought they were seeing a ghost. He said, "Why are you afraid? Look at my hands and my feet. It is I. Touch me and see." They were amazed and filled with joy. Then he asked them, "Do you have anything to eat?" And they gave him a piece of baked fish. He took it and ate it in front of them.

Based on Luke 24:36–43

All: Praise the Lord, O Jerusalem. Praise your God. Alleluia!

Leader: Who is so great as God? You, O God, alone work wonders.

All: You are so great, O God.

Leader: You made known your power to the nations and saved your people with your might.

All: You are so great, O God.

Leader: Remember the Lord's deeds. Remember all his works.

All: You are so great, O God.

Leader: O Jesus, our Savior, your Resurrection changed our whole universe. You have raised all of us up to new life. O Lord Almighty, glory to you!

All: Amen.

Based on the Byzantine Catholic Celebration of Easter

Holy Days

Those who seek the Lord will offer praise. May our hearts enjoy life forever!

Based on Psalm 22:27

The Exaltation of the Holy Cross

From the beginning of the Church, Christians revered the cross on which God's Son was crucified. But many wondered what had happened to Jesus' cross. Today in the Church we have a special holy day for celebrating the cross. Every year on September 14, we celebrate the Feast of the Exaltation of the Holy Cross. Sometimes this holy day is also called the Triumph of the Holy Cross. The word *exalt* means "to lift up by praising" or "to glorify." This means that we give something the special importance that it is due. It is certainly important that we honor the cross upon which our Lord gave his life for us.

There are many legends connected with the finding of the cross. The first is about Saint Helena, the mother of the great emperor Constantine. Helena was kind and generous. She was a woman of great faith. When she was about eighty, she decided to go to Jerusalem to see if she could find the cross. It is said that in A.D. 326, three crosses were found on Mount Calvary. One by one the crosses were brought to a woman who was very ill. When she touched the third cross, she was cured. Helena was so happy to hear about this that she had a church built in Jerusalem and placed part of the cross there. She also sent parts of the cross to Rome and Constantinople, the capitals of the empire.

The Church of the Cross, Jerusalem

Another legend is about the emperor Heraclius I. About A.D. 612 the city of Jerusalem was conquered by a Muslim army and the part of the cross was taken from the church that Helena had built. Heraclius fought a long war to get Jerusalem back. He made the Muslim leaders give him back the part of the cross.

In A.D. 629, Heraclius returned the piece of the cross to Jerusalem, carrying it on his shoulders. But it got heavier and heavier and Heraclius had difficulty carrying it. The bishop Zachary reminded him that only the poor and humble are like Jesus. So Heraclius took off his kingly robes and put on the clothes of a poor man. Then he was able to bring the cross back to Jerusalem. Many miracles happened there once it was returned.

Exalting the Cross

Today, to honor the cross, many people go to Jerusalem to visit the Basilica of the Holy Cross. But we don't have to journey to Jerusalem to remember the meaning of the cross. How can you exalt the holy cross?

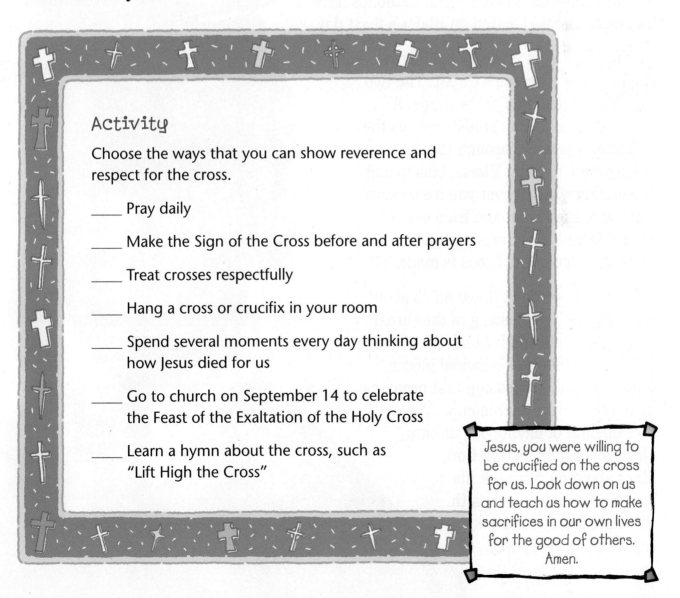

Activity

Choose the ways that you can show reverence and respect for the cross.

_____ Pray daily

_____ Make the Sign of the Cross before and after prayers

_____ Treat crosses respectfully

_____ Hang a cross or crucifix in your room

_____ Spend several moments every day thinking about how Jesus died for us

_____ Go to church on September 14 to celebrate the Feast of the Exaltation of the Holy Cross

_____ Learn a hymn about the cross, such as "Lift High the Cross"

Jesus, you were willing to be crucified on the cross for us. Look down on us and teach us how to make sacrifices in our own lives for the good of others. Amen.

The Feast of Saint Blaise

Every year on February 3, Catholics can have their throats blessed on the Feast of Saint Blaise. Very little is known about Saint Blaise. Some say he was a doctor before he became a bishop in Armenia. Others say that he was a martyr. Another legend tells how he hid in a cave when Christians were being persecuted. He healed the sick and the wounded wild animals that he found. In A.D. 316, hunters saw Blaise and brought him before the governor who later had him beheaded.

In one story, Saint Blaise stopped a young boy from choking to death on a fishbone. This is why we pray to Saint Blaise when we have throat trouble. Since the Middle Ages, Catholics have had their throats blessed on Blaise's feast day.

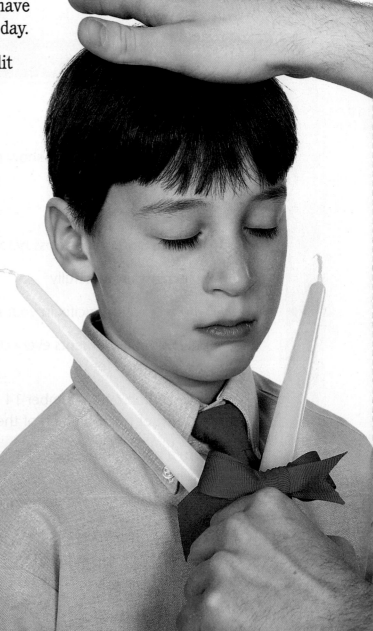

The blessing is given by holding two unlit candles near a person's throat. The two candles are held in a cross shape. A priest, deacon, or lay minister prays the following prayer: "Through the intercession of Saint Blaise, bishop and martyr, may God deliver you from every disease of the throat and from every other illness" (*Book of Blessings*). Then the Sign of the Cross is made.

Although we don't know much about Saint Blaise, the blessing of the throats has been practiced for hundreds of years. It is a sacramental—a sacred object, prayer, action, or blessing that prepares us to receive the Sacraments. The sacramental of having our throats blessed reminds us that God cares about us. We seek his blessing for our good health. We depend on God to take care of us in every way.

Blessings

Catholics seek God's blessing in many different ways. On Saint Blaise's day, we can have our throats blessed. Also, every day we pray before meals to ask for God's blessing on the food we eat. We may bless ourselves and our loved ones before an important event. We may bless our homes and our cars. There are many times when we ask for God's blessing. When do you and your family pray blessings?

Activity

Write a prayer for the Feast of Saint Blaise. Remember to include something that Saint Blaise is known for and what you want to ask the saint for.

_____

_____

_____

_____

_____

_____

_____

_____

_____

_____

_____

Saint Blaise, just as you saved a boy from choking, take care of us. Keep us and our friends and family healthy. Help us to avoid sore throats and other throat problems. Amen.

The Feast of Pentecost

When the Jewish feast of Pentecost came, the followers of Jesus were in Jerusalem. They had locked themselves in an upstairs room out of fear.

Suddenly, there came a noise like a strong wind blowing. What appeared to be tongues of fire rested on each person's head. All were filled with the Holy Spirit. The disciples were no longer afraid. The Helper promised to them by God had come. They began to speak of Jesus and his teachings with great courage to all who had come to Jerusalem for the feast.

Based on the Acts of the Apostles 2:1–11

The Holy Spirit Is Our Helper

On Pentecost, we celebrate the coming of the Holy Spirit. The Scripture passage above tells us that the Holy Spirit was sent to the early Church on the Jewish feast of Pentecost. It was on this day that God fulfilled his promise to send a Helper. The Holy Spirit would help Jesus' friends remember all that he had taught them. The Holy Spirit would help them live their lives in imitation of Jesus, the Lord.

In our Church today, many call the Feast of Pentecost the birthday of the Church. On that first Pentecost, the disciples began to teach and preach with great courage about Jesus of Nazareth and all that took place through his Death and Resurrection.

Everyone Needs a Helper

When you were a very young child, you needed help with
almost everything. Now that you are older, you can
do many more things on your own. But even as
an adult, there will be times when you need
a helper. The Holy Spirit is our Helper.

Activity

Complete the activity by filling in the blanks.

The Holy Spirit is my Helper especially when I

_____

_____ .

The Holy Spirit will help anyone when

_____

_____ .

The Holy Spirit helps us to

_____

_____ .

When I need someone's advice and no one is around I can

_____

_____ .

The most important thing I learned from the story of
Pentecost is

_____

_____ .

Spirit of Hope, help us
always to be a Church
committed to following
the Gospel of Christ in
doing the Father's will.
Amen.

Mary

God, who is mighty, has done great things for me.

Based on Luke 1:49

Mary Gives God Praise

Mary set out to a town of Judah to the house of her cousin, Elizabeth. When Elizabeth heard Mary's greeting, the baby inside her leaped for joy. Elizabeth was filled with the Holy Spirit and sang out, "Blessed are you among all the women of the world and blessed is the baby inside you."

Mary responded to her cousin with a prayer of praise to God.

"My whole being shouts out how great is the Lord,
my spirit finds great joy in God who saves me.

"For God has looked upon me, his servant, in her humility;
all generations to come will call me blessed.

"God who is mighty has done great things for me;
holy is his name."

Based on Luke 1:39–49

Mary understood that by making her the Mother of God's own Son, God had blessed her with the most wonderful gift any person would ever receive. She praised God for having chosen her to be the Mother of the Savior. Mary praised and thanked God throughout her life for every blessing.

The prayer of praise that Mary sang out when she greeted Elizabeth is called the Magnificat. The word *magnificat* is a Latin word that means "magnificent." Mary was telling God that what he had done for her was magnificent and worthy of great praise.

Giving Praise to God

To praise someone means to tell a person how great he or she is. When we praise God, we tell God how great he is. We praise him for being a kind and loving God. We praise God for blessing our lives with good people and with all that we need to live happy and healthy lives.

Activity

Complete the activity by listing the people and things you wish to praise God for.

I praise you, God, for these things in my life.

_____

_____

_____

_____

_____

I praise you, God, for these people in my life.

_____

_____

_____

_____

_____

Mary, our mother, teach us to be ready to do what God asks of us. Keep us faithful to your Son, Jesus Christ. Amen.

Saint Catherine Labouré and the Miraculous Medal of Mary

Zoe Labouré was born in France in 1806. She had ten brothers and sisters. When she was eight, Zoe's mother died and she had to help take care of her family. When she was a teenager, she felt called to become a nun, but her father would not let her. He wanted her to get married, but Zoe refused.

When Zoe was twenty-four, her father changed his mind. Zoe entered the Daughters of Charity of Saint Vincent de Paul. She took the name of Catherine. After several months, Sister Catherine began to have visions of Mary. In one vision, a child woke her up and led her to the convent chapel, where she saw Mary. On November 27, 1830, Sister Catherine Labouré had a vision in which she saw the images of a medal. This medal has the image of Mary on one side with the words "O Mary, conceived without sin, pray for us who have recourse to thee." On the other side of the medal is the letter *M* with a cross above it and the hearts of Jesus and Mary below it. Mary told Sister Catherine to have medals made like this, and said to Sister Catherine "Those who wear it will receive great graces." Sister Catherine had this vision several times during 1831.

Sister Catherine told a priest about her visions. He asked her many questions to make sure she was serious. Sister Catherine was so serious that she made him promise not to tell anyone who she was. She did not want to become famous. Then he got the permission of the archbishop to have the medals made.

The Miraculous Medal became known to Catholics throughout the world, and many Catholics have been wearing it since. As for Sister Catherine, she lived a quiet life as a nun. She looked after the chickens that her convent raised for food. She also helped take care of the elderly nuns. She died in 1876. Sister Catherine was canonized in 1947, and her feast day is November 25.

Why Catholics Wear Medals

The Miraculous Medal of Mary is one of the most common medals that Catholics wear. But there are others. Most have images of saints on them. Why do Catholics wear medals? To remind us of holy people, such as Mary and the saints, who can help us and pray for us. When we think of Mary and other holy people, we are reminded what it means to lead good lives.

Activity

Draw a picture of a scene from the story of Saint Catherine Labouré and the miraculous medal. Then write a sentence about why you chose this scene. Share your picture and sentence with a partner.

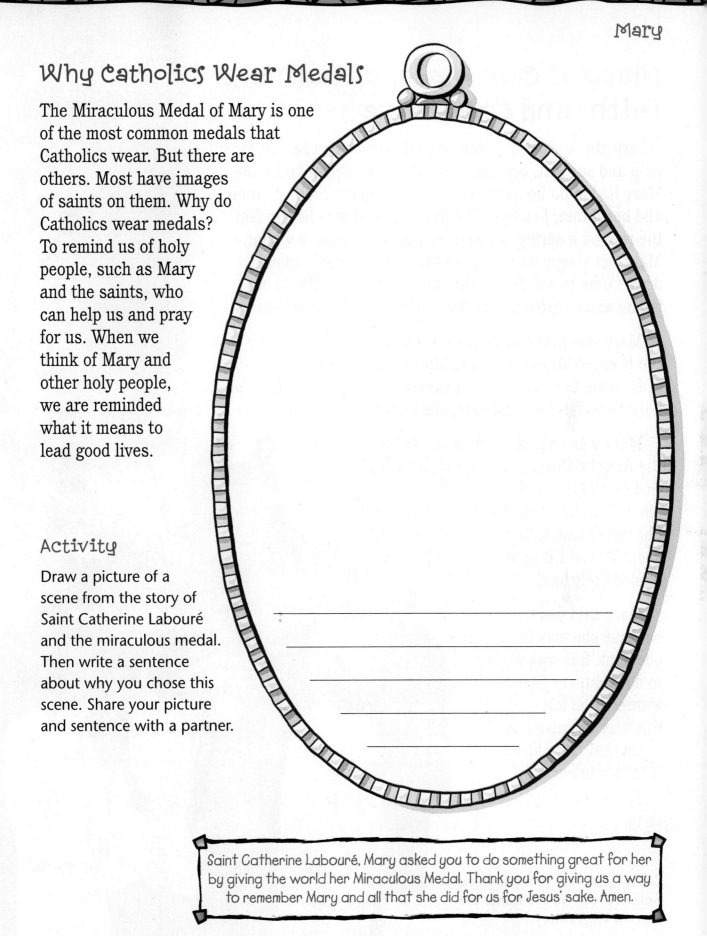

Saint Catherine Labouré, Mary asked you to do something great for her by giving the world her Miraculous Medal. Thank you for giving us a way to remember Mary and all that she did for us for Jesus' sake. Amen.

Mary Is Our Model of Holiness, Faith, and Obedience

Mary, the Mother of Jesus, is someone we can call on for help and support. She understands what life is like for us. Mary had to do household chores to help her mother, Anne, and her father, Joachim. She knew what it was like to feel the rain on a spring day and the cold of a night in winter. Mary felt sleepy when she was tired and hungry when it was time to eat. She understands what it is like to be young and to grow up and have to take on responsibilities.

Mary was much more than one of us. She is Our Lady, the Blessed Virgin Mary, the Mother of God, and the Queen of Heaven. She is a perfect example of what it means to be holy, to be faithful, and to be obedient to God's will.

Mary was only about fourteen years old when the Angel Gabriel asked her if she would follow God's will for her. She knew that God's plan might be hard, but she never hesitated. She never said to Gabriel, "Let me think about it, and I'll get back to you." She immediately said, "Yes."

Mary said yes to God because she was faithful and obedient. She was willing to do whatever God wanted. She felt this way because she loved God. This love is what made her holy.

Catholics in East Timor, Indonesia, walk in procession to honor the Blessed Virgin Mary.

Mary is the perfect model for us. If we are not sure if we can do something that is good but difficult, Mary's example reminds us that we must accept the challenge. If we wonder if what we are told about God is true, we can recall that Mary loved God and did not doubt. If we think that holiness is impossible for us, we can always rely on Mary to guide us.

A Source of Love and Support

Many people pray to Mary and remember to celebrate her feast days. When do you turn to Mary in your everyday life?

Activity

Answer the following questions in complete sentences.

When was Mary obedient to God?

_____

_____

What does it mean to be faithful?

_____

_____

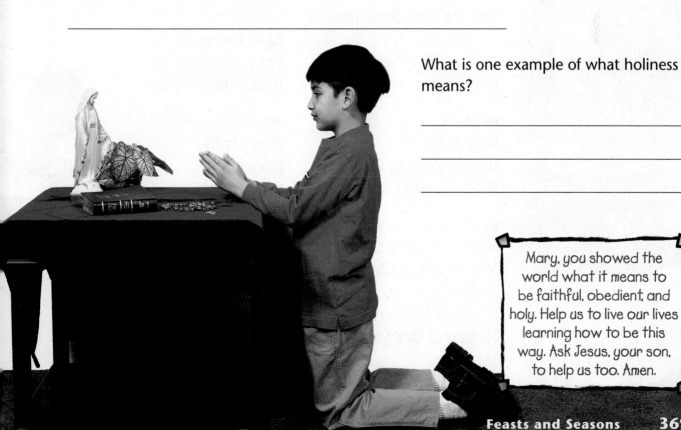

What is one example of what holiness means?

_____

_____

_____

Mary, you showed the world what it means to be faithful, obedient, and holy. Help us to live our lives learning how to be this way. Ask Jesus, your son, to help us too. Amen.

Prayer Celebration in Honor of Mary

Litany of the Blessed Virgin Mary

One of the ways Catholics honor Mary is by praying the Litany of the Blessed Virgin Mary. A litany is a prayer that calls on God, Jesus, the Holy Spirit, Mary, or the saints.

The Litany of the Blessed Virgin Mary is centuries old. When we pray the Litany we are giving honor to Mary and asking her to lead us to her Son, Jesus.

Reader 1	**All**
Lord, have mercy.	Lord, have mercy.
Christ, have mercy.	Christ, have mercy.
Lord, have mercy.	Lord, have mercy.

Reader 2	**All**
God our Father in Heaven,	have mercy on us.
God the Son, Redeemer of the world,	have mercy on us.
God the Holy Spirit,	have mercy on us.
Holy Trinity, one God,	have mercy on us.

Reader 3	**All**
Holy Mary,	pray for us.
Holy Mother of God,	pray for us.
Most Honored of Virgins,	pray for us.

Reader 4	**All**
Mother of Christ,	pray for us.
Mother of the Church,	pray for us.
Sinless Mother,	pray for us.
Model of Motherhood,	pray for us.
Mother of Our Savior,	pray for us.

Reader 5

	All
Queen of Angels,	pray for us.
Queen of Prophets,	pray for us.
Queen of Apostles and Martyrs,	pray for us.
Queen of All Saints,	pray for us.
Queen Conceived without Original Sin,	pray for us.
Queen Assumed into Heaven,	pray for us.
Queen of the Rosary,	pray for us.
Queen of Peace,	pray for us.

Reader 6

	All
Lamb of God, you take away the sins of the world,	have mercy on us.
Pray for us, holy Mother of God,	that we may become worthy of the promises of Christ.

All

Mary, Mother of God, help us to live holy lives. Give us the strength to make good choices for ourselves. Lead us to your Son, Jesus. Amen.

Based on the Litany of the Blessed Virgin Mary

Saints

Turn from evil, and do good.

Based on Psalm 34:15

Saint Martin de Porres

Martin de Porres was born in Lima, Peru, in 1579. Martin was not accepted in his town because he was a child of a man from Spain and a black woman freed from slavery. People made fun of him. They teased him. They called him names.

When Martin was a teenager, he became an assistant to a man who was a pharmacist, doctor, and surgeon. Martin soon was able to help others with the skills he learned. He wanted to do more for people who were hurting, so he decided to join the Dominicans. The Dominicans are an order of priests and brothers who work with the poor, the sick, and those who need schooling. Martin asked if they would take him in as a helper. But the priests and brothers soon recognized that Martin was a holy man who had many gifts to offer their order and the poor of Peru. They asked Martin to be a lay brother. Martin eagerly agreed. This opportunity was more than he had ever hoped for.

Martin spent much of his time tending to the sick and injured. He worked with the poor and spent many nights praying and fasting.

Because Martin suffered from the cruelty of others, he could see when people were sad. Martin spent his life caring with compassion and love for those who were hurting.

The Feast of Saint Martin de Porres is celebrated on November 3.

Treating Others Fairly

Saint Martin de Porres is known for treating others fairly because he suffered much injustice when he was growing up. Think about how you treat others. Is it the way you would like to be treated?

Activity

Saint Martin de Porres knew how much it hurt to be made fun of. He also knew what it was like to be treated unfairly because of who his parents were. How do you respond when someone does not accept you? Decide what you would do in the following examples.

A classmate says mean things about your family. What do you do?

____ Punch your classmate

____ Say mean things about your classmate's family

____ Walk away

____ Talk with that person and share how you feel

____ Tell your teacher how much you are being hurt

Why did you choose this action?

_____

_____

What do you think Saint Martin de Porres would have done? Why?

_____

_____

Saint Martin de Porres, we can learn from you what it means to be gentle and kind to all people. Pray with us for those who are hurting this day. Amen.

Saint Clare

Clare was born in A.D. 1194. When she was eighteen, she heard Saint Francis of Assisi preach during Lent. She talked to him and told him she wanted to become a nun. He encouraged her. On Palm Sunday, she was too shy to go and take some palms. The bishop was in the church and saw how shy she was, so he gave her some palms. Clare took this as a sign. That very night she left her family and went to the monastery where Saint Francis and his followers lived.

As a sign of Clare's humility, Francis cut off her hair and gave her a sackcloth to wear with a rope. Then, because Francis had not yet started a convent for women, Clare went to live with some Benedictine nuns.

Later on, Francis made Clare the mother superior of the women who wanted to follow his simple life of poverty. At first, they were known as the Poor Ladies. They later became known as the Poor Clares. Eventually, Clare's sister and her mother joined her. Clare started monasteries of nuns in Italy, France, and Germany. Clare and her nuns wore no shoes and slept on the ground. They never ate meat and spoke as little as possible.

Clare led her nuns for forty years. One time an army invaded Italy and attacked the convent. The story is told that Clare defended her nuns. She put a consecrated host in a monstrance and placed it on the convent wall. When the invaders saw the monstrance, they turned and left without harming anyone. Jesus had protected Clare and her nuns through the Eucharist.

Clare died when she was sixty, but her religious order still exists today. Her feast day is August 11.

Facing Challenges

When Clare decided to live a holy life of poverty, she faced many problems, but she never gave up. When do people today find it difficult to do the right thing?

Activity

Complete the word search puzzle below.

Clues:

Time of the year when Clare heard Saint Francis preach _____

What Clare wanted to be _____

The place where Saint Francis and his community lived _____

Clare wanted to live a simple life of _____.

Clare started monasteries in Italy, France, and _____.

Clare led her nuns for _____ years.

Clare protected the convent by placing a _____ on the convent wall.

Clare and her nuns never ate _____.

The month of Clare's feast day is _____.

Clare's age when she died _____

```
p m o n a s t e r y v p y m d
x o e l o y n m q p o n t o d
b u r i t l e n t v i u r n o
g o k t n s h z e q d n o s i
f b y z i h u r w p g z f t l
c g v s d u t g x u k u d r x
w h e k y y n j u m a y i a l
l c v i t y e c d a e g d n d
u s h x z n g f u e j a r c g
l s i g q v c v e l w j t e a
w s f f a f g y y n a m r e g
```

O Saint Clare, you bravely led a life of poverty and holiness. You knew how to lead your nuns and protect them. Protect us from danger in our world. Teach us how to live simple lives. Amen.

Saint Jean de Brébeuf and Companions

Before the voyages of Columbus and other explorers, Native Americans were the only ones who lived in North America. Then European traders and settlers began to arrive. Some of the Europeans were nice to the Native Americans. Other Europeans tried to take advantage of the Native Americans and caused trouble. In the 1600s, Jesuit missionaries arrived to teach the Native Americans about Christianity. It was a dangerous time. There were many misunderstandings between Europeans and Native Americans. Many Native Americans wanted the Europeans to go back to their own countries.

Between 1642 and 1649, eight Jesuit missionaries were killed for their faith. We call them the North American Martyrs. They had been working among the Huron people, Native Americans who lived in what is now upstate New York and Canada. The missionaries baptized them and spread the Good News of Jesus Christ. The Hurons called the holy water used in Baptism "the waters of importance." Father Jean de Brébeuf was one of the first missionaries to work among the Huron.

Another Native American people were the Mohawks. They were the enemies of the Hurons. The Mohawks were also unfriendly to Europeans. They did not want to hear about God from the missionaries. One day they attacked and captured Father Isaac Jogues, Father Charles Garnier, and René Goupil, a Jesuit lay brother. The Mohawks tortured them and made them slaves. René Goupil was tomahawked in 1642 for making the Sign of the Cross over some children. Father Isaac Jogues escaped.

Bravely, the Jesuits tried to work with Native Americans again, but they paid a heavy price.

A Jesuit missionary preaches to Native Americans and fur traders.

Father Isaac Jogues and lay man Jean de Lalande were killed in 1646 by Mohawks. Fathers Jean de Brébeuf, Antoine Daniel, Charles Garnier, Noel Chabanel, and Gabriel Lalemant were killed in 1648 and 1649. We celebrate their feast day on October 19.

Sharing the Faith

Sometimes those who want to spread the Good News of Jesus Christ are martyred. They are killed for the work they are doing. Missionaries today still work in dangerous areas of the world, such as Africa and Southeast Asia. What can you do to help them?

Activity

Describe what you have learned about missionaries in three or four sentences below.

_____

_____

_____

Choose two things you can do to help missionaries in their work

_____ Pray for them every day

_____ Read about religious orders that send missionaries around the world

_____ Give money to the missions

_____ Help when missionaries are trying to collect food, clothing, and medical supplies

_____ Attend Mass on October 19 in honor of the North American Martyrs

_____ Learn more about the people who missionaries are trying to help

Lord, remember the people who are martyred while spreading the Good News about your Son, Jesus. Take care of the missionaries who are serving you in dangerous places around the world. Amen.

Saint Monica

Saint Monica lived between A.D. 332 and A.D. 387. She was a Christian. Monica was married to a non-Christian named Patritius, and they lived in northern Africa in the town of Tagaste. Patritius was much older than Monica, and he had a violent temper. His mother lived with Patritius and Monica and was often mean to Monica. Monica, was very unhappy. She tried to be a good person. She prayed every day and gave money away to the poor. This only made Patritius angry and he treated her badly, but Monica continued to hope that he and his mother would become Christians.

Other women in the town of Tagaste had unhappy marriages, too. They looked to Monica for help. They knew she suffered as they did, but she was always patient and kind. Her words helped them to tolerate much suffering.

Monica and Patritius had three children—Augustine, Navigius, and Perpetua. Monica prayed that her children, her husband, and his mother would become Christians. In A.D. 370, Patritius and his mother became Christians. Monica's children Perpetua and Navigius also became Christians and led good lives, but Augustine would not become a Christian.

Monica prayed for Augustine for seventeen years. It seemed hopeless. Augustine was very lazy and sinned a lot. This upset Monica very much. She prayed and prayed for him. She asked priests to pray for him, too. One of them told her, "God will surely hear you. The son of those tears will not be lost." Augustine moved to Rome, and Monica followed him. When she got there, she found out he had moved to Milan. So she followed him there. Finally, Augustine agreed to be baptized. Augustine and Monica were happy together for about six months, and then she died as they were traveling back to their home in Africa. Augustine went on to become a Catholic bishop and one of the early Fathers of the Church.

Saint Monica is known for never giving up on her family members. She is remembered especially because she had such strong faith in the power of prayer. Her feast day is August 27.

The Power of Prayer

Saint Monica teaches us that all things are possible through God. When everyone else thought that Augustine was a sinner who would never change, Saint Monica depended on God in prayer. How often do you pray?

Activity

Think of ten words that describe Saint Monica. Write them here.

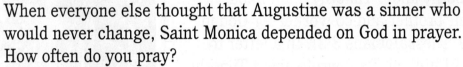

_____

_____

_____

_____

_____

Write a poem about Saint Monica's life. Remember, your poem does not have to rhyme.

_____

_____

_____

_____

_____

_____

Saint Monica, you never gave up on praying for members of your family to become Christian. Help us to be patient and kind with those who hurt our feelings. Teach us to pray more. Amen.

Saint Timothy and Saint Titus

Timothy and Titus were good friends of Saint Paul. They traveled with Paul on his journeys to spread the Good News of Jesus Christ. We read about both Timothy and Titus in the New Testament of the Bible.

Timothy is one of the people we read about in the Acts of the Apostles, a book in the New Testament. He is an early leader among the Christians. There are also two letters in the New Testament that were sent to him. These two letters are called 1 Timothy and 2 Timothy. Paul liked Timothy and called him "brother and co-worker for God in the gospel of Christ" (1 Thessalonians 3:2). In a letter to Christians in the city of Phillippi, Paul wrote about Timothy, "I have no one like him. He cares about you. You know how wonderful he is" (based on Philippians 2:19–24).

Later on, Timothy became the first bishop of the city of Ephesus. In A.D. 97 he made a group of non-Christians angry by telling them not to worship the goddess Diana. So they killed him.

Titus used to travel with Paul. One time, Titus traveled to Jerusalem with Paul and another Christian friend, Barnabas. Another time, Paul sent him to the city of Corinth to help the community there. The Corinthians were not getting along with one another, and they were not listening to Paul's advice. So Paul thought that Titus was a person they would listen to. He was right. Titus helped the Church in Corinth unite as a community.

Later, Titus went to Crete, a Greek island in the Mediterranean Sea. He helped lead the early Church there and later became the first bishop of Crete. Paul sent Titus a letter giving him advice for the Christians of Crete. This letter is found in the New Testament. In the letter, Paul explained to Titus how Christians could get along better together.

The feast day of Saint Timothy and Saint Titus is January 26.

Saint Timothy

Saint Titus

Being a Leader

Timothy and Titus were leaders in the early Church. They helped the Christians in their communities grow close to one another and to God. Who are the leaders in your parish and diocese?

Activity

Pretend you are about to do a TV interview with either Timothy or Titus about being a leader in the early Church. What kinds of things would you like to ask? What do you admire most about their lives? Write your questions here.

_____

_____

_____

_____

_____

_____

_____

_____

_____

_____

_____

_____

_____

Saints Timothy and Titus, help our Church choose good leaders to guide us and unite all the Christians in the world. Teach our Church leaders to help us grow closer to God. Amen.

Holy People

Children, let us love in action and in truth.

Based on 1 John 3:18

Blessed Teresa of Calcutta

Agnes Gonxha Bojaxhiu (boi yah jee oo) was born in Skopje, Macedonia, in 1910 to parents who were from Albania. Along with many of her friends, Agnes belonged to a Catholic group for young girls that was dedicated to Mary.

While she was still a teenager, Agnes knew that God was calling her to serve him in a special way. She eventually joined an Irish order of religious sisters and volunteered to do mission work in India. Agnes took the name Teresa as her religious name and taught high school in Calcutta. Sister Teresa loved her life as a sister and as a teacher. But soon Sister Teresa felt that God was calling her to do more.

Sister Teresa decided to start an order of sisters of her own. These sisters would do the hardest work of all. They would care for those who were very poor and had no one to care for them. Sister Teresa became known as Mother Teresa. Soon her order grew to several thousand women from India and around the world who wanted to serve the poorest of the poor. The sisters also cared for children who had no families, were very ill, or had been neglected. The sisters loved all these people with the same love as Jesus.

In 1997, Mother Teresa died, but her order, the Missionaries of Charity, continues her important work throughout the world. The Feast of Blessed Teresa of Calcutta is celebrated on September 5.

Loving Others As Jesus Did

Mother Teresa taught her sisters to love others the way Jesus did. She encouraged them to live simple lives of service. How can you be of service to others in your life?

Activity

Read the list below and choose two actions that you will do this week to help you grow in holiness.

_____ Spend some time each day in prayer

_____ Not complain when my parents ask me to do something

_____ Give part of my allowance to the missions

_____ Offer to help my teacher

_____ Treat each person I meet with respect and kindness

_____ Not lose my temper

_____ Help out at home without my mom or dad having to ask me

_____ Thank God each day for all the blessings in my life

_____ Be respectful to my teacher and to my classmates

_____ Be friends with someone in my class who doesn't have many friends

> Mother Teresa of Calcutta, we believe that you are with God in Heaven. Pray for us that we may see Jesus in the poor as you did, and love him and care for him in serving them. Amen.

Blessed Miguel Pro

Miguel Agustin Pro was born in Mexico in 1891. His father was an engineer who worked in the mines. His family was well off and were devout Catholics. When he grew up, Miguel entered the Jesuit order to become a priest. During this time, the rulers of Mexico tried to persecute the Catholic Church. So Miguel went to Spain and then to Belgium to finish his education. He was ordained to the priesthood in 1925.

Father Pro returned to Mexico to help his people, but the Catholic religion was outlawed. So Father Pro had to be careful. Secretly, he celebrated the Sacraments, taught and preached, and helped people who were poor. He avoided the police and stayed only in houses that were safe. He used disguises so that he would not be arrested. Sometimes he dressed like a poor beggar and carried the Gospel book and chalice in an old bag. Other times, he would dress in a business suit and pretend to be an important salesman. He even visited prisons dressed as a policeman. When arranging meetings with Catholics he didn't know, he used passwords or wore a flower in his lapel.

After just two years, Father Pro was arrested. He was charged with trying to kill the president of Mexico. He was innocent, but the government wanted to get rid of him. He was killed by a firing squad in 1927. They offered him a blindfold, but he turned it down. His last words were *Viva Cristo Rey*. This means "Long live Christ the King."

Thousands of people went to his funeral even though they were forbidden to do so. More than 500 cars were in the procession to the cemetery. A miracle even occurred. A woman who had been blind regained sight. Father Miguel Pro was beatified in 1988. His feast day is November 23.

Taking Risks for Faith

Father Miguel Pro risked his life more than once to help Catholics live their faith. Sometimes we forget that in many places in the world, people are not free to live their faith. We are used to having religious freedom. Yet, we too may one day be called upon to take risks for our faith. Will you be ready?

Activity

Color and decorate the banner below to remember the last words of Father Miguel Pro.

Blessed Miguel Pro, you led a secret, dangerous life so that others might have faith. Help us to be strong in our faith when we are tempted to forget what we believe. Amen.

Blessed Luigi and Maria Quattrocchi

Luigi and Maria Quattrocchi (quah traw cheei) were married in 1905 and lived in Rome. Luigi was a lawyer, and Maria raised their four children and wrote textbooks and magazine articles about education. Most people probably thought Luigi and Maria were nice people, but very few would have known that God was leading them to become saints.

For example, Luigi and Maria went to Mass and received the Eucharist every day. They prayed the Rosary. They went on retreats and took courses to deepen their knowledge about their faith. They met with their spiritual advisors. They gave their time and money to help others in need. They helped to start the Catholic University of the Sacred Heart in Rome. They taught the faith to children and started a scout troop for poor children. They helped other Catholics prepare for marriage and raise their families.

Luigi and Maria were good people. They were also willing to be heroic and make great sacrifices for their faith. When Maria was expecting their fourth child, she became ill. The doctor told Maria that she could have the baby but she might die. They put their trust in God. They would accept what he wanted. Maria suffered much during the pregnancy. But in the end, she gave birth to a healthy baby girl. Maria was fine too. Luigi and Maria named their daughter Enrichetta.

The good lives that Luigi and Maria lived meant that they raised their children well. In fact, three of them entered religious life. Their two sons became priests, and one of their daughters became a Benedictine nun.

Luigi died in 1951. Maria died in 1965. They were beatified by Pope John Paul II in a ceremony in 2001.

Holiness in the Family

Luigi and Maria Quattrocchi were holy not because they did extra special things but because they did regular things well to serve God. This is what it means to be holy: to do everything we do for God. Do you do good because you love God?

Activity

Complete the matching activity below. Draw lines from each problem to the correct solution.

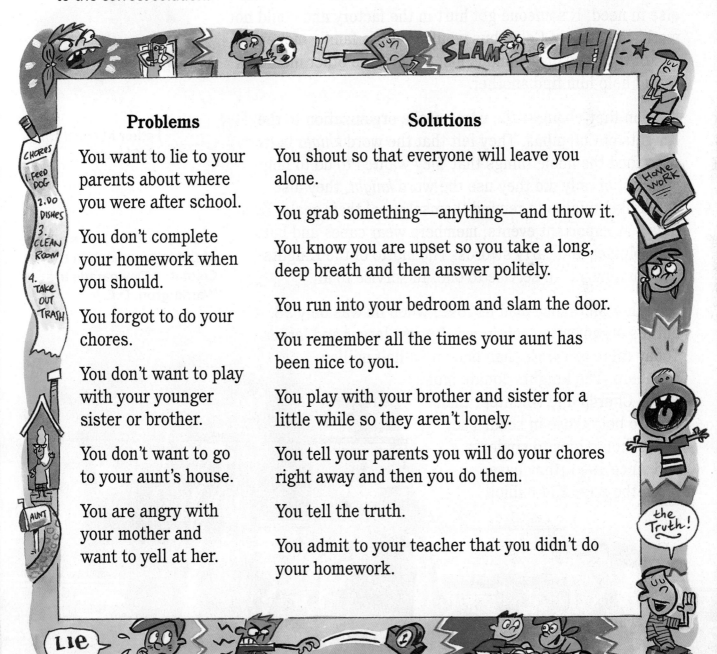

Problems	**Solutions**
You want to lie to your parents about where you were after school.	You shout so that everyone will leave you alone.
	You grab something—anything—and throw it.
You don't complete your homework when you should.	You know you are upset so you take a long, deep breath and then answer politely.
You forgot to do your chores.	You run into your bedroom and slam the door.
	You remember all the times your aunt has been nice to you.
You don't want to play with your younger sister or brother.	You play with your brother and sister for a little while so they aren't lonely.
You don't want to go to your aunt's house.	You tell your parents you will do your chores right away and then you do them.
You are angry with your mother and want to yell at her.	You tell the truth.
	You admit to your teacher that you didn't do your homework.

The Knights of Columbus

More than one hundred years ago, there was a priest who lived and worked in New Haven, Connecticut. His name was Father Michael J. McGivney. At that time, most Catholics were very poor and worked in factories. The work was hard and the wages were small. Father McGivney wanted to help the people in his parish to have better lives. In 1882, he met with twenty-four men of his parish and started an organization they called the Sons of Columbus.

The Sons of Columbus would help each other and anyone else in need. If someone got hurt in the factory and could not work, the Sons of Columbus would give his family money. If one of the Sons of Columbus lost his job, the other members would help him find another.

Soon they changed the name of the organization to the Knights of Columbus. They felt that the word *knight* better described the noble things that they wanted to do to help others. Not only did they use the word *knight*, they also acted like knights to remind themselves of their goals. Even today, at important events, members wear capes and hats with plumes and carry swords. The motto of the Knights of Columbus is "In service to one. In service to all."

Father McGivney died in 1890, when he was only 38, but his organization continued. It grew larger and larger. Today there are more than one-and-a-half million members. The knights donate money to the Church and volunteer their time to help those in need. They give scholarships to students, and since 1981, they have given the pope $34 million.

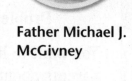

Father Michael J. McGivney

Members of the Knights of Columbus march in the Columbus Day parade in Washington, D.C.

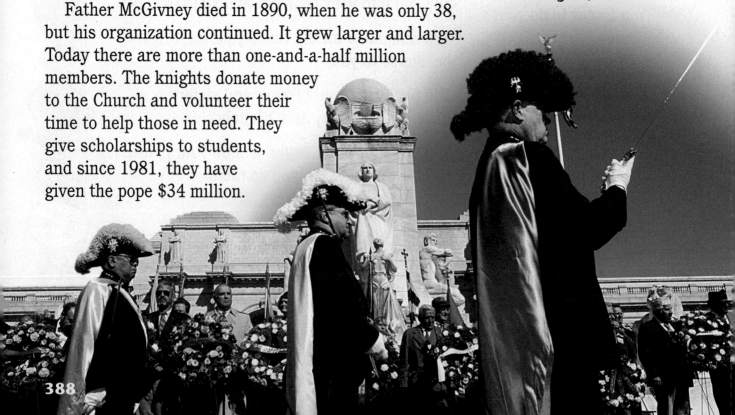

In 1939, the Columbiettes was formed. This is the women's group of the Knights of Columbus. The Columbiettes also collect money, spend time helping others, and look for ways to make the Catholic Church stronger. In 1925 the Columbian Squires, an organization for Catholic boys ages 12 to 17, was founded. They prepare for leadership roles in the Church.

Although it started as a tiny organization, the Knights of Columbus has grown to become one of the largest and most influential group of laypeople in the Church today.

The official symbol of the Knights of Columbus

Helping Others

The Knights of Columbus live Jesus' call to serve others. Today they work on behalf of those in need in several countries throughout the world. They are a great example of service for us. In what ways do you serve others?

Activity

Complete the following statements.

At home, I serve others by _____
_____.

Sometimes I help my friends by _____
_____.

At school, I serve others by _____
_____.

One of the hardest things about serving others is
_____
_____.

When I am helping others, I feel
_____
_____

Heavenly Father, bless the Knights of Columbus, the Columbiettes, and the Columbian Squires for the many good works that they do. Bless them for their generosity and their dedication. Amen.

Feasts and Seasons Wrap-up

Find the answers to the puzzle in the titles of the Feasts and Seasons lessons.

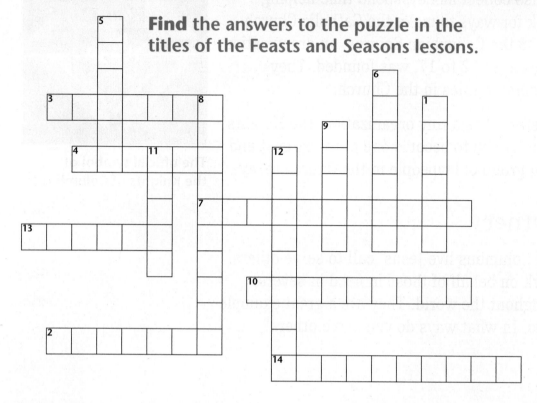

Across

2. Jesus raised _____ from the dead.

3. The three days between Holy Thursday and Easter Sunday are called the _____.

4. A _____ is someone who is killed because the person refuses to deny the Christian faith.

7. Easter is the Church's greatest _____.

10. Christmas is a time to remember, believe, and _____.

13. Catholics can have their throats blessed on the Feast of Saint _____.

14. On September 14th, we celebrate the _____ of the Holy Cross.

Down

1. The Advent wreath is an example of an Advent _____.

5. Saint _____ was the mother of Saint Augustine.

6. Today, many Catholic men belong to the _____ of Columbus.

8. Saint Catherine Laboure gave us the _____ Medal of Mary.

9. After his Resurrection, Jesus appeared to the disciples on the _____.

11. During Advent we celebrate the _____ comings of Jesus.

12. Mary is our model of holiness, faith, and _____.

OUR CATHOLIC HERITAGE

WHAT CATHOLICS BELIEVE

We believe in all that our Church teaches.

ABOUT
REVELATION

God speaks to us through Sacred Tradition and Sacred Scripture.

Sacred Tradition

Sacred Tradition includes the Church's official teachings and customs that have been handed down by the Apostles over the centuries.

Sacred Scripture

Sacred Scripture, or the Bible, is the written Word of God. We believe that the Holy Spirit inspired the writers of the Bible. Sacred Scripture is made up of the Old Testament and the New Testament.

ABOUT
THE TRINITY

We believe that there is one God in Three Divine Persons. We call the mystery of one God in Three Divine Persons the Holy Trinity. The Three Divine Persons are the Father, the Son, and the Holy Spirit.

God, Our Father

God the Father, the First Person of the Holy Trinity, is the Creator of all life. Jesus, God's only Son taught us to call God "Father." Through our Baptism, we become children of God. Jesus told us that our Father in Heaven loves us always.

Jesus Christ

Jesus Christ is the Son of God. By the power of the Holy Spirit, Jesus was born of the Blessed Virgin Mary. He suffered and died on the cross to save us from sin and death.

The Holy Spirit

After he returned to his Father in Heaven, Jesus sent the Holy Spirit to his disciples. The Holy Spirit will guide the Church until the end of time. We receive the Holy Spirit at Baptism and in the other Sacraments.

ABOUT
THE CATHOLIC CHURCH

We believe in one, holy, catholic, and apostolic Church.

The Church is one. We believe in one God. We believe in one faith and in one Baptism. We believe that the Catholic Church is one because we are joined together when we believe in Jesus Christ.

The Catholic Church is holy because Jesus Christ, with the Father and the Holy Spirit, is holy. It is by God's grace that we are holy.

The Church is catholic, or universal, because we welcome all people as Jesus does.

The Church is apostolic. Apostolic means that the Church is founded on the teachings of Jesus Christ and the Apostles. We believe the chief teacher of the Church is the Pope. When he speaks for the Church about faith or morals, we believe that the Pope represents Jesus on earth.

ABOUT
MARY AND THE SAINTS

Mary, the mother of Jesus, is our greatest saint. Mary was filled with grace from the first moment of her life. She lived a life without sin. Mary loved and cared for Jesus, and she loves and cares for us. Catholics honor Mary, Mother of Jesus and the Mother of the Church.

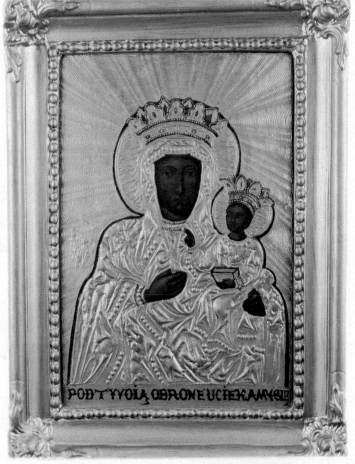

The Black Madonna

We believe that we are joined with all those who believe in Jesus Christ. We believe that the lives of the saints show us how to live as Jesus taught us. We honor the saints and ask them to pray for us. We believe that one day we will live with all the saints forever with God.

HOW CATHOLICS WORSHIP

We celebrate our faith in worship when we give honor and praise to God. Worship is so important to the Catholic Church that the Church calls it the first "work" of God's people.

ABOUT
THE SACRAMENTS

As Catholics, we gather in community to worship when we celebrate the Seven Sacraments. The Sacraments are the sacred signs that celebrate God's love for us. The Sacraments join us with Jesus Christ. Each Sacrament has special words and actions. Through these words and actions, God becomes present to us in the Church.

The Seven Sacraments are divided into three groups to help us understand their words and actions. The first group is called the Sacraments of Christian Initiation.

ABOUT
THE SACRAMENTS OF CHRISTIAN INITIATION

We become full members of the Catholic Church through the Sacraments of Baptism, Confirmation, and Eucharist.

Baptism

Baptism is the Sacrament of welcome into the Church. When we are baptized, we receive the Holy Spirit. We are anointed and marked with the Sign of the Cross. We begin our journey of faith and begin to grow in holiness.

At Baptism the priest or deacon baptizes the person, saying, "I baptize you in the name of the Father, and of the Son, and of the Holy Spirit" (*Rite of Baptism*).

394

The priest or deacon pours water over the head of the person being baptized or immerses the person in the water. This is a sign that we are one with Jesus Christ, through his life, Death, and Resurrection.

Confirmation

Confirmation is the Sacrament that helps us grow in holiness. In Confirmation, the Holy Spirit strengthens us in the faith and helps us share the Good News of Jesus with others.

The bishop or priest lays his hands on the head of the person being confirmed and anoints his or her forehead with Sacred Chrism.

When we are confirmed, the bishop or priest prays, "Be sealed with the gift of the Holy Spirit" (*Rite of Confirmation*).

Eucharist

The Eucharist is the Sacrament in which Jesus Christ gives himself to us in a unique way. At Mass the bread and wine become the Body and Blood of Christ through the power of the Holy Spirit and the words of the priest. The priest takes the bread and says, "TAKE THIS, ALL OF YOU, AND EAT OF IT, FOR THIS IS MY BODY." He then takes the wine and says, "TAKE THIS, ALL OF YOU, AND DRINK FROM IT, FOR THIS IS THE CHALICE OF MY BLOOD" (*Eucharistic Prayer*). During the Communion Rite at Mass we receive Jesus Christ in the Eucharist.

At Mass Jesus is also present to us in the readings from Sacred Scripture, in the priest, and in the people gathered for worship.

THE SACRAMENTS OF HEALING

The Sacraments of Penance and Reconciliation and Anointing of the Sick are called the Sacraments of Healing. They celebrate God's forgiveness and healing.

Penance and Reconciliation

Penance and Reconciliation, also referred to as the Sacrament of Conversion, Confession, or Penance, is the Sacrament that celebrates God's forgiveness. God always forgives us when we are sorry. Through this Sacrament, we examine our conscience, we admit our sins, we express our sorrow, and we receive absolution.

When we celebrate the Sacrament of Penance and Reconciliation, the priest prays, "I absolve you from your sins in the name of the Father, and of the Son, and of the Holy Spirit" (*Rite of Penance*). The priest makes the Sign of the Cross as he prays this prayer of absolution.

The Anointing of the Sick

The Sacrament of Anointing of the Sick celebrates God's love and healing. It is for those who are either very sick or elderly. Through the prayers of the Church and the grace of this Sacrament, people can be healed in both mind and body.

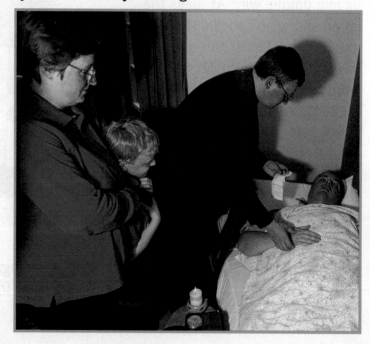

In Anointing of the Sick, the priest anoints the person's forehead and hands with the Oil of the Sick. First the priest anoints the person's forehead as he prays, "Through this holy anointing may the Lord in his love and mercy help you with the grace of the Holy Spirit." Next the priest anoints the person's hands as he prays, "May the Lord who frees you from sin save you and raise you up." (*Rite of Anointing of the Sick*).

ABOUT
THE SACRAMENTS AT THE SERVICE OF COMMUNION

The third group of Sacraments is called the Sacraments at the Service of Communion. These two Sacraments are Holy Orders and Matrimony. They celebrate two special ways that people serve God by sharing their gifts with others.

Holy Orders

Holy Orders is the Sacrament that celebrates the ordination of bishops, priests, and deacons to serve the Church. Bishops and priests are ordained to lead and serve the Church by celebrating the Sacraments and teaching God's Word. Deacons help bishops and priests. They preach homilies, preside at the celebration of some of the Sacraments, and help direct the work among the poor.

Matrimony

The Sacrament of Matrimony celebrates the commitment that a baptized man and a baptized woman make to each other. Their commitment to each other is for a lifetime. Through the grace of this Sacrament, the married man and woman are strengthened in their ability to be faithful to one another. They are called to conduct their family life as though it were a model for the whole Church.

In the celebration of the Sacrament of Matrimony, the man says to the woman, "I take you to be my wife." The woman says to the man, "I take you to be my husband" (*Rite of Marriage*). In the Sacrament of Matrimony, the couple make these promises to each other in the presence of a priest or deacon and the Catholic community.

ABOUT
THE MASS

Introductory Rites

At Mass, we come together to worship God with our parish community.

Entrance Procession and Opening Hymn

As the priest and those assisting him in the Mass enter in procession, we stand and sing the opening hymn.

Greeting

We make the Sign of the Cross. The priest welcomes us. He says, "The Lord be with you." We answer, "And with your spirit."

Penitential Act ▶

We think about our sinfulness. We ask for God's forgiveness and the prayers of the Church.

Gloria ▶

We sing the Gloria, which is a hymn of praise to God.

Opening Prayer

We pray an opening prayer.

Liturgy of the Word

First Reading ▶

The lector reads a story or a lesson usually from the Old Testament.

Responsorial Psalm

We sing the responses to a Psalm from the Old Testament.

Second Reading

The lector reads from one of the books in the New Testament, other than the Gospels.

Gospel Acclamation

We sing "Alleluia" or another acclamation of praise as the priest or deacon prepares to read the Gospel.

Gospel ▶

We stand in reverence as the priest or deacon proclaims the Gospel.

Homily ▶

The priest or deacon tells us about the meaning of the Gospel and the other Scripture readings.

Profession of Faith

We recite the Nicene Creed to profess our belief in what the Church teaches.

Universal Prayer

We pray for the Church, the Pope and bishops, and for the needs of all God's people. We also pray for the needs of the members of our parish community.

Liturgy of the Eucharist

Preparation of the Altar and Gifts ▶

We bring our gifts of bread and wine to the altar. We also give gifts for the poor and donations of money for the Church.

Eucharistic Prayer

The priest begins with a prayer of praise and thanksgiving to God the Father for the wonderful gifts of creation and for the greatest gift of his Son, Jesus Christ. We sing, "Holy, Holy, Holy."

The priest recalls with us the story of the Last Supper. We hear Jesus' own words "FOR THIS IS MY BODY" and "FOR THIS IS THE CHALICE OF MY BLOOD." We sing or say, "We proclaim your Death, O Lord, and profess your Resurrection until you come again," or a similar acclamation.

At the end of the Eucharistic Prayer, we sing, "Amen."

Communion Rite

The Lord's Prayer

We pray together the prayer that Jesus taught us, The Lord's Prayer, or the Our Father.

Sign of Peace

We share the Sign of Peace with those around us.

Breaking of the Bread ▶

We sing the Lamb of God prayer as the priest and deacon prepare for the distribution of Holy Communion.

Holy Communion

We receive the Body and Blood of Christ. We say, "Amen."

Concluding Rite

Blessing

We make the Sign of the Cross as the priest blesses us.

Dismissal ▶

The priest or deacon tells us to go in peace. We sing a hymn of thanks and praise.

ABOUT
RECONCILIATION

In the Sacrament of Penance and Reconciliation, we celebrate God's forgiveness. We ask the Holy Spirit to help us better live as Jesus taught us.

Rite of Reconciliation of Individuals

Preparation

I examine my conscience by thinking of things I might have done or said on purpose that were harmful to myself or others. I remember that I may have sinned by not doing something good when I should have.

Priest's Welcome ▶

The priest welcomes me in the name of Jesus and the Church community.

Reading from Scripture

The priest may read from the Bible or may tell me a story from the Gospels.

Confession

I tell the priest my sins. The priest asks me to do a kind act or say a prayer to show that I am sorry for my sins and to remind me to be more loving.

Prayer of Sorrow ▶

I tell the priest that I am sorry for all my sins. The priest asks me to pray an act of contrition. I pray aloud the prayer of sorrow or I can make one up of my own.

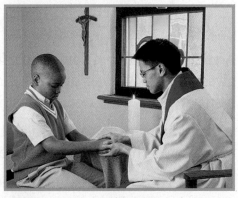

Absolution ▶

Acting on behalf of the Church, the priest extends his hands over me and asks God to forgive me. The priest gives me absolution in the name of the Father, Son, and Holy Spirit.

Prayer of Praise and Dismissal

With the priest, I pray a prayer of praise. The priest tells me to go in peace. I answer, "Amen."

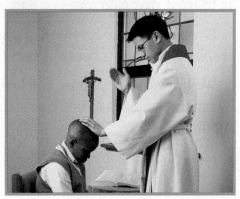

HOW CATHOLICS LIVE

Living as Jesus taught us is not easy, but God helps us. God gives us our conscience and three special gifts. When we turn away from sin and make good choices, we live as children of God.

ABOUT
CONSCIENCE

Our conscience is a gift from God.
Our conscience helps us to know
what is right and what is wrong.
As Catholics, we have help in developing a good conscience.
We have the Beatitudes, the Ten Commandments, and the
teachings of Jesus to help us. Through the Church, the
Holy Spirit guides us to understand what is right and to
turn away from what is sinful.

ABOUT
FAITH, HOPE, AND LOVE

A **virtue** is a habit of doing good. Three special virtues that God
gives to us at Baptism are faith, hope, and love. These virtues
help us to believe in God, to trust in his promises, and to love him.

Faith helps us to believe in all that the Church teaches. It helps
us to grow in truth and knowledge of God.

Hope helps us to trust in God no matter what happens. It helps
us to trust that God loves us and is always guiding us.

Love helps us to love God, ourselves, and others. We treat all
people with respect because God created and loves each person.

We grow in faith, hope, and love by practicing them every day.
By making choices to live these virtues, we please God and grow
in holiness.

ABOUT
THE BEATITUDES

Jesus taught us the Beatitudes to help us live as witnesses to God's Kingdom. When we live the Beatitudes, we help others understand what God wants for all people.

The Beatitudes	Living the Beatitudes
Blessed are the poor in spirit, for theirs is the kingdom of heaven.	We are poor in spirit when we know that we need God more than anything else.
Blessed are they who mourn, for they will be comforted.	We try to help those who are in sorrow or those who are hurting. We know God will comfort them.
Blessed are the meek, for they will inherit the land.	We are gentle and patient with others. We believe we will share in God's promises.
Blessed are they who hunger and thirst for righteousness, for they will be satisfied.	We try to be fair and just toward others. We share what we have with those in need.
Blessed are the merciful, for they will be shown mercy.	We forgive those who are unkind to us. We accept the forgiveness of others.
Blessed are the clean of heart, for they will see God.	We try to keep God first in our lives.
Blessed are the peacemakers, for they will be called children of God.	We try to bring God's peace to the world. When we live peacefully, we are known as God's children.
Blessed are they who are persecuted for the sake of righteousness, for theirs is the kingdom of heaven.	We try to do what is right even when we are teased or insulted. We believe we will be with God forever.

Matthew 5:3–10

THE COMMANDMENTS

The Ten Commandments are God's laws of love. God gave us the commandments as a gift to help us live in peace. Jesus told us that we must always obey the Commandments.

The Ten Commandments	Living the Ten Commandments
1. I am the LORD your God. You shall not have other gods besides me.	We believe in God. We only worship God. We love him more than everyone and everything else. We offer God prayers of adoration and of thanksgiving.
2. You shall not take the name of the LORD, your God, in vain.	We never use the name of God or Jesus in an angry way. We use the names of God, Jesus, Mary, and the saints with respect at all times.
3. Remember to keep holy the LORD's Day.	On Sunday we honor God in special ways. We worship him by attending Mass with our family and friends.
4. Honor your father and mother.	We love, honor, respect, and obey our parents and all adults who care for us.
5. You shall not kill.	We believe that God gives us the gift of life. We must protect the lives of children not yet born, the sick, and the elderly. We respect the life and health of others. We must live peacefully and prevent harm from coming to ourselves and others.
6. You shall not commit adultery.	God created man and woman in his image. God calls each to accept his or her identity. The Church teaches that chastity is important for us to be healthy and happy. We must respect our bodies and the bodies of others. We honor the lifelong marriage covenant.
7. You shall not steal.	We take good care of the gifts that God has given us and share them with others. We want others who come after us to have them, too. We do not cheat.
8. You shall not bear false witness against your neighbor.	We must not tell lies, or mislead others on purpose. We must not hurt others by what we say. If we have misled somebody, we must correct what we have said.
9. You shall not covet your neighbor's wife.	We respect the promises married people have made to each other. We must always dress and act in a decent way.
10. You shall not covet anything that belongs to your neighbor.	We are to be satisfied with what we have. We are not to be jealous, envious, or greedy. The Gospel teaches us to place God first in our lives.

Based on Exodus 20:2–17

God's Laws for Today

When God created the world, he gave people two commands—take care of the world he created and build the human family. When God gave us the Ten Commandments through Moses, he did so to remind us that his laws are based on the nature of Creation.

We follow the Fifth Commandment when we protect all that God created, especially human life. Destroying the life of an innocent, unborn child (abortion) or as a sick or elderly person (euthanasia) is against God's Law because it is against God's Creation.

The Church believes that the family is at the heart of the human community. And so the Sixth Commandment teaches that husbands and wives must be faithful to each other for life. Families welcome children and help them grow.

God created people in his own image. Because of this, the Eighth Commandment requires us to always be truthful as God is Truth.

At Creation, God asked us to increase and multiply and care for the earth. We are reminded of this responsibility when we think about God's Commandments.

The Great Commandment

Jesus told us that the Ten Commandments could be summed up in what is known as the Great Commandment. "Love God with all your heart, with all your mind, and with all your strength, and love your neighbor as yourself" (based on Mark 12:30–31).

The New Commandment

Jesus told us that besides giving us the Great Commandment, he wanted to give us the New Commandment. The New Commandment Jesus gave us is, "Love one another as I love you" (based on John 15:12). Jesus' love for us is the perfect example of how to live. When we love others and treat them as Jesus taught us, we live in happiness and freedom.

ABOUT
VOCATIONS
Many Ways of Serving

Laypersons Most Catholics live out their baptismal vocation as **laypersons**. Laypersons usually hold jobs in society and are either single or married. As part of their Christian vocation, laypersons often volunteer their time and skills in serving their local parish community or diocese. They may help care for the poor, teach as a catechist in religious education classes, help with parish and school organizations, or invite others to join the Church. In these and many other ways, laypersons help their parish community fulfill the Church's mission to reach out to all in the spirit of Jesus.

Religious Sisters and Brothers Some men and women choose to devote their entire lives to the ministry of the Catholic Church. These people join religious communities of sisters or brothers. Vows or promises of poverty, chastity, and obedience are taken so that the sisters or brothers can be completely devoted to their ministries and become closer to God in community. Each religious community chooses a particular ministry, such as teaching, working with the poor, preaching, prayer and contemplation, nursing work, or parish work.

Ordained Ministers In the Catholic Church, there are also ordained ministers—bishops, priests, and deacons. Baptized men who are called to ordained ministry have the special vocation of leading the community in worship, as well as serving in a wide variety of ministries within the Church.

Bishops are the chief teachers of the faith. They administer dioceses and celebrate the Sacraments.

Diocesan priests serve in positions such as pastors of parishes, educators, and counselors. Priests who belong to religious communities may be assigned as pastors or teachers, or they may work in the particular ministry of their communities.

Most deacons that serve in parishes are called "permanent deacons." These men usually assist the pastor of a parish by leading the celebrations of Baptism and Marriage, preaching at Sunday Mass, and helping with parish management. Unlike priests, permanent deacons can be married and have families.

HOW CATHOLICS PRAY

When we pray, we are expressing our faith in God. As Catholics, we can pray privately by ourselves. We can also pray with others in the Church community when we gather to worship.

ABOUT
PRAYER

Prayer is listening and talking to God. We can pray to praise and thank God. We pray to ask God for special blessings for ourselves and for others. We can pray to express sorrow for our sins. Sometimes we call upon Mary or one of the saints to pray to God for us.

We believe God always hears our prayers. We believe God always answers our prayers in the way that is best for us. Jesus said, "Whatever you ask the Father in my name, he will give you" (based on John 16:23).

ABOUT
THE KINDS OF PRAYER

Just as we have different ways of talking and listening to our friends, we have different ways of praying.

It is always possible to pray. We can pray without saying words. When we are quiet and we think about God, we are praying. This is a very good way to pray because the Holy Spirit speaks to our hearts. Another way to pray is to quietly think about a Bible story. We can try to imagine ourselves being in the crowd when Jesus preached. This kind of prayer helps us to think about what our faith means to us. We can also use church music or instrumental music to help us pray. Music can help us focus on prayer when it is easy to get distracted.

Beautiful sights in nature remind us of God's wonderful gifts. When we see a sunrise or sunset, smell the ocean or a flower, see the colored leaves in autumn, or even play with our pets, we can pray a quiet prayer of thanks to God.

Our   Father   who art

in   heaven   hallowed be

thy   name.

Thy   kingdom   come.

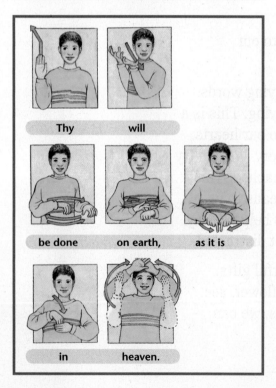

Thy   will

be done   on earth,   as it is

in   heaven.

THE LORD'S PRAYER

Jesus taught his followers to pray. He gave us the Lord's Prayer so that we can honor God and remember God's love for us. This prayer teaches us many important lessons about how God wants us to live.

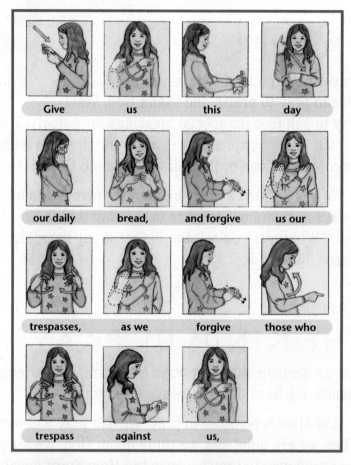

Give   us   this   day

our daily   bread,   and forgive   us our

trespasses,   as we   forgive   those who

trespass   against   us,

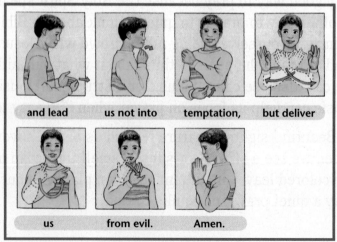

and lead   us not into   temptation,   but deliver

us   from evil.   Amen.

The Lord's Prayer

Our Father who art in heaven, hallowed be thy name.

God is our Father. We praise and thank God for all the wonderful gifts he has given us. We pray that God's name will be spoken with respect and reverence at all times.

Thy kingdom come.

Jesus told us about God's Kingdom in Heaven. We pray that everyone will live as Jesus teaches us to live. We look forward to the day when God's Kingdom will finally come.

Thy will be done on earth, as it is in heaven.

We pray that everyone will obey God's laws. We know that Jesus has taught us how to live as his followers. We wish to show others how to live as Jesus taught.

Give us this day our daily bread,

God cares for us. We know that we can pray for our needs. We know that we must pray for the needs of the poor. We ask God for the good things we can share with others.

and forgive us our trespasses,
as we forgive those who trespass against us,

We ask God for forgiveness when we have done something wrong. We forgive those who have hurt us.

and lead us not into temptation,

We pray that God will help us make good choices and do what is right. When we have difficult choices to make, we can pray to the Holy Spirit for guidance.

but deliver us from evil.

We pray that God will protect us from what is harmful. We know that we should care for our own health and the well-being of others.

Amen.

When we say "Amen," it means "I believe."

ABOUT
MEDITATIVE PRAYER

Meditation is praying without words. In meditative prayer, we pay close attention to our thoughts and our feelings. We pray silently so that God can speak to us in our hearts.

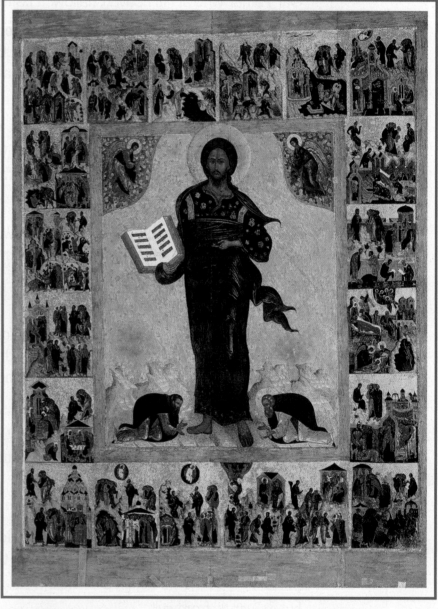

Meditative prayer begins by thinking about one single subject. We may begin by reading a Bible story. Or we can think about a holy person whom we respect. Another thing we might pay very close attention to is something beautiful in the world around us such as a sunset or the ocean waves. As long as we are paying very close attention to our relationship with God while we do this, we are beginning to pray in a meditative way.

Another way to meditate is to call upon the Holy Spirit to help us think about how we are living with God. Are we truly living as a follower of Jesus? Are there some things we think we need to correct? Think about how you can better show your love for God in your everyday life.

Then, we think about what God wants us to do. We use our imagination to think about different ways we can serve God. We now have a better understanding of what God wants us to do as followers of Jesus.

CELEBRATING CATHOLIC SCHOOLS WEEK

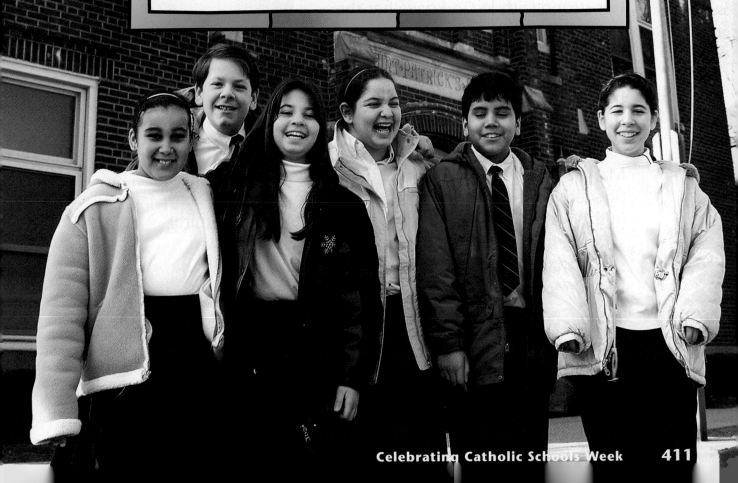

CATHOLIC SCHOOLS IN AMERICA
Mother Joseph of the Sacred Heart

Woman of Faith

Esther Pariseau was born April 16, 1823, in Quebec, Canada. When she was twenty, she joined the religious community of the Sisters of Providence. She later became known as Mother Joseph of the Sacred Heart. In 1856 she and four other sisters traveled 6,000 miles to their new home in the Washington Territory. They were asked by the bishop to care for the poor and sick. They also taught the young. Mother Joseph established schools as well. She knew that a good education made people good citizens and good Catholics.

Mother Joseph cared deeply for the people of the Washington Territory. Her strong faith in God gave her the strength to overcome any challenge that she faced. Whatever was needed to help the poor she did. She also received help from many people who lived in the area. Mother Joseph used her gifts to establish schools and hospitals in the region.

Many children in this region had no parents. Mother Joseph opened homes and cared for them. During her forty-six years in the Washington Territory, she opened more than thirty schools, hospitals, and homes. Mother Joseph told her sisters that whatever concerns the poor should always be their concern.

The people of Washington State knew that Mother Joseph helped so many people there that in 1980, they honored her by making a statue of her. Today the statue stands in the U.S. Capitol in Washington, D.C.

Activity

Mother Joseph believed that a good education could help people become good citizens and good Catholics. Think of ways your school helps you and your classmates develop these qualities. Then work with a partner to complete the chart below.

Anthony Quiroz 1-29-13 Qr.3

How Our School Helps Us to Grow

	As Good Citizens	As Good Catholics
Ways we practice our faith	care foo them, Care	hope faith in God
Subjects about which we learn	LA math	history religion
Activities we do	drawing	church
Celebrations or events in which we participate	church Parties	babtisms

CATHOLIC EDUCATION TODAY

Cristo Rey High School Network

Cristo Rey is a Spanish phrase that means "Christ the King." The Cristo Rey Network is an organization of Catholic high schools. These schools provide an education for young people who live in poor neighborhoods in cities across the United States. Cristo Rey schools offer a good Catholic education that is affordable for the high school students. The mission of these schools is to ensure that the young people are well prepared for college.

To accomplish this, every Cristo Rey high school has a work-study program. This means that its students have jobs that help to pay for their education. The jobs also prepare the students for a career. The students work in their jobs five days each month. Corporations make agreements with the schools to provide the students with jobs. Cristo Rey schools also have a longer school day and more time spent in school each year than other schools.

The first Cristo Rey school opened in a Chicago neighborhood in 1996. It began with 80 students, but now has more than 500 students. Leaders in other communities saw how much the school helped the young people. They wanted to establish Cristo Rey schools in other cities.

Today, there is a network of Cristo Rey high schools throughout the United States. The schools receive financial support from donations and are run by members of religious orders.

Cristo Rey high schools have very few dropouts. Almost all Cristo Rey graduates enroll in college.

Activity

The mission of Cristo Rey schools is to educate young people with limited opportunities and to prepare them for college. Their motto is "Schools that work." Their logo is a cross with a crown to represent Christ the King.

Think about how you would describe the mission of your school. Then, in the space below, write a motto for your school and draw a logo to go with it.

Go to SAIC School you will learn a lot of stuff.

MY CATHOLIC SCHOOL

Be a Detective:
Investigate Your School's History!

Imagine that you are a detective whose mission is to uncover the history of your school. Discover the details requested below, and write your findings on the lines provided.

School name ___Saint Anthony___ ___Immaculate conception___

Founded by _____

Year it was built _____

Date it first opened _____

Number of students when it first opened _____

Number of students today _____

Grade levels when it first opened _____

Grade levels today _____

Subjects taught when it first opened _____

Subjects taught today _____

Notable person or people in school's history

_____

Most surprising or interesting historical fact

_____

What I Like About My School

Use the items below to help you create on the screen below an advertisement about your school.

- The best things about the parish community of which your school is a part

- What you most admire about those who teach or lead your school

- Some of the things your school does to help others

- Some of the ways your school celebrates the Catholic faith

- The most valuable things you have learned as a student

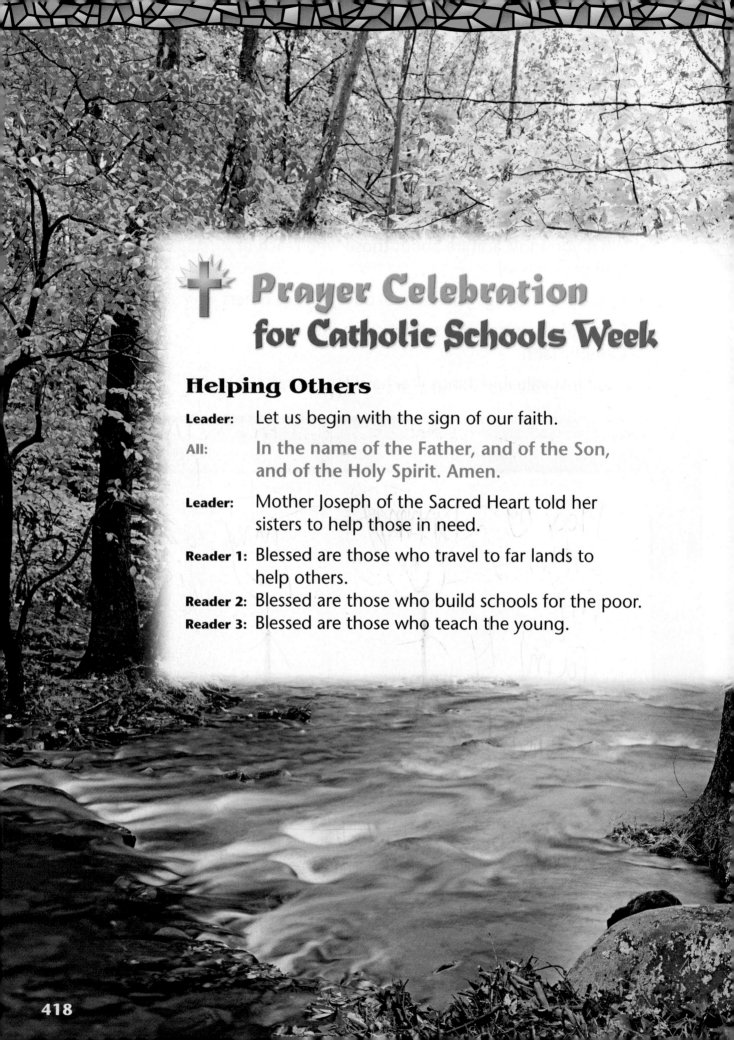

✝ Prayer Celebration for Catholic Schools Week

Helping Others

Leader: Let us begin with the sign of our faith.

All: In the name of the Father, and of the Son, and of the Holy Spirit. Amen.

Leader: Mother Joseph of the Sacred Heart told her sisters to help those in need.

Reader 1: Blessed are those who travel to far lands to help others.

Reader 2: Blessed are those who build schools for the poor.

Reader 3: Blessed are those who teach the young.

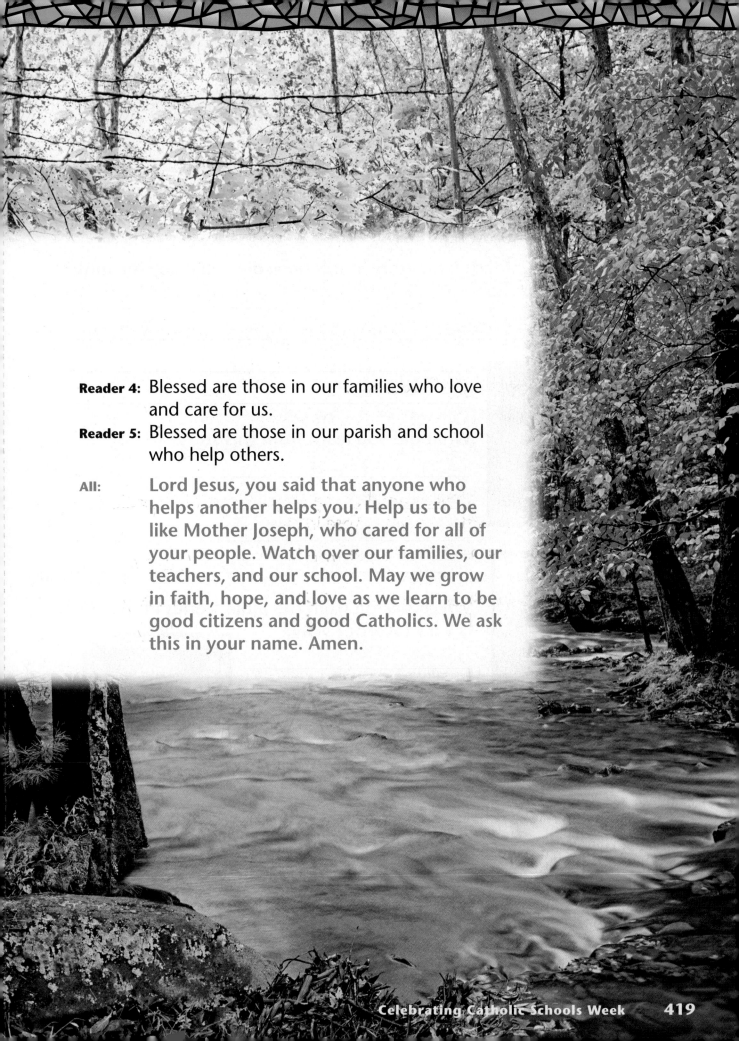

Reader 4: Blessed are those in our families who love and care for us.

Reader 5: Blessed are those in our parish and school who help others.

All: Lord Jesus, you said that anyone who helps another helps you. Help us to be like Mother Joseph, who cared for all of your people. Watch over our families, our teachers, and our school. May we grow in faith, hope, and love as we learn to be good citizens and good Catholics. We ask this in your name. Amen.

GRADE 4 FAVORITES

The school year is just about over. You have learned a lot in your religion classes. Think about the things you have studied and celebrated this year, and respond to the following.

Which Bible story in this book did you enjoy the most?

_____

_____

_____

What did you learn from this story?

_____

_____

_____

Which person from the Bible stories in this book is your favorite? Why?

_____

_____

_____

_____

_____

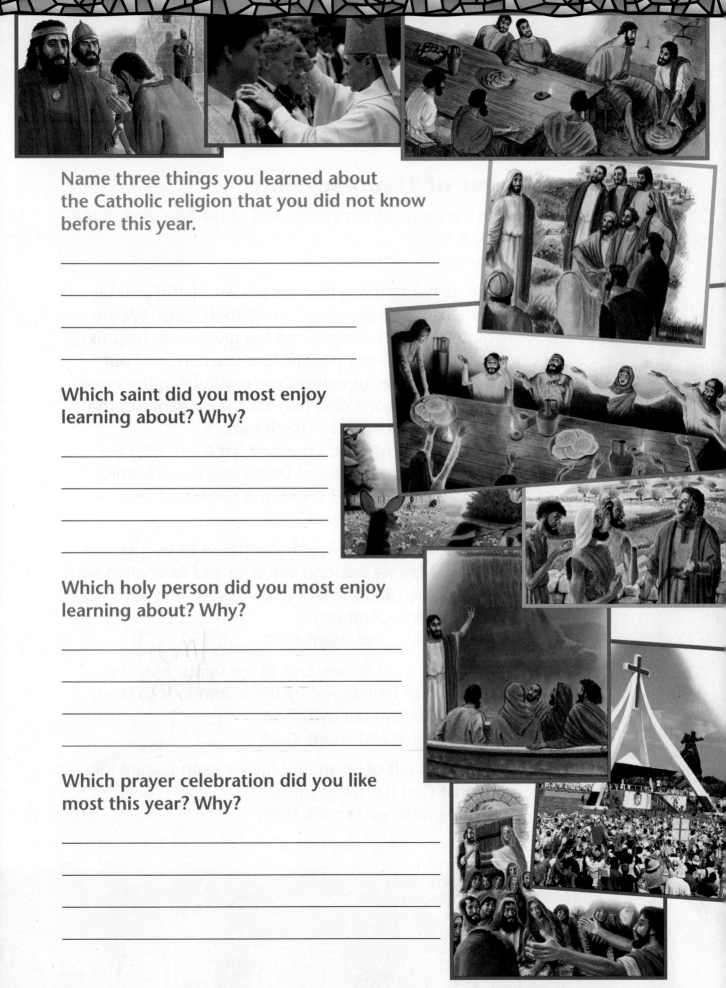

Name three things you learned about
the Catholic religion that you did not know
before this year.

_____

_____

_____

_____

Which saint did you most enjoy
learning about? Why?

_____

_____

_____

_____

Which holy person did you most enjoy
learning about? Why?

_____

_____

_____

_____

Which prayer celebration did you like
most this year? Why?

_____

_____

_____

_____

END-OF-YEAR PRAYER

A Prayer of Thanksgiving

Leader: In the name of the Father, and of the Son, and of the Holy Spirit.

All: Amen.

Leader: We gather to thank God for the wonderful year we have had learning about our Catholic faith. We are grateful for the people God has given us to help us grow in faith—our parents, our teachers, and our parish staff. Let us express our gratitude in the name of Jesus, our Lord, and pray for the guidance of the Holy Spirit, now and in the future.

Reader 1: For Jesus Christ, God's greatest gift to us. May we learn to appreciate Jesus' Death and Resurrection, and the new life that it brought to each of us,

All: let us praise and thank God.

Reader 2: For the Holy Spirit who challenges us to be just and loving. May we respond in justice and love when we see injustice and the lack of love present in our lives and the lives of others,

All: let us praise and thank God.

Reader 3: For Mary, our Mother, and all the saints. May we continue to be inspired by them, and look to them for guidance in our own lives,

All: let us praise and thank God.

Reader 4: For God's gift of creation. May we learn to care for all that God has given us,

All: let us praise and thank God.

Reader 5: For the Ten Commandments and the Beatitudes. May we continue to be guided by the Ten Commandments, and live by the Beatitudes as we love and serve God,

All: let us praise and thank God.

Reader 6: For the gift of Baptism. May we truly believe that God's life in us will make us a sign of the Kingdom of God,

All: let us praise and thank God.

Reader 7: For the gift of the Eucharist, the Body and Blood of Jesus Christ. May we continue to participate at Mass over the summer, and listen to God's Word,

All: let us praise and thank God.

Reader 8: For the gift of reconciliation and forgiveness. May we always be willing to offer forgiveness and be reconciled to those we have hurt or those who have hurt us,

All: let us praise and thank God.

Leader: All these petitions of praise and gratitude we offer to you, O God our Father as a sign of our belief in your Son, Jesus Christ, and the Holy Spirit, who is with us always helping us to live as true disciples.

All: Amen.

Leader: Let us offer each other a sign of peace.

Glossary

absolution Absolution is the prayer and declaration of forgiveness for sins prayed by the priest in the Sacrament of Reconcilation. *(page 217)*

Adoration Adoration of the Blessed Sacrament is a special devotion that gives thanks and praise to Jesus Christ in the Blessed Sacrament. *(page 182)*

anointed Being anointed means that the person receives God's grace to spread Christ's message. We are anointed with Sacred Chrism when we are baptized and confirmed. *(page 99)*

Ascension The Ascension is the moment when Jesus, in his resurrected body, entered Heaven. *(page 87)*

assembly An assembly is a gathering of Catholics to celebrate the Eucharist and the other Sacraments. *(page 275)*

Baptism Baptism is the first Sacrament of Christian Initiation that welcomes us into the Church and frees us from all sin. *(page 99)*

Beatitudes The Beatitudes are Jesus' teachings about how to live and find real happiness in God's Kingdom. *(page 113)*

bishop A bishop is the leader of a diocese. Bishops are the chief teachers of the Catholic Church. *(page 156)*

Bible The Bible is the Word of God. The Holy Spirit guided people to write all that is contained in the Bible. *(page 29)*

Blessed Sacrament The Blessed Sacrament is another name for the Eucharist kept in the tabernacle. *(page 181)*

Body of Christ The Body of Christ is the People of God, the Church. *(page 203)*

Christ's mission Christ's mission is to bring the Kingdom of God to all people. The Church guides us in spreading God's peace and love to the world. *(page 202)*

Communion of Saints The Communion of Saints is the community of all people, living and dead, who believe in Jesus Christ. *(page 263)*

Confirmation Confirmation is the Sacrament of Christian Initiation in which the Holy Spirit strengthens our faith and helps us become fuller members of the Church. *(page 157)*

conscience Our conscience is our ability to know what is right and what is wrong. God speaks to us in our conscience and helps us make responsible decisions. *(page 227)*

Corporal Works of Mercy The Corporal Works of Mercy are ways the Church takes care of the basic physical needs of others. *(page 285)*

covenant A covenant is an agreement between people or groups of people. God made a sacred covenant with the Hebrew people. *(page 53)*

deacon A deacon is a baptized man who is ordained to serve the parish community in many ways. *(page 397)*

divine The word *divine* means "of God." Jesus Christ is both human and divine—that is, both true God and true man. *(page 87)*

Eucharist The Eucharist is the Sacrament of the Body and Blood of Jesus Christ. *(page 40)*

examination of conscience In an examination of conscience we decide whether our words and actions show love for God and others. *(page 169)*

faith Faith is belief in God. *(page 65)*

Gifts of the Holy Spirit The Seven Gifts of the Holy Spirit are wisdom, understanding, knowledge, right judgment, courage, reverence, and wonder and awe. These Gifts help us know and love God and live as his followers. *(page 156)*

Gospel The word *gospel* means "Good News." At Mass, we listen to readings about Jesus' life and teachings from the four Gospels in the New Testament. *(page 275)*

grace Grace is God's life within us that fills us with his love. *(page 157)*

Holy Orders Holy Orders is the Sacrament in which bishops, priests, and deacons are ordained to serve the Church. *(page 261)*

Holy Trinity The Holy Trinity is one God in Three Divine Persons. The Three Divine Persons are God the Father, God the Son, and God the Holy Spirit. *(page 31)*

homily A homily is the talk a priest or deacon gives at Mass to help us understand God's message in the Gospel and other readings. *(page 275)*

immersed Immersed means being placed in water for Baptism. *(page 98)*

justice Justice means treating everyone fairly and with respect by following Jesus' teachings. *(page 123)*

Kingdom of God The Kingdom of God is God's promise of justice, peace, and joy that all his people will share at the end of time. *(page 65)*

Law of Love The Law of Love is the loving message in which Jesus united the Ten Commandments and the Beatitudes into one. It is also known as the New Commandment. *(page 169)*

layperson A layperson is any Catholic who is not a bishop, priest, deacon or a religious sister or brother. *(page 406)*

Liturgy of the Eucharist The Liturgy of the Eucharist is the part of the Mass in which the bread and wine become the Body and Blood of Christ. *(page 41)*

Liturgy of the Word The Liturgy of the Word is the part of the Mass in which we hear the Word of God in the Scriptures. *(page 41)*

Mass The Mass is the celebration of the Eucharist. *(page 41)*

Matrimony Matrimony is the Sacrament that celebrates the marriage commitment that a baptized man and a baptized woman make to each other. *(page 397)*

mercy Mercy is the loving kindness that God shows to sinners. *(page 65)*

monastery A monastery is a place where members of a religious community live. *(page 30)*

moral decisions Moral decisions are choices between what is right and what is wrong. *(page 227)*

mortal sin A mortal sin is a serious violation of God's Law. It separates us from God's grace until we ask for forgiveness in the Sacrament of Reconciliation. *(page 217)*

mystery A mystery is what cannot be fully understood about God. *(page 30)*

New Commandment The New Commandment is the loving message in which Jesus united the Ten Commandments and the Beatitudes into one. It is also known as the Law of Love. *(page 169)*

Original Sin Original Sin is the sin of Adam and Eve that has been passed on to all human beings. Because of this sin, we are weakened in our ability to resist sin and to do good. *(page 101)*

parable A parable is a story that teaches a moral or religious lesson. Parables use everyday events and objects to explain important truths. *(page 239)*

Paschal Mystery The Paschal Mystery is the life, suffering, Death, Resurrection, and Ascension of Jesus Christ. *(page 87)*

peace Peace follows forgiveness. It is the calm, good feeling of being together with God and with others. *(page 241)*

Pentecost On Pentecost, Jesus sent the gift of the Holy Spirit to his first disciples. This event marks the beginning of the Church. *(page 147)*

petition A petition is a prayer in which we ask for God's help for others and ourselves. *(page 297)*

priest A priest is a baptized man ordained in the Sacrament of Holy Orders to lead the community in worship and to serve in a wide variety of ministries in the Church. *(page 43)*

Rosary The Rosary is a special devotion that honors Mary. The Rosary helps us to meditate on events in the lives of Jesus and Mary. *(page 15)*

Sacraments The Sacraments are the seven sacred signs that celebrate God's love for us and Christ's presence in our lives and in the Church. *(page 203)*

Sacrament of Anointing of the Sick Anointing of the Sick is the Sacrament of Healing that brings Jesus' comfort to people who are very sick, elderly, or near death. *(page 215)*

Sacraments at the Service of Communion The Sacraments at the Service of Communion are Holy Orders and Matrimony. These two Sacraments celebrate two special ways that people serve God by sharing their gifts with others. *(page 397)*

Sacraments of Healing The Sacraments of Healing are Reconciliation and Anointing of the Sick. *(page 215)*

Sacraments of Christian Initiation The Sacraments of Christian Initiation are Baptism, Confirmation, and Eucharist. *(page 159)*

Sacrament of Reconciliation Reconciliation is the Sacrament of Healing that celebrates the gift of God's love and forgiveness. *(page 215)*

Sacred Chrism Sacred Chrism is perfumed oil that has been consecrated by a bishop. *(page 99)*

sacred images Sacred images are statues or pictures that help us to pray to God, Mary, and the saints. *(page 54)*

sin A sin is any thought, word, or action that turns us away from God and the way God wants us to live. *(page 216)*

Spiritual Works of Mercy The Spiritual Works of Mercy are loving actions that describe how to respond to people's basic spiritual needs. *(page 287)*

tabernacle A tabernacle is the special container in church where the Blessed Sacrament is kept for distribution to those unable to come to Mass due to illness and for personal prayer. *(page 181)*

Ten Commandments The Ten Commandments are the laws God gave to Moses. They help us live in peace by loving God, ourselves, and others. *(page 53)*

venial sin A venial sin is a sin less serious than a mortal sin. It weakens our love for God and others and can lead to mortal sin. *(page 217)*

virtue Virtue is the ability to make morally good decisions that lead to the habit of doing good. Christian virtues are considered gifts from God that we can develop into habits of Christian living. *(page 402)*

vocation A vocation is the work we do as members of the Church. We are called by God to use our talents to carry on Christ's mission in the world. *(page 261)*

worship To worship is to give honor, thanks, and praise to God, especially as a community. *(page 54)*

Index